WINNING
ARMAGEDDON

Titles in the Series

Airpower Reborn: The Strategic Concepts of John Warden and John Boyd

The Bridge to Airpower: Logistics Support for Royal Flying Corps Operations on the Western Front, 1914–18

Airpower Applied: U.S., NATO, and Israeli Combat Experience

The Origins of American Strategic Bombing Theory

Beyond the Beach: The Allied Air War against France

"The Man Who Took the Rap": Sir Robert Brooke-Popham and the Fall of Singapore

Flight Risk: The Coalition's Air Advisory Mission in Afghanistan, 2005–2015

The History of Military Aviation
Paul J. Springer, editor

This series is designed to explore previously ignored facets of the history of airpower. It includes a wide variety of disciplinary approaches, scholarly perspectives, and argumentative styles. Its fundamental goal is to analyze the past, present, and potential future utility of airpower and to enhance our understanding of the changing roles played by aerial assets in the formulation and execution of national military strategies. It encompasses the incredibly diverse roles played by airpower, which include but are not limited to efforts to achieve air superiority; strategic attack; intelligence, surveillance, and reconnaissance missions; airlift operations; close-air support; and more. Of course, airpower does not exist in a vacuum. There are myriad terrestrial support operations required to make airpower functional, and examinations of these missions is also a goal of this series.

In less than a century, airpower developed from flights measured in minutes to the ability to circumnavigate the globe without landing. Airpower has become the military tool of choice for rapid responses to enemy activity, the primary deterrent to aggression by peer competitors, and a key enabler to military missions on the land and sea. This series provides an opportunity to examine many of the key issues associated with its usage in the past and present, and to influence its development for the future.

WINNING ARMAGEDDON

CURTIS LeMAY AND STRATEGIC AIR COMMAND, 1948–1957

TREVOR ALBERTSON

Naval Institute Press
Annapolis, Maryland

Naval Institute Press
291 Wood Road
Annapolis, MD 21402

Library of Congress Cataloging-in-Publication Data

Names: Albertson, Trevor, date, author.
Title: Winning armageddon : Curtis LeMay and Strategic Air Command,
    1948–1957 / Trevor Albertson.
Description: Annapolis, Maryland : Naval Institute Press, [2019] | Series:
    The history of military aviation | Includes bibliographical references and
    index.
Identifiers: LCCN 2018060112 (print) | LCCN 2019001252 (ebook) | ISBN
    9781682474471 (epdf) | ISBN 9781682474228 (hardcover : alk. paper)
Subjects: LCSH: LeMay, Curtis E. | First strike (Nuclear strategy) | United
    States—Military policy. | Nuclear warfare—United States—History—20th
    century. | United States. Air Force. Strategic Air Command—History.
Classification: LCC UA923 (ebook) | LCC UA923 .A43 2019 (print) | DDC
    355.02/17097309045—dc23
LC record available at https://lccn.loc.gov/2018060112

∞ Print editions meet the requirements of ANSI/NISO z39.48-1992 (Permanence
of Paper).
Printed in the United States of America.

27 26 25 24 23 22 21 20 19   9 8 7 6 5 4 3 2 1
First printing

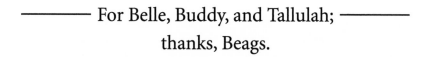 For Belle, Buddy, and Tallulah;
thanks, Beags.

Contents

Foreword

M y favorite elective to teach when I was a professor of history at West Point was entitled "Generalship and the Art of Command." The course examined great captains such as Alexander and Napoleon but also focused on commanders classified as "transformational leaders" who turned losers into winners in tough circumstances. Examples included Philippe Petain, who rejuvenated the French army after the mutinies of 1917, and Matthew Ridgway, who restored the fighting spirit of the U.S. Eighth Army in Korea in early 1951 after the longest retreat in U.S. military history. The course also included an examination of selected naval and air leaders, including Curtis LeMay. No U.S. general better fits the definition of transformational leader. LeMay inspired outstanding performance in the units he commanded in the Eighth Air Force and the Twentieth Air Force during World War II and in the postwar Strategic Air Command. His unique operational expertise and leadership skills were well recognized by his superiors, who consistently gave him the hardest jobs in the most critical places. He was the most renowned problem solver in the Army Air Forces/U.S. Air Force. As Brig. Gen. Lauris Norstad, Twentieth Air Force chief of staff, remarked when LeMay was given command of all bombing operations against Japan out of the Mariana Islands in early 1945, "LeMay is an operator, the rest of us are planners."

One of LeMay's greatest attributes was his ingenuity. No airman in history has been more innovative. He did not just think outside of the box; to him, there was no box. He envisioned no restrictions beyond those imposed by technological limitations. During World War II in Europe, he came up with the optimal design of staggered bomber formations to increase defensive fire-power, implemented the nonevasive action bomb run to improve targeting accuracy, and initiated the training of selected lead crews to specialize on each objective. He pioneered the use of after-action reviews and systems analysis. In the Pacific, he resorted to low-level night fire-bombing of Japanese cities that decimated indus-try there while killing hundreds of thousands of civilians—one of the key blows that prompted Japan's surrender. After that dev-astating war, he became the main architect of the Berlin airlift, shifting easily from dumping incendiaries on Japanese children to dropping candy to German ones, and executing many "extralegal" actions to circumvent peacetime rules of European allies. And he transformed the postwar Strategic Air Command into the most competent and deadliest military force on the planet.

It is not surprising then, as Trevor Albertson so thoroughly reveals, that LeMay intensely analyzed the problem of winning the nuclear war he would have to fight. And again his solution was unique, shaped by his evaluation of the capabilities of the weap-ons at his disposal. His plan for a preemptive war was a counter-force strategy that would take away most of the enemy's capability to fight back, leaving them with the decision of whether to expand the war into the countervalue realm of indiscriminately destroy-ing cities. While often inaccurately compared to the character of Gen. Jack D. Ripper in the movie *Dr. Strangelove*, who launches his bombers at the Soviet Union without permission, LeMay more closely resembled the character of Gen. Buck Turgidson, with a plan to limit civilian casualties as much as possible when war became inevitable, "depending on the breaks." Exhibiting great political sensitivity to the impact of his ideas, however, LeMay was very careful how he promulgated them. Albertson clearly explains their origin and logic.

In this era of increasing nuclear threats from rogue nations and terrorists, it may well be time to relook at LeMay's thinking about the use of nuclear weapons. We do not need the Bulletin of Atomic Scientists moving the hands of their doomsday clock closer to midnight to remind us all that we are getting closer to seeing another nuclear explosion somewhere; there are plenty of other signs. It would behoove U.S. leaders and the public to rethink the possible utilization of such weapons of mass destruction; our enemies do. LeMay's method of examining the problem can provide a model about how to structure such an analysis. The final answers will probably be different than his were, but the process will still require the same clear, realistic, and innovative thinking that Curtis LeMay demonstrated so well.

Conrad C. Crane
U.S. Army Heritage and Education Center

Preface

The completion of this manuscript and the beginning of Strategic Air Command (SAC)—at least as it was known under Curtis E. LeMay's command and thereafter—occurred in the same location: above Tokyo. The process of editing the manuscript began on the thirty-sixth floor of a Tokyo hotel, where a realization struck, that LeMay's bombing of the city led, at least in part, to the building of the modern world. For LeMay, his time at SAC also began over Tokyo, with his decision to firebomb the city. In so doing, LeMay built the modern concept of strategic bombardment; he also laid the groundwork of modernity through the destruction of Tokyo, allowing it to reemerge as the prototypical modern metropolis. It was a practical end to a practical concern. Through violence, LeMay forced a new beginning—though he simply wanted to force an end to World War II. The new creation, the concept of massive destruction in short order and on a scale never before seen, presaged what came later with atomic weapons and SAC. The command was the embodiment of the Cold War; it was also representative of the hopes and fears of the United States. Its rise signaled the Cold War's start, and its demise was a harbinger of that conflict's conclusion.

In a practical sense, LeMay's tenure at SAC was the beginning of U.S. Cold War nuclear policy. LeMay's time at the nuclear command predated many of the policy decisions that have been used as milestones to define the conflict—Harry S. Truman's National Security Council Report 68, Dwight D. Eisenhower's New Look, and John F. Kennedy's Flexible Response were prime examples. The pragmatic foundation of those ideas, however, was LeMay's efforts to build an effective defense against a new kind of war. He did it before the policy leaders made decisions to do so. As a result, LeMay's efforts toward a workable defense highlighted his practical nature. Pragmatism drove LeMay, personally and professionally. LeMay wanted the solution to work—the first time.

The debate by U.S. historians over the end of the Cold War and the credit for its demise in many ways discounts the very history of the conflict. Whether Ronald Reagan, Mikhail Gorbachev, or a host of others in the 1980s and 1990s brought an end to the Cold War was less salient to the discourse than the role of the ideas, practices, policies, and actions of those in critical positions at its outset. Truman, George Kennan, Dean Acheson, Paul Nitze, LeMay, and Eisenhower had more to do with the end of the Cold War than those in power at its actual conclusion because they created the conditions that defined what the conflict meant—and the conditions to be met in order for it to be called off.

General Curtis E. LeMay was the second and most influential commander of SAC, and his tutelage gave teeth to the political-diplomatic edicts of the period. The command's nuclear bomber force, through its ability to deliver such weapons against distant targets, gave the Cold War its early and ominous overtones. Bookending the conflict were LeMay's arrival at SAC in 1948, and the stand-down of that organization's nuclear bomber alert force in 1991 and the command as a whole in 1992. The existence of SAC gave as much reason for the conflict to begin as it did for it to end; no one wanted a nuclear war—especially one born of the military construct shaped by LeMay. But that was only part of the account. A story of greater importance revolved around preemption.

As SAC commander from fall 1948 until summer 1957, LeMay advocated for justified preemption of Soviet military forces. Preemption—military strikes undertaken in an effort to preclude an imminent enemy attack—differed from the notion of preventive war—a conflict undertaken with a conviction that while no imminent threat is present, delaying war would only increase the eventual danger from an enemy threat. Rather than arguing for preventive war, LeMay maintained support for preemptive strikes in response to an imminent Soviet attack against the United States. The story of LeMay's argument for preemption paralleled the development of U.S. policy toward the Soviet Union. While national leaders talked deterrence, LeMay, sometimes quietly and at other times more forcefully, made his own case for something different. His staid argument, made repeatedly, gave life to a message that was not in step with the one preached by U.S. policy leaders. That dissonance called into question the nature of U.S. foreign policy during the early Cold War and the reasons the nation took the stance it did. At the same time, LeMay's push for preemption did not alter the publicly declared U.S. policy of deterrence.

That LeMay sought first strikes does not automatically place him among the pantheon of historical warmongers. Rather, LeMay's pursuit of preemption was a result of fear of a widespread nuclear war expanding into an all-consuming situation that killed millions of civilians, destroyed their cities, and leveled commerce in short order. LeMay believed that he could prevent that from happening for the United States and, in a subsidiary sense, for the Soviet Union as well. If the elimination of enemy strategic air-power before its employment but after a foe's decision to go to war led to the capitulation of that enemy, then not only were targets in the United States saved, but there would also be no need to attack the opponent's cities, people, and industry. It was an ambitious hope that spoke volumes for who LeMay was and how he viewed the world. This is the story of his advocacy.

Acknowledgments

First and foremost, I want to thank God for His grace in making this book happen. To my wife Katie goes much of the credit for getting my dissertation, the antecedent to this work, completed and this book to print. Her kindness, her gentleness, and her compassion over the years have reminded me constantly that I am a lucky man. I couldn't have asked for a better wife.

I hope this book helps build a better world for my children than the one I grew up in. Although the Cold War is part of history, fear and the weapons that drove it are still with us. To my children: Don't let fear govern your decisions and thoughts. Be understanding, but also be courageous and stand up for what you believe in. More than likely, as the Cold War informed us, the other side shares the same fears, hopes, and dreams—but do not sacrifice yours willingly.

My parents deserve a share of the credit for this project and for much of the success I have been blessed with in life. From an early age, they helped me to understand many lessons of history and the character of the Cold War. They put up with me when I was a tough kid to raise—thanks for not giving up on me. My grandparents were the best anyone could have wanted. They taught me the practice of taking the long view and thus made me a better historian. They showed me love for many years, and I miss them dearly.

Many thanks to Dr. Gregg Herken for his patience while serving as my doctoral and dissertation advisor. He helped me through many tough spots in research and writing. I wish for every graduate student an advisor with the wisdom, knowledge, humor, and forbearance that Gregg had with me. His friendship and advice since graduation have been equally appreciated.

Dr. Paul Springer has been one of the best supporters I have known, and this book would not have happened without him. Dr. John Terino has been a great department chair, personal cheerleader, and supporter who helped make this work a reality. Dr. James Forsyth, dean of the Air Command and Staff College, changed the trajectory of my career. One of the sharpest minds I have ever had the chance to probe is that of Dr. Edwin Redman. His counsel, humor, and insights were instrumental in making this book a better product than it otherwise would have been. Dr. Sebastian Lukasik has been a wise colleague and good friend while also serving as a cheerful writing partner. Dr. Jordan Hayworth is someone I will be able to say I knew before he was a big-name scholar. Jordan, you were a huge help. Dr. S. Michael Pavelec is a wonderful scholar and friend who shepherded me to a successful conclusion. You are a good man, Mike. To the entire Department of Airpower, thank you! You are fantastic colleagues to have. Thanks for letting me join the "flying circus."

My life in academia started with Dr. Willard Hardman, to whom I owe much; thanks for all the advice over the years. At the University of California, Merced, Dr. Robin DeLugan, Dr. Ruth Mostern, and Dr. Christopher Viney all were the best dissertation committee members I could have asked for. Their advice—academic, professional, and personal—was valuable, and I wish I had been a better listener. Donald Barclay and Eric Scott at the UC Merced library were also instrumental to my success as a student and growth as a scholar. Dr. Sean Malloy afforded me a grounded understanding of the canon of airpower history that few others would have been able to provide. Dr. James Ortez was a good friend and mentor. Dr. Sam Traina helped immeasurably with numerous administrative decisions as the dean of graduate studies. Dr. Keith Alley was a friendly face when I needed a smile. Dr. Bradford Johnston and Dr. Richard Ravalli were good friends among the graduate student ranks, and I owe them both so much for their advice, support, and companionship.

To the staff of the Library of Congress, I owe a word of thanks. You were the kind of archivists every researcher deserves and few will get. The Library of Congress Manuscript Division is an amazing public resource that deserves more funding, staff, and support than it receives. Because of you all, the nation's story can be told and truth spoken to power.

If not for the folks at the Air Force Historical Research Agency (AFHRA), this work would be less complete. Barry Spink, Dr. Dan Haulman, Tammy Horton, and Dr. Charles O'Connell: you all made a big difference, and I really appreciate it. Although the Air Force at times had a troubled past, it also had its share of true heroics. History should remember the totality of the Air Force experience, and AFHRA makes examinations of that history possible.

To my Norwich classmates of 2002: do not give up the fight! You are amazing folks who make a real difference in the world. I am proud to have stood at attention in formation with you. I also owe a great debt of gratitude to the faculty at Norwich: Dr. Gary Lord, Dr. Christine McCann, Dr. Reina Pennington, Dr. Thomas

Taylor, Dr. Mark Byrnes, and everyone else. To the deputy commandant, Col. Eric Braman, USA: I guess those "tours" finally took hold. Lastly, to Christopher Hoover, USMC: I get it now. The discipline you instilled in me was a constant refrain throughout this and many other trying events in my life: "Don't quit." Thanks, Drill Sergeant Hoover.

The staff of the Naval Institute Press deserves special credit, particularly Paul Merzlak. Thank you for your guidance and direct advice. A special thanks to my editor, Lisa Yambrick. She was patient with me *and* my writing.

Thanks as well to Col. Joseph "Batman" Battaglia, Col. Douglas Drakeley, and Col. Carl Magnusson. Dr. Jerome Martin and Dr. Vince Giroux were larger than life in my personal growth as a historian. Thank you for investing so much in me so early on. It has made a real difference, and you infused me with an expansive interest in airpower history.

Finally, I offer a note of appreciation to Dr. Conrad Crane, an impressive scholar and now a good friend. He helped guide my efforts at the earliest stages of this work and provided critical feedback throughout.

I know there are other friends and colleagues that deserve mention. Please accept my apologies for failing to acknowledge your contributions; your absence is not intended as a slight. Know that your positive influence on me is written across the better pages of this manuscript. Any errors are my own.

Reasons for Fear

Events from late 1948 to mid-1950 gave many in the U.S. military and government, including Curtis LeMay, plenty of cause for fear. Ever since the first confrontation with the Soviet Union over Berlin in early 1948, events had been creating a sense of coming conflict that overshadowed U.S. efforts at stabilizing its place in the postwar world. This fear was magnified by the sense of the unknown that pervaded the era. The Cold War represented a wholly new challenge for the United States and its fledgling Air Force. The nation was not interested in fighting another war, no matter how ideologically opposed the U.S. and Soviet systems appeared; but the United States had no desire to abdicate the international role it had gained as a result of World War II. Striking a delicate balance between the two was a problem left to the Air Force and, specifically, Strategic Air Command.

For LeMay, the period was one of problems and surprises. In the late 1940s and early 1950s, SAC was hardly able to meet the mission with which it had been charged. It was also an era that stressed—but did not break—LeMay's concept of the purpose of the Air Force in general and SAC in particular.[1] Getting to know his command, LeMay was given other reasons to be fearful of what the future held. When LeMay took command from Gen. George Kenney in October 1948, SAC was not in a position to do much of anything; "The downward spiral that had gripped SAC since its inception had never been arrested."[2] Kenney's roughly two years leading SAC were uneventful. The impetus for LeMay's selection as SAC's new commander began in mid-1948 at a meeting of high-level service leaders, including Kenney, that was called by Secretary of Defense James Forrestal.[3] After Kenney gave a substandard presentation to the attendees, Lauris Norstad, who directed Air Force operations, "insisted that Vandenberg [Chief of Staff Hoyt Vandenberg] name a new SAC commander."[4] Vandenberg asked Norstad for his recommendation for the position. "Norstad responded with a question: 'Who would you want in command of SAC if war broke out tomorrow?' . . . The chief of staff quickly replied: 'LeMay.'"[5] Late in August 1948 Vandenberg and Secretary of the Air Force Stuart Symington traveled to Europe and met with General LeMay.[6] The visit took place during the aerial resupply of the besieged city of Berlin and amid the rapidly escalating tensions between the Americans and Soviets. Vandenberg and Symington "found [LeMay's] organization, USAFE [U.S. Air Forces in Europe], ready for the emergency facing them in Germany."[7]

In the eyes of senior Air Force leadership, LeMay was the perfect person for the job of building SAC. In the early years of the Cold War, the Air Force controlled the most realistic means of delivering the U.S. nuclear arsenal against Soviet targets. It needed a sharp commander to ensure its force was capable of carrying out that mission. During World War II in Europe and the Pacific, and then during the postwar period of growing international tensions, LeMay had shown a talent for achieving rapid results. He would need to do the same at SAC.

Getting to Know SAC

LeMay arrived on October 19 and wasted little time in assessing his new command to determine what changes needed to be made.[8] Not all of the changes were directly related to combat capability. In late 1948 LeMay made an inspection tour of various SAC bases, including living conditions on them. This initiative was an early indication of his style of leadership at SAC and his enduring interest in the welfare of the people serving under him. The records from such visits are rich with the details of LeMay's concerns and specific curiosities. They also provide some insight into life in SAC in the late 1940s, and they offer a touchstone against which the changes initiated by LeMay during his command were measured.

On December 10, 1948, LeMay made a stop at Topeka Air Force Base in Kansas. He appeared just as interested in the living conditions for those stationed there as he was in the base's combat readiness. In the notes from his trip, LeMay commented on several issues, chief among them being concerns about quality of life issues. LeMay noted that in the base mess hall, "arrangement is poor. Drainage and new food are too close together. Should be separated. Mess Hall needs improving." With regard to the status of housing, the base commander reported to LeMay that "a project was begun last September. I tried to contact civilian contractors, sign about 250 men to buy homes, work on houses after duty. It would cost about $100 down payment plus labor. Rental about

$45 a month. 2 or 3 bedrooms. I tried to contact Air Installations Officer and get his assistance. Air Installations and FHA [Federal Housing Administration] cannot get together."[9] Nonetheless, LeMay's airmen needed places to live.

Three days later, LeMay visited Kearney Air Force Base in Nebraska and repeated his query as to progress on housing: "When are they going to start and finish?" The reply came that "they are going to start in March. They don't know when they will finish," prompting LeMay to ask: "How many people have unsatisfactory places to live or no place at all?" His notes on the response he received told of the types of issues faced by military members of the era: "One hundred and eight married men who don't have families here. I assume 90 percent would like their families here. Off base, 233 enlisted and 95 officers. Maybe one hundred are living in satisfactory places in town. Sixty dollars a month pays for a basement apartment with inadequate heat and light."[10] Taking on a more delicate topic, LeMay queried the rate of venereal disease infection, which he was informed was zero. In his typical manner— blunt and almost comical—the general dug deeper: "No women around town?" LeMay was told that "some men are getting civilian care. Kearney [the nearby town] is well controlled. The town of Grand Island is not so well controlled. North Platte is a fairly wide open town. There are houses [presumably of ill repute] there. Men in uniform will be picked up if they are found in them."[11] LeMay was no fool and knew that the services in question could be found somewhere nearby—and that venereal disease existed to some extent among the troops. He also knew how the effects of venereal disease could impact his troops and the command as a whole.

Three days later, on December 16, LeMay visited Carswell Air Force Base, Texas, a major bomber base located in the

Fort Worth area that was home for the new B-36 bomber. The record of LeMay's visit to Carswell offered further insight into his approach to making life better for his airmen. During a ride with the base commanding officer in a staff car, LeMay inquired about the status of civilian housing. The commander replied, "It has improved a little. We have built quite a few apartments and some smaller houses. It's just the price." LeMay responded, "Still too high for enlisted men? What rent do NCOs [noncommissioned officers] have to pay off base?" The answer: "About 50 to 80 dollars for a one-bedroom apartment," no small price in 1948. Finally, LeMay offered some advice that reflected his savvy in community relations and in dealing with the reality of running a large organization: "Convince the local community we are going to stay in this area. Try and get the community to build low-cost houses. They worry whether a base is going to stay or not."[12] LeMay may not have known it at the time, but his admonition was in keeping with the truth; Carswell was an active base into the 1990s and remains open as a joint reserve base to the present day.

Regarding the Carswell mess hall, LeMay commented that "the food from Quartermaster is pretty good, but cooks sometimes spoil it. Try and work up a program to have Mess Officer, Mess Sergeant and even cooks go to some big hotel and see how they prepare food. Cut down on your waste. No reason why you can't do it. Good example of a mess hall was Cadet Mess at Kelly Field [near San Antonio]. Food was so good, no one wanted to eat in town. How many people do you feed?"[13] The mess sergeant replied, "About 230 people, sir." LeMay queried: "Plenty of ice box space?" to which the response was, "Yes sir." Just as had been the case with housing, LeMay offered a suggestion, stating that "a tablecloth on the tables will dress up the mess, as long as they can be kept clean."[14] LeMay was concerned with even the simplest of refinements related to quality of life for his airmen.

A discussion with the base commander gave a glimpse into LeMay's concern for the national security environment of the period. LeMay told the commander that "you have a pretty good place here. Got to get something done. Lay down the law to your officers. Training and service club in particular. No reason why we shouldn't be on the ball everyplace. Some people are satisfied with a mediocre performance. We can't be satisfied with a mediocre performance. People will have to snap to. Crack the whip a couple times and these people will snap to. We're fools if we are not ready shortly."[15]

The circumstance for which LeMay most likely wanted to be "ready shortly" was a potential war with the Soviet Union. To fight such a war, LeMay needed a long-range bomber to strike targets inside the Soviet Union directly from the United States— without relying upon overseas bases in either Europe or Africa.[16] In the late 1940s through the mid-1950s, that airplane was the B-36 Peacemaker. A sizable machine, the B-36 faced a number of maintenance complications.[17] These problems were particularly acute; the B-36 was as important to SAC and the overall U.S. defense scheme as it was large. Making the machine actually work as a weapon fell to LeMay.

The Carswell commander told LeMay that "the problem as far as putting B-36Bs [bombers] into operation is training for our radar people. As far as operating personnel, I think we have enough to do the job." LeMay's simple yet encouraging response was, "Let's get this thing going. . . [as it] takes time to train people to be instructors."[18] Without cutting the commander slack but still demonstrating a level of compassion, LeMay offered an insight that drove to the core of his approach to leadership and management of an organization:

> When you run up against a stone wall and you have to have help from Eighth Air Force or SAC, start screaming. Don't be satisfied with mediocre performances from my staff people. All you have to worry about is fighting or getting ready to fight. Nothing makes me madder than to have staff officers with directives from Washington who pass it on, instead of doing something about it themselves. If staff is passing work on to combat units that they should be doing themselves, I want to know about it. If they are not helping, they are not doing their job. I want the Inspectors Department to contain an expert on all phases of activities; personnel, supply, procedures of supply, so that you can call on him to help with something that is wrong. Call on these inspectors. He is to correct the mistakes that exist in the outfit. Get him on the telephone and have him come down and give you a hand, not to make inspections and gig [the] hell out of you. Some of these inspectors get too damn snotty. Let's get rid of them.[19]

Housing, however, remained a prime concern for LeMay, and he did not waste much time in elevating concerns about the problem—or in proposing an innovative solution. In a January 14, 1949, letter to Chief of Staff Hoyt Vandenberg, LeMay stated, "You are well aware of the deplorable housing conditions facing our married airmen and officers at almost every Strategic Air Command station."[20] Although there was word that Congress would take some action to partially rectify the problem of "low-cost housing," the SAC commander had no faith that the nation's legislative body would fully resolve the issue: "Whatever they do will hardly begin to meet our present urgent requirements."[21] LeMay explained to Vandenberg a solution that was used at an Army base in Texas:

> It seems to me that the only method of securing positive and prompt results lies in adopting a plan similar to the so-called "Fort Bliss Low-Cost-Housing-Plan". . . . Under this plan an association of enlisted men has been formed whose purpose is to provide the members small, low-cost housing units, to be erected by members, on property of the station leased by the association from the Government for fifteen years. Two hundred units have been ordered from Sears, Roebuck at a cost of $1,400.00 each. Each member pays $300.00 down ($250.00 of which can be obtained on loan from the Army Emergency Relief) and $40.00 a month rent. The purchase of the 200 units has been financed by a local bank and is amortized in four years. Utilities and roads are to be brought to the housing units from existing station facilities by civilian contractors hired with Department of the Army funds.[22]

LeMay told Vandenberg that "one or two of our bases have been working on a plan of this type" and that he was working with the rest of the command to determine whether such a plan would be practical to employ throughout the organization. After asking Vandenberg for his "tentative backing," he concluded his letter by reminding the chief that "the plight of our airman and the hardship brought about by the general shortage of family housing more than justify our initiating this plan."[23]

Inspections of other SAC bases highlighted additional complications that were representative of the disjointed, lax approach pervading much of the command.[24] One report, dated March 24, 1949, chronicled the inspection of Smoky Hill Air Force, Kansas: "This Base has a serious maintenance deficiency, caused by a shortage of parts due for change. . . . maintenance hangar needs policing. Private aircraft stored to be removed."[25] Not only were the technicalities of maintenance a problem there, but basic concepts of proper military usage were also a concern. That private aircraft were stored in a SAC maintenance hangar would have been incomprehensible to SAC personnel in the decades that followed. That was a result of the no-nonsense attitude LeMay instilled in SAC during his command; incidents such as these may have been the impetus behind LeMay's approach. A report from May 4 at Mountain Home Air Force Base, Idaho, revealed a mix of conditions, though there were some notable low points. According to the document, "It was stated that the Control Tower presently being used was unsafe in high winds of this area. . . . A guard tower built near the main gate is apparently in good condition and is available. Its removal to replace the present Control Tower might be considered."[26] This creative suggestion belied LeMay's reputation as a black-and-white thinker.

LeMay's interest in the welfare of his airmen spoke to the investment he made in them over the roughly nine years he spent at SAC. It also suggested LeMay knew that he was in it for the long haul; these visits gave LeMay plenty of reason to believe that the problems at SAC were widespread and pervasive and would take years to resolve. It also lent credibility to an argument that LeMay believed that wars were won as much behind the front lines as they were in the skies over an enemy. Troops that were well fed, properly housed, and free of undue administrative impediments would undoubtedly perform better than those subsisting on poor rations, living in ratty conditions, and bearing the burdens of bureaucratic processes.

LeMay attended to the basic needs of his men and their families without losing sight of other strategic organizational matters. An ability to manage details while also attending to macro-level concerns was a hallmark of LeMay's leadership and was essential to his success at SAC. Not only were living conditions a challenge, but also SAC's combat preparedness was abysmal. The Dayton raid provided some impetus for concern in the latter regard.

_____

Dayton and Joe One

LeMay conceived the Dayton raid as a large-scale test of the command's ability to carry out "a simulated radar bombing mission against Dayton, Ohio" in January 1949.[27] The results were dreadful: "Of 303 [bombing] runs, nearly two-thirds were more than 7,000 feet off target. The average error was 10,090 feet. Such an error, even with an atomic bomb over Hiroshima would have left the target unscathed."[28] Roughly five months later, a subsequent "smaller-scale mission . . . showed little improvement."[29] The results of the Dayton raid must have been sobering for LeMay, leaving him with little room but to conclude that in the late 1940s SAC was, operationally speaking, in shambles.

From the U.S. perspective, the world was turned on its side when the Soviet Union detonated its first atomic device, nicknamed Joe One, in August 1949, and the responsibility for keeping it from tipping over rested on LeMay's shoulders. The end of the U.S. monopoly on nuclear weapons meant that the nation's perceived security advantage in such devices had been cracked. It also spelled problems for U.S. prospects for defeating the Soviet Union in a war without receiving an unacceptable amount of damage. More than anything, however, the detonation of Joe One created a sense of urgency among U.S. defense officials and a belief that a war with the Soviet Union could spell disaster for the United States; this led to more aggressive preparations for war by the defense establishment.[30]

The Harry S. Truman administration's "illusion of calm had begun to shatter, inwardly, only weeks—if not days—after the Russian bomb was confirmed, and the assumptions on which the policy of monopoly had been based were proved wrong."[31] Predictions that the Soviets would not have the bomb until well into the 1950s also carried with them the belief that U.S. nuclear superiority sufficed for preventing a war with the Soviet Union. With Joe One, all plans and expectations were disrupted. In an effort to stave off Soviet nuclear parity, the United States undertook an effort to build a new type of nuclear weapon, the hydrogen or "super" bomb, the development of which had been debated since prior to Joe One. However, "the pall left by the Soviet atomic test and the changed perception of the Russian threat made the prospect of abandoning the 'Super' all but unthinkable."[32] Even if the United States was able to effectively field a hydrogen bomb, the damage to its sense of security superiority was done. At the same time, however, the United States had the ability to assuage concerns over the rising nuclear power of the Soviet Union. This came as a result of a belief, however faulty, that SAC was ready for war.

Nonetheless, according to historian John Lewis Gaddis, the U.S. loss of the nuclear monopoly was supplanted by another monopoly that did not involve a new type of atomic device. Gaddis argued that "because of superior long-range bombing capabilities, the United States retained an effective monopoly well into the 1950s."[33] This is an important point that has been overlooked by many U.S. Cold War historians. This point also meant that LeMay was responsible for the maintenance of the U.S. monopoly, whether perceived or real, on security in the early Cold War. This effective monopoly also meant that had the United States chosen to preempt the Soviets—in other words, to strike the Soviet Union first if a Soviet attack was thought imminent—it could do so with relative impunity. Approval for such a plan was what LeMay sought from Vandenberg at the close of 1949.

An Appeal to Vandenberg

A letter from LeMay to Vandenberg on December 12 was, in a sense, an appeal to the chief of staff to help assuage LeMay's pervasive fears. It also directly addressed LeMay's opinion on preemptive and preventive war. LeMay's letter, classified top secret when written, specifically spoke to the issues of preemptive and preventive war as a response to a potential threat posed by the Soviet Union to SAC ability to respond when required. It demonstrated that even following the test of the first Soviet atomic bomb, there was discussion among some of the most senior leaders in the Air Force of a first strike against the Soviet Union. LeMay's letter was a response to one Vandenberg sent the preceding October in which LeMay felt that Vandenberg had "stressed the importance of accelerating our readiness to conduct effective atomic warfare."[34] In his December reply LeMay noted that

> our readiness in this regard will depend materially upon our ability to avoid or absorb the effects of enemy attempts to immobilize our atomic striking force before it can be committed to combat. . . . I further realize that the magnitude of the problem of improving our means of coping with such attempts is so great, considering the limited resources available to meet all USAF commitments, that the possibilities of achieving an adequate overall solution in the near future are extremely limited.[35]

What LeMay referred to was the dilemma that SAC and the United States faced in being prevented from or impeded in launching a nuclear strike against the Soviets. Specifically, LeMay worried that "the information available to us indicates that the [Soviet Union] has the capability of penetrating all Strategic Air Command stations to the extent required to immobilize through sabotage the combat units based thereon."[36] Such a chilling assessment from a respected commander of one of the Air Force's major commands—let alone the nation's primary nuclear command—likely had an impact upon the decision-making process, which may have been LeMay's intent in phrasing the letter as he did. But this danger also left LeMay an opening to propose his solution to the problem. LeMay pointed out that

> no matter how much active defense we provide for ourselves, it is unlikely that we can prevent the Soviets from

attaining a measure of success in any attacks against our striking force.... The size of our striking force is so closely tailored to fit the task with which it is charged that we have little or no margin of safety within which we can absorb the effects of a successful enemy attack. *Under these circumstances, it would appear economical and logical to adopt the objective of completely avoiding enemy attack against our strategic force by destroying his atomic force before it can attack ours* [emphasis added].[37]

As this letter shows, LeMay advocated some form of first strike to the Chief of Staff of the Air Force. Whether he was suggesting a preemptive or preventive strike was a distinction he went on to address: "Assuming that as a democracy we are not prepared to wage a preventive war, this course of action poses two most difficult requirements: (1) An intelligence system which can locate the vulnerable elements of the Soviet striking force and forewarn us when attack by that force is imminent, and (2) Agreement at top governmental level that when such information is received the Strategic Air Command will be directed to attack."[38]

On February 1, 1950, Vandenberg responded to LeMay in a letter signed in his absence by Vice Chief of Staff Muir S. Fairchild: "Your letter of 12 December 1949 expressed your concern about the defensive aspects of your stations, and the combat units based on them,"[39] a reference to LeMay's expressed apprehension of Soviet subterfuge. With regard to LeMay's proposal for the establishment of a policy of preemptive attack, Vandenberg informed LeMay that "I will discuss with you personally your ideas as set forth in the next to last paragraph of your letter."[40] What was eventually said between Vandenberg and LeMay is unknown. What is known is that LeMay continued to push for some sort of policy of preemption. In the meantime, national policy evolved as well.

NSC-68

In the spring of 1950 the National Security Council (NSC), the body responsible for advising the president on matters related to national security, completed a document that came to shape U.S. Cold War policy. Entitled NSC-68, this document was intended to clearly identify the Soviet Union as the enemy and to establish that some sort of military solution to the problem had to be undertaken. LeMay's efforts at SAC dovetailed with those actions called for under NSC-68.

In his 1980 joint article with one of the principal authors of the document, Paul Nitze, historian John Lewis Gaddis stated that "NSC-68 represented something new in the American political-military experience: It was nothing less than an attempt to set down in the unforgiving medium of cold type a comprehensive statement of what United States national security policy should be."[41] What Gaddis did not address was that within the singularly most vital element of the military during the early Cold War, SAC, actions were already being taken to do something about the perceived threat from the Soviet Union. For his part, Nitze, in speaking of World War II and its aftermath, argued that "the United States had won a tremendous war at great cost, even if at less real cost than suffered by any of the other participants. Although the country was returning successfully to domestic prosperity, international developments appeared exceedingly ominous. There was a feeling that the United States was losing the peace."[42]

It was a cost that LeMay certainly understood, having lost many of his airmen in the skies over Europe and the Pacific. The experience of combat during World War II heavily colored his perception of what peace and war meant. In LeMay's case, however, losing the peace meant something different than what Nitze proposed; for the general, it was a more narrowly defined question of being ready during a perceived period of peace for the time when, undoubtedly, war would shatter the quiet. Nitze stated that "it is untrue to claim that we [the authors of NSC-68] thought the Russians were about to attack."[43] LeMay clearly did not share the authors' sentiments on the subject.

The Joint Chiefs of Staff unanimously endorsed NSC-68 and sent it to President Harry S. Truman on April 17, 1950.[44] The approval of NSC-68 was a tacit vindication of the steps LeMay had already taken—or would take—in readying SAC for war. It was also a de facto nod to LeMay's fears. From the military's perspective, the Soviet Union clearly was the enemy, and something had to be done about it. LeMay's thinking was in line with the larger policy movement being orchestrated in Washington in 1950. He was not the only one in the U.S. national security apparatus who was concerned. In many ways, NSC-68 set the stage for the arms race and general competition between the United States and the Soviet Union that came to define the Cold War. What the authors of NSC-68 did not directly acknowledge was that LeMay was already preparing to be a key actor in this potentially destructive and deadly play.

Commanders Conference

In April 1950 LeMay used a commanders conference, a periodic meeting of the Air Force's senior staff and major command leaders, as a forum in which to again raise his concerns about pre-emptive strikes against the Soviet Union. The conference served as a coordinating meeting, whereby policy guidance could be given by senior military and civilian officials within the Air Force to those commanders whose responsibility it was to carry that policy out. Commanders conferences also were a roundtable for airing grievances and proposing new ideas about Air Force doctrine, strategy, and operations. On April 26 LeMay took full advantage of the opportunity afforded him. One of his subordinates, Brig. Gen. John B. Montgomery, made the initial presentation, an explanation of SAC's role in a nuclear war.[45] What followed Montgomery's presentation further illuminated the issues LeMay had raised to Vandenberg concerning a preemptive strategy. Offering thoughts on SAC's nuclear role and some of the weaknesses he saw in the ability of the command to perform its mission, LeMay turned to "the future."[46] He began with an indication that "Vandenberg has raised the point that our loss of monopoly in atomic weapons has serious implications on our plans for national security. I would like to tell you how severely it affects the Strategic Air Command mission."[47] Clearly, the Soviet acquisition of nuclear weapons had a significant impact upon the command's plans, and that reality drove the shaping of future operations and plans at SAC; LeMay exploited the issue and used it as an opportunity to further his advocacy of a preemptive strike policy. But as he had done with Vandenberg, LeMay first needed to appropriately set the stage to make his argument about the necessity of a preemptive policy: "As the Soviet stockpile grows and their capability to deliver that stockpile grows, there comes a time when the entire picture changes radically. It is about this period and what we must do about it that I would like to say a few words."[48]

LeMay then argued that once the Soviets had amassed enough weapons to launch a sufficiently large nuclear strike against the United States, the nation would "no longer have military superiority as we know it today. The enemy, even though possessing fewer bombs than we may have, will have enough either to destroy our striking force or the major cities of this country or both."[49] He pointed out that the Air Force's plans for the air defense of the nation against such an attack would be limited in utility and that "the proposed air defense can only reduce the damage inflicted upon us. It certainly cannot eliminate all of the damage to us by a long shot."[50]

But LeMay had a plan in mind. He turned to a report released by the Joint Chiefs, citing an argument that once relative nuclear parity had been reached, the nation that initiated a nuclear strike, under conditions of surprise, would likely benefit greatly in a war.[51] This was the logic behind LeMay's belief in the necessity for preemptive action in the case of an impending Soviet attack. In citing the Joint Chiefs' report, LeMay established the logical imperative for preemption before the group of officials whose support he needed for the strategy he was intent upon carrying out. LeMay continued: "In other words, unless we take steps now that are not presently programmed, we are pretty apt to lose the next war. In my mind, we now face a basic change in our concept."[52] The change that LeMay was about to propose, in this top secret forum of peers and superiors, mirrored the sentiments he had shared in his letter to Vandenberg. Now with the Air Force Chief of Staff, Secretary Finletter, and others assembled before him, LeMay argued that the changes he sought required that "we must not only plan to destroy the enemy industrial power but we must be capable at the same time of destroying his force before it destroys us."[53]

LeMay continued with a frank assessment of critical problems in the pursuit of preemption as a possible solution to the Soviet threat, eventually admitting that "we are a long way from possessing the capability of destroying the Soviet striking force. . . . As General [Charles] Cabell stated, there is so little intelligence available on that force today as to its size and location that it is not possible to estimate what we can do about it."[54] Nonetheless, LeMay anticipated a resolution and noted that "from our experience in building an atomic striking force, we know that sensitive spots do exist which, if attacked, would drastically reduce the striking power. . . . As a matter of fact, we believe that a well-planned attack based on sound intelligence might well eliminate that threat. Not only am I thinking of aircraft, but I am thinking of sites like Able, Baker, and Charlie."[55] LeMay then brought up the next problem: "In addition to our intelligence shortcomings today, too small a portion of our striking force has sufficient range to enable us to strike promptly from this country without deploying to forward bases."[56]

Though LeMay had introduced some curious and acute issues related to the question of preemption, he was undeterred, saying that regardless of "weaknesses on our part, I am convinced that we have no alternative. We must achieve the capability of destroying the enemy's long-range striking force."[57] LeMay concluded by urging national leaders to "re-examine present policies which imply that we must absorb the first atomic blow."[58] In LeMay's mind, there was no sense in waiting to be the recipient of a nuclear attack; a first strike was the best option.

LeMay's advocacy for a policy of preemptive attack during the April 1950 commanders conference was certain in its meaning. He had expressed similar thoughts to Vandenberg in his December

1949 letter, and it was highly likely that the SAC commander's recounting of comparable ideas at the commanders conference implied some degree of acceptance by Vandenberg of the concepts LeMay proposed. If Vandenberg had any concerns about LeMay's ability to appropriately carry out set national policy objectives in light of his comments at the commanders conference—namely, deterrence and retaliation—he surely would have relieved him of his command. Instead, LeMay's ongoing command of SAC and Vandenberg's apparent confidence in him indicated a degree of de facto consent to his ideas. Subsequent events only steeled LeMay's concerns.

6.25: Getting Ready

While the detonation of Joe One provided a reason to fear the Soviets, the communist invasion of South Korea brought those fears into vivid relief for LeMay and others in the nation's defense establishment. In truth, Joe One and the North Korean invasion did not dramatically alter the actual balance of international power. They did, however, suggest to the Americans that the momentum of that balance was shifting toward international communism and led to efforts to at least stabilize that balance— if not swing the momentum more favorably for the United States. These actions aided in the implementation of paranoid, but generally benevolently intended, deeds that came to define the duration of the Cold War. Behind many of these actions was Curtis LeMay. Had the Korean War not occurred, LeMay might not have come into his own as a postwar personality and leader, and, perhaps, the Cold War would not have become the conflict generations knew it to be. The Korean War was essential to LeMay—as was LeMay to the Cold War. In this sense, North Korea's invasion fostered a strategic defeat for communism.

The communist invasion of South Korea on June 25, 1950, known in the country as 6.25, was a shocking event. The march of North Korean forces into South Korea represented what many in the United States believed was the first strike in a larger war. For LeMay, such meant a nuclear war with the Soviet Union. He was as surprised as anyone by the timing and place of the invasion. In the days and weeks before the invasion, LeMay's office diary indicated no particular concern of coming military action, though it did contain an interesting reference to an aerial mishap in which he was involved. The entry from May 25–26 indicated LeMay was on an aircraft that performed an undesired overflight of the area near the White House after departure from Bolling Air Force Base. This overflight occurred despite the fact that LeMay warned air traffic controllers about it.[59] Apparently in late May LeMay was more worried about drawing the ire of the White House than he was about a potential conflict in a distant corner of the world. In the period that followed the invasion, however, everything changed.

The days after the invasion were filled with a degree of panic and a number of critical decisions that exposed LeMay's general sense of fear. They also showcased his relationships with other key Air Force personalities. LeMay's office diary reported that at 4 a.m. on June 25:

North Korean forces declared war on South Korea and attacked all along the 38 parallel. This situation has been greeted very seriously by the U.S. and the President of the U.S. has returned from a vacation in Missouri to give his personal attention to the problem. In the U.S. the Air Defense command has ordered its activities on a 24 hour alert basis and has dispersed several of there [*sic*] units to locations such as Chicago, Cleveland Bangor Maine etc and has ordered all unidentified aircraft to be intercepted and forced to land if entering the U.S. from the North, East or West or from Ocean areas. SAC agencies have been alerted for special security precautions.[60]

As the diary revealed, provisions were made for potential military activity by actors other than North Korea, which had no ability to attack the United States with its own air force; the alerting of Air Defense Command to possible airspace intrusions was preparation for something well beyond a North Korean attack, which, particularly from the east of the United States, would have been a practical impossibility. The United States feared the Soviet Union and a general war, and LeMay wasted little time getting ready.

At 6 p.m. on June 25, LeMay convened "a meeting of his staff heads at his home" on Offutt Air Force Base near Omaha, Nebraska, for the purpose of discussing the events taking place in Korea. After the meeting, he phoned his subordinated numbered Air Force commanders, those individuals who would have been responsible for carrying out SAC war plans had the order been given. According to LeMay's office diary, he "told them to read the papers, tighten up base security, and be ready for any eventuality."[61] If war was coming, LeMay had no intention of being caught unprepared. To LeMay's credit as a commander, his directive was uncomplicated and straightforward. He left it to his subordinates to figure out what to do next with their individual commands. There was probably little doubt in the minds of his numbered Air Force commanders as to what potential eventualities LeMay referred to.

For LeMay, the invasion of South Korea was the tocsin of the larger conflict with communism and, ultimately, the Soviet Union, for which he had been waiting. With communist forces spilling over the border between the two Koreas, LeMay's fear appeared to be evolving into reality. On June 26 the final item in LeMay's office diary reported that the "latest info on the Korean situation indicates that the capital SEOUL is about to fall in the face of heavy tank attacks. The govt claims American aide [*sic*] was to[o] little and to[o] late."[62] Things were not looking good for the nominally democratic south and its U.S. backers. In the fight between communist and democratic states, it appeared the West was about to receive its first defeat.

Early on June 27, LeMay was briefed on the events in Korea. His papers reported there was word that according "to all indications the situation is improving in the Seoul area" and that the South Korean government had "decided not to move there [*sic*] Headquarters."[63] This bit of good news did not stand the test of time, however. Eventually, Seoul fell, the North Korean military occupied the city, and the South Korean government moved south. For his part, LeMay had no intention of finding his command or country in the same predicament as the South Korean government and military, and he had begun taking steps to prepare SAC for what he assumed was coming next.

SAC was the primary U.S. nuclear force in the early 1950s, but it did not have custody of the very weapons it, and especially LeMay, was intent on delivering if the need arose. Rather, custody of nuclear weapons was entrusted to the Atomic Energy Commission (AEC), a civilian agency that was the successor to the Manhattan Project of World War II. This arrangement came about following the end of war and the dropping of nuclear weapons on the Japanese cities of Hiroshima and Nagasaki. Recognizing the unique power of nuclear weapons, the United States chose to invest control of those weapons in the hands of civilians and not the military. Had the decision been made to launch a nuclear attack, SAC would have first needed to take custody of the weapons from the civilian authorities at the AEC and then mate the weapons with the aircraft. This procedural separation, which ensured the weapons were released to military control only under the proper authorities, created a logjam in the process by which attack sorties would have been launched. It also meant that if enemy action impeded or prevented the transmission of orders from Washington to release the stockpile to LeMay, no nuclear attack would have taken place. It was the perfect operational bottleneck; it was also a point of paranoia and frustration for LeMay.

On the afternoon of June 27, 1950, just two days after the beginning of the war in Korea, LeMay held an important meeting at Offutt attended by some key players from SAC and Headquarters Air Force, as well as the commander of the Sandia Missile Base near Albuquerque, Gen. Robert Montague. Montague was also associated with the Armed Forces Special Weapons Project, the agency responsible for military aspects of nuclear weapons operations not directly associated with combat. While a meeting between these parties might not have drawn significant attention under normal circumstances, the outbreak of hostilities in Korea and the fear of a larger war did suggest something important was at hand. LeMay's records from that day only indicated that the "main subject of the meeting [was] to

Bring Montinque [*sic*] up to date on any alternate plans that we may have to meet the situation in Korea."[64] A subsequent memorandum, however, provided more detail concerning the meeting and the larger purpose behind it. It also offered some insight into the fear LeMay experienced at the time—and the lengths to which it drove him.

Approximately three weeks later, on July 20, LeMay met with Gen. Delmar Spivey, chief of plans for the Air Force deputy chief of staff for operations. During this meeting, LeMay explained an arrangement he had made on June 27 with General Montague. According to a memorandum for record written by LeMay's chief of staff, Maj. Gen. August "Augie" Kissner, LeMay had crafted with Montague a plan to secure the release of nuclear weapons to SAC without explicit authorization "in the event that Washington was destroyed before we had received word to execute our war plan."[65]

According to LeMay's plan, in the event that Washington, DC, was destroyed, "in the absence of communications with the alternate Headquarters USAF, Mitchel Field, General LeMay would contact General Montague, identifying himself by a system of code words and attain release of the bombs to our bombardment crews."[66] In other words, the U.S. nuclear response could have occurred without the approval of the nation's political leadership. Remarkably, the arrangement between LeMay and Montague had apparently been concluded without the prior knowledge or approval of LeMay's superior, Chief of Staff Hoyt Vandenberg, any of the civilian leadership of the AEC, or the president. In effect, LeMay had, on his own, circumvented the procedures of civilian control and custody. Per Kissner's memorandum, "General LeMay told General Spivey that he considered it important that General Vandenberg recognize and approve the arrangement he had effected with General Montague."[67] While "General Spivey approved the arrangement made," Spivey "stated that he would endeavor to bring the arrangement to the attention of General Vandenberg."[68] According to Kissner, Spivey "implied that although he could see the desirability of such approval, he did not believe joint approval was either necessary or desirable."[69] Whether Vandenberg ever learned of the specifics of this arrangement is not clear, based on the historical record.

The implications of LeMay's agreement with Montague were meaningful. Not only had LeMay avoided the edicts that governed the custody of nuclear weapons, but he had also established, in effect, predelegated authority for the execution of a nuclear war. Had a war begun and LeMay's plan gone into effect, the outcome could have resulted in the deaths of millions and would have been the most significant national security decision in U.S. history—all without prior approval of the nation's civilian authorities. The fear that drove LeMay's decision to undertake such an agreement must have been intense. Had Vandenberg or the White House learned of the agreement and not found it acceptable, a political firestorm could have erupted that would have shaken the entire government and paralleled the nuclear one LeMay was worried he may not be able to deliver.

Weapons custody was a recurring theme for LeMay. Referring to the problem in a June 30 letter to Vandenberg, LeMay pointed out that "the current international crisis together with the Soviet development of atomic weapons highlights a major weakness in our planning for the atomic offensive. I refer to the process by which the execution of such an air offensive might be ordered and *the necessary atomic weapons made available to me*" [emphasis added].

. . . the authority to launch the atomic offensive must be disseminated concurrently through two different channels—the Atomic Energy Commission and the United States Air Force."[70] LeMay then warned Vandenberg that "if either of the chains of command is disrupted, the offensive would be delayed. Every day that passes makes more possible the total destruction of Washington by several atomic bombs or a single hydrogen bomb, leaving our nation temporarily without top level direction."[71] Interestingly, LeMay's mention of a hydrogen weapon preceded the actual development and fielding of such a weapon by either the United States or the Soviet Union and indicated a potential gap in U.S. intelligence as to Soviet capabilities.

LeMay concluded his letter to Vandenberg by pointing out that "regarding the release of atomic bombs, it would appear that a positive system could be established which would insure that a deputized Atomic Energy Commission representative on the spot would release bombs at my personal request unless he received from higher authority specific instructions to the contrary."[72] What LeMay did not tell Vandenberg was that he had already put into place such an agreement.

The surprise and exigencies of the early days of the Korean War captured the general sense of fear and paranoia that gripped the U.S. military and LeMay, particularly since the detonation of Joe One. Though LeMay had believed that a war was coming even before the Soviets acquired their first nuclear weapon, the combined effect of these events pushed LeMay's concern to a higher level. The more immediate and pragmatic issues related to Korea took a lion's share of his time and attention, but LeMay did not lose sight of what he saw as his singularly most important mission and concern. The fight to protect his command's ability to fight a broader nuclear war became LeMay's greatest battle for the remainder of the year, if not for the balance of the Korean War.

Launching the Fleet

One challenge LeMay faced in building and retaining the combat capability of SAC was the unwanted dispersal of assets from his command in response to events in Korea. LeMay, like other senior Air Force officers of the period, understood the importance of SAC and its mission to the overall defense of the United States. Building the command to support that mission and objective was challenge enough; defending it against degradation at the hands of a regional war was another concern altogether.

The Korean War left the United States in a difficult position. As the leader of the democratic world, it could not sit idly by and do nothing in the face of the North Korean invasion; at the same time, it initially possessed an insufficient conventional capability for halting or repelling the onslaught. Beyond these immediate concerns, the United States also faced the fear that a broader war was on the horizon. Historian Walton Moody notes that "the global implications of the Korean war were evident from the outset. Not only did Kim's [North Korean leader Kim Il Sung] regime bear all the earmarks of a Soviet satellite with a Soviet-trained army, but the attack probably had at least [Joseph] Stalin's tacit approval."[73] To be certain, both the immediacy of the fight in Korea and the broader fear of a war with the Soviet Union doubtless drew the potential use of nuclear weapons into the milieu of possibilities. No matter what shape those possibilities took or the purpose of their being leveraged, LeMay and SAC were certain to be involved—both as a weapon and as an implied threat.

Though closely (and at times infamously) associated with nuclear weapons and even known as an advocate for their use, LeMay was not the first to propose the deployment of nuclear weapons to Asia. Historian Conrad Crane noted that LeMay had failed to win a "battle to prevent the deployment of ten nuclear-capable B-29s of the Ninth Bombardment Wing to Guam in addition to the 98th and 307th Groups, the first prepositioning of such potential in the Far East" and that the Joint Chiefs of Staff "first examined the use of atomic weapons in Korea in early July." Crane points to the belief that "in a foreshadowing of things to come, this initial discussion may have been a result of the prodding of Gen. Dwight Eisenhower."[74] Though in agreement on many issues, particularly later when Eisenhower became president, LeMay and the well-respected general had a difference of opinion on this point. The driving force behind LeMay's interest in not seeing nuclear-capable bombers deployed was rather simple: bombers playing a regional role were unavailable to prepare for, deter, or participate in the war for which they were actually intended.

Transcripts of phone conversations between LeMay and other senior Air Force officers revealed interesting details about the decision to send SAC bombers to the Pacific and the process for doing so, LeMay's objections and his rationale for them, and the complexity of deploying these aircraft. In the years before twenty-four-hour nuclear alert in SAC, the procedures for executing plans for war were more amorphous and less formal; these calls provided a level of visibility on how the decision to go to war would have filtered to the forces that would have fought it and the likely confusion that would have buffeted the process. In a certain sense, they offered a window into how the Cold War would have become a hot one.

On July 1, 1950, five days after the start of the war, LeMay had a call with Gen. Roger Ramey, a senior officer associated with servicewide operations for the Air Force. Ramey informed LeMay that "we have just gotten a directive to send ten of your standard mediums, that are not specially trig modified, that will hurt you the least." With LeMay acknowledging this, Ramey said that he would need to send along "full crews plus the 30 day mobilization, I mean fly away business." Ramey's reference to the aircraft not being "specially trig modified" meant they were not equipped with the special triggers needed to employ nuclear weapons. This meant the first batch of aircraft deployed was not even intended to be nuclear capable and, at best, could serve as an insubstantial bluff of such intent. It also meant that LeMay's nuclear war plan would not be degraded, though his overall war plan and force would be infringed upon. At the same time, Ramey's directive that the package being sent include the components needed for "30 day mobilization" and "fly away business" meant that it would include the maintenance material needed to operate from a forward location for a more extended period. This was to be an issue that LeMay did not let pass lightly, and it was a major point of discussion during a subsequent call that day.[75]

At this juncture, however, LeMay began to ask questions and became a bit agitated, asking, "Now, do you want to send just that number or a unit?" to which Ramey replied, "No, send only that number and not a unit for various political reasons at the moment." LeMay responded with an interesting comment: "Well, we are doing just exactly what we shouldn't do, Roger, you know that?" Ramey responded, "I agree with you. However, that particular point was brought up and argued out." What exactly LeMay saw wrong in this proposition was unclear. Most likely, he either did not want to destroy unit integrity by deploying only part of an organization, or he was concerned about the overall degradation of SAC's ability to carry out its major war plan and did not want to jeopardize it by having to support a regional war. LeMay's previously expressed fear over a larger conflict on the heels of the Korean invasion gave some credence to the latter supposition. Nonetheless, LeMay smartly replied, "O.K.—To be there yesterday, I suppose?" Even in this seemingly dire situation, LeMay's characteristically witty humor came out.[76]

After some discussion of which unit forces would be drawn from, Ramey reassured LeMay, "Now I will again present your views on the unit proposition, but they have been presented but we were told that the political and other considerations at the moment were against that." This was not LeMay's only concern going into this mission; he raised another issue, asking Ramey, "Now, are we going to get replacements on these people?" Ramey explained to the SAC commander, "Just as soon as we can, yes," prompting LeMay to ask, "What do you mean by that?" Ramey responded, "Well, I mean that that will be asked for immediately because the result of taking them is realized. There has been some money available to get them out of storage, so that shouldn't present any particular problem." Then, in a comment emblematic of LeMay and his priorities, he told Ramey he was "wondering more about people than airplanes," to which Ramey replied, "Yes, I know you are, and we will certainly follow that through as fast as we can, and concurrent with this request."[77]

Later on July 1, LeMay had a call with Gen. Richard Nugent, the acting deputy chief of staff for personnel for the Air Force. In this role, Nugent was responsible for overall personnel policy and management in the Air Force and was one of the individuals most able to help LeMay in both caring for his people and getting the replacements he had told Ramey he wanted. Though personnel issues were the purpose for LeMay's call to Nugent, other issues made their way into the conversation, as LeMay explained to Nugent that "we are sending out ten crews. Of course, I object violently to this frittering away of our effort. We can do this, of course, but we are afraid it isn't going to be the last."[78] LeMay's remarks suggest why he was concerned with deploying crews to support operations over Korea. It is nearly impossible that LeMay had an organic aversion to backing up U.S. forces engaged on the peninsula. Instead, and as his further comments revealed, LeMay's concern was related to his fear that the loss of the assets would impact his command's ability carry out its "effort," the larger mission of deterring and, more specifically, bombing the Soviet Union. In this instance, and in a larger sense—despite the intense paranoia that was filling the military and government following the start of the Korean War—LeMay remained focused on his overarching, strategic task.

The conversation returned to core personnel issues, with LeMay asking Nugent, "Now, can you give us replacements for these people right now, order them in to MacDill Field so that we can get transition on them so that we can recover as quickly as possible?"[79] Nugent responded, "I will look into that and see exactly what I can do and let you know, Curt."[80] Hackles raised, the SAC commander responded: "You mean you haven't thought of it up until now? Who was in on the deal on this anyway when they decided to send these people?" to which Nugent responded, "Well I haven't been in on it yet." LeMay shot back, "Well, can you give me an answer, Dick?"[81] Nugent replied, "Well, I will have to go down to Ramey and see what this is all about first, and then see what it is. I haven't heard about it yet."[82] LeMay explained to Nugent—again making the point about the degradation of SAC's greater mission—"Well, what's happening is Strat [Lt. Gen. George E. Stratemeyer, commander of Far East Air Forces] wants help and we are sending ten crews. Now when we do, we just fritter away our striking force."[83]

LeMay continued his petition in a similar call with Lauris Norstad, deputy chief of staff for operations and acting vice chief of staff of the Air Force. The call with Norstad summed up LeMay's concerns and fears about where the issue was headed. LeMay stated that "[Ramey] told me that everything had been argued out. I just wondered if Van [Hoyt Vandenberg] knows that we can fritter away this force pretty quickly. Is this going to be the last or not?"[84] LeMay echoed his worry about the force he commanded being hurt by the piecemeal deployment of assets to a secondary conflict, apparently hoping his sentiments would be shared by the chief of staff. Without directly answering his question—perhaps not wanting to go on record with LeMay on the issue or suspecting what was to come— Norstad offered that "there is the one thing that has got to be done and that is build that thing up to strength and keep it there, otherwise we are going to forfeit that unit out there, and we don't want to do that, we don't want to do that. This is the cheapest way out of it and the most effective. . . . I talked to Van last night. We don't want to send a group out there. We don't want to send a squadron out there."[85] LeMay curtly replied, "You are ruining a Group, and by taking the fly-away kit. Why do they have to have that?" Norstad pled ignorance, and additional discussion ensued.[86] LeMay returned to the issue of further deployment of his command and revealed the depth of his anxiety, again bluntly asking Norstad whether he was "going to call on us any more then?"[87] Again taking the middle road, Norstad stated, "Not unless the situation changes."[88] The point of the conversation was clear: LeMay did not want his forces to go, but he was not going to be relieved of the mission by anyone on the air staff, and there was nowhere else to feasibly lodge an appeal.[89] The war was officially on for SAC.

Turning Point

This period in LeMay's career, and for the Air Force in general, was one of chaos and being on the defensive on many levels. The lack of achieved standards in the command, of depth of employable resources, and of custody of the very weapons that defined the service's purpose were all problems that needed resolution, which fell to LeMay. Having to safeguard SAC's assets from being diverted to other missions and the country from a larger onslaught, both the Air Force and SAC were stuck in response mode. In the months that followed, changes began that continued throughout the balance of LeMay's tenure at SAC.

02

When It Became Real

Although SAC's war in Korea was under way, the "real" war with the Soviet Union that LeMay feared remained a threat. The planning and preparation for this war that had been ongoing in the first year and a half of LeMay's tenure at SAC took on new life following the North Korean attack. From mid-1950 to the end of 1951, LeMay faced myriad challenges in turning the command into an organization physically ready for and capable of fighting a nuclear war. Although rectifying the basic policy and management problems that SAC faced was important, LeMay was concurrently making preparations to carry out a nuclear war in the immediate future. As a result, the operational details of what a nuclear war between the Soviet Union and the United States during the early 1950s would have looked like were exposed. Despite being beset by repeated concerns that fell outside his initial interests for the transformation of the command in the fashion he imagined, LeMay was able to proceed as planned.

A Time for War

Late on the morning of July 10, LeMay received a phone call from Norstad to inform him of some developments. During the call,

Norstad told LeMay, "Reference my redline to you this morning . . . Item 1 on that redline . . . Chiefs approved item 1 this morning and the item has gone up from here. The Secretary is doing all he can to get the thing approved immediately, but you will just have to wait." LeMay responded that "the delay already has cost us one day and I think we should tell the units to start take off Wednesday morning now. . . . Approve this if you will." LeMay explained to Norstad that he had issued a "field order" and had "approved another" and that he "would like to put this [the item under discussion] in there [*sic*] hands and then tell them which one to execute." Norstad approved this proposal, but LeMay was told to "keep the distribution down to a minimum" and to "be sure that no PIO [public information officer] release gets out." The subject under discussion was not for public knowledge. As the conversation wound down, LeMay made a final entreaty with Norstad and drove home "the necessity for speed on the decision as the units are already delayed one day and if they don't get the word soon it will be more."[1] LeMay wanted to be ready for something.

Although notes on the call were cryptic, some clarity about what the two generals discussed could be divined from the context of the call and discussions that followed. In LeMay's office diary entries from that day, deployments, specific units, and even the number of bombs to be used in a war with the Soviet Union were noted. One entry on the status of LeMay's aide-de-camp and whether he was to move to another job exposed the real issue weighing on LeMay's mind that day. The determination was made that "if war comes now you [the aide] will stay for duty until such time as the Atomic Offensive is over and we can catch our breath, if the thing diddles around until August or Sept we will get a replacement in and allow him to spend three or four months getting ready and then send you to unit."[2] Given world events and the nature of the conversation, Norstad and LeMay were likely discussing operational planning for war.

That afternoon, LeMay held a meeting in his office to discuss recent modifications to SAC's nuclear war plan in light of the world situation. According to LeMay's office diary, the meeting began with his director of plans, Walter Sweeney, pointing out that "no change from the present War plan should be made until such time a[s] the units in the field had a chance to look the plan over and get there [sic] detailed instructions out to the units and to the crews. This he [Sweeney] estimated would take some thirty days after the plan was approved at this level." A description of some of the details ensued: "Under the new plan the Far East now in possession of the 22 and 92nd BG [bomb groups] would be augmented by 10 Bomb Carriers from the 9th Wing and would [be] operated against those targets in that area from Okinawa."[3] The discussion continued:

In the UK would be the presently planned 301st, 93rd and 97th BGs with the 31st fighter unit. . . . In the Goose Bay [Canada] area would be the 43rd Bomb Group with 40 tankers at Goose and one Bomb Squadron, and two Bomb Squadrons at Harmon field [Canada]. They would operate against Leningrad from Goose and land in the North African theatre for future operations. . . . The B-36s from Ft Worth [probably Carswell AFB] 14 in number would [be] operated from Ft Worth direct to Moscow and land in the UK or as alternate [and] were time available deploy to Limestone and operate from there. . . . The 509th [Bomb Group] with 40 tankers and 3 Bomb Squadrons would deploy to the Azores and Santa Maria for there [sic]

operations against the targets they are now assigned. . . .
The command post for the first strike under these conditions would be in Omaha and after the first strike would
move to Port Liodi [Port Lyautey, Morocco] for continued effort. . . . An alternate command post will be set up
in the UK on case operations are centered there. . . . Gen
[Emmett] Odonnell in the Pacific and Gen [Thomas]
Power would move on the initial advon [advance team]
to the Port Liodi [Lyautey] area with Gen LeMay holding in Omaha for the initial strike. . . . This is a prelimi-
nary plan and will be firmed up and taken to Washington
next Friday morning. . . . Port Liodi [Port Lyautey] This
plan minus the 509th Bomb Group will place approx 80
Bombs on the target.[4]

The details of the SAC plan for a war with the Soviet Union that
the meeting revealed were significant in several regards. While the
discussion was terse, the gravity of the information was immense.
It offered a rare and vivid glimpse into the mechanics of a potential nuclear war in the early 1950s—the assets involved, basing,
command and control, targets, and weapons.

Though a large portion of the modified SAC bomber and
tanker force would have been forward based in Europe under the
proposed plan, the meeting notes revealed that some of the strike
force was based in the continental United States. LeMay and SAC
placed their trust in the B-36 intercontinental bomber to strike
the crucial target of Moscow. This proposal brought some clarity to questions about SAC's confidence in the B-36. LeMay and
his staff had little doubt about the ability of the politically dis-
puted bomber, which was assigned one of the most critical targets,

to achieve its mission. For the majority of the force, however, a nuclear raid against the Soviet Union meant a somewhat shorter flight. This was particularly the case for forces stationed in the United Kingdom and, to a lesser degree, those being launched from Atlantic islands and Canada. The basing of SAC forces represented a solution to the quandary faced by early war planners. On the one hand, SAC was forced to forward base units on account of the limited range of the majority of aircraft then in its bomber and tanker force (another result of which was shorter flight times to targets); on the other hand, it wanted the greatest assurance possible that neither sabotage nor a preemptive/preventive Soviet attack would suddenly disarm the command—hence a desire for basing in the continental United States. At the same time, domestic posting eliminated the complicated diplomatic requirements that accompanied overseas deployment of nuclear weapons. What resulted was a relatively balanced lay-down plan.

Command and control of nuclear forces, an enduring theme for SAC throughout the Cold War, was not neglected in SAC's modified war plan. In his book *Command and Control*, Eric Schlosser wrote that "one of LeMay's greatest concerns was the command and control of nuclear weapons—the system of rules and procedures that guided his men, the network of radars and sensors and communications lines that allowed information to travel back and forth between headquarters and the field, the mechanisms that prevented accidental detonations and permitted deliberate ones, all of it designed to make sure that orders could be properly given, received, and carried out."[5] LeMay's approach demonstrated that he understood from early in the nuclear era that being able to adequately effect command and control over nuclear weapons would both engender the successful execution of the mission and prevent their inadvertent use. This latter issue was a major concern, particularly in the early days of the Cold War, to both the nation's military and its political leadership. Regarding nuclear weapons, President Harry S. Truman reportedly said that he did not want "to have some dashing lieutenant colonel decide when would be the proper time to drop one."[6] Though the meeting offered little detail regarding specific command and control processes other than a possible location shift of poststrike headquarters, the information about the location of command and control hubs offered some definition of how the process was intended to evolve. The initial basing of LeMay's command and control headquarters in Omaha suggested a desire to either bury the command as far inside U.S. territory as imaginable in an effort to avoid or at least slow the impact of a Soviet strike or to keep LeMay as close to his supporting staff as possible (or both). In any case, SAC headquarters would be the initial nerve center for the second U.S. nuclear war. For its part, the regional command of overseas forces provided an additional echelon of command and redundancy in case LeMay's Omaha core facility was destroyed. Both of the principles remained essential to SAC operations for the duration of the Cold War.

While the full target set was not discussed, a rough picture of the strike force developed, and some targets were named. A meaningful portion of the forces discussed under the plan focused on striking two of the population centers of the Soviet Union: Leningrad and Moscow.[7] As LeMay's office diary described, a portion of the strike force was to fly nonstop from Texas to bomb Moscow and return to bases in Great Britain.[8] In striking the Soviet capital, LeMay's forces would not only stand to kill a great number of Soviet citizens but also to potentially eliminate a mass of Soviet political and military leaders. While the document did not make clear the exact purpose of striking Leningrad and Moscow, such attacks would have continued LeMay's controversial approach to war by targeting cities—as had been the case with his firebombing of Japanese cities during World War II.

Though not specifically spoken of as atomic or nuclear weapons, the mention of the "plan minus the 509th Bomb Group will place approx 80 Bombs on the target" likely referred to nuclear weapons.[9] Interestingly, timing of the strike from beginning to end was not discussed; however, based on the discussion of recovery bases, these eighty bombs were probably to be dropped in a single onslaught. Compared to the contemporary size and scale of the U.S. nuclear arsenal, the SAC arsenal of 1950 appears somewhat quaint. Nonetheless, eighty atomic weapons, even if marginally stronger in power than those used against Japan in 1945, represented a catastrophic force if employed. Whether it would force Soviet capitulation could not be reliably said.

Finally, it was clear that SAC's plan for nuclear war was not quite a robust one, though the command's leaders and planning process could dynamically respond to changes in the international situation. This response indicated a degree of flexibility that later, more rigid plans did not possess—or that the flight times of intercontinental ballistic missiles would permit. At the same time, the SAC staff treated the process with great seriousness, as it was the general belief that the war plan was not an academic exercise; rather, it was a real plan for a real war that, at least in LeMay's mind, was likely to occur. While memories of such seriousness and general tension have faded in the post–Cold War years, the record of this meeting stands as a silent reminder of a time when nuclear war seemed a likely aspect of the near future. Despite all the excitement, however, nuclear war did not come.

Rhetoric Was Reality

The fall of 1950 brought its own series of interesting and important developments for LeMay, though a certain degree of normalcy prevailed. Remaining as focused on the small concerns as the large ones, LeMay conducted a personnel inspection at Offutt on the morning of September 30; his office diary reported that "the troops were in blue uniforms for the first time, and looked good."[10] Few details escaped LeMay.

Another matter that arose days later was one of more immediate operational significance. News on October 2 that challenged the notion of near-invincibility of the SAC force was likely received by LeMay with a mixture of chagrin and disbelief: "A letter received on Operation Whipstock indicates that 50% of the SAC bombers taking part in the exercise were intercepted by ConAC [Continental Air Command] fighters."[11] While some losses were to be expected in such a war game (and in a real assault on the Soviet Union), losses of this magnitude would have crippled the SAC bomber force. That also meant that if the Soviets were able to launch a surprise attack against SAC bases or incapacitate aircraft on the ground through sabotage, even fewer would be able to make it to their target. This information may explain some of LeMay's interest in surprising the Soviets through a preemptive attack.

LeMay was asked directly about a first strike in the context of preventive—not preemptive—war during an interview with Scripps-Howard newspapers on October 20. When asked, "What is your feeling on a preventive war, and do you think it should be discussed with the public now?" LeMay's response was somewhat enigmatic: "Any responsible Air Force officer will not advocate a preventive war, but you do have to risk it and be ready to fight." In a seeming nod to mutual deterrence with the Soviet Union, LeMay continued: "We don't want a war and I don't think Joe [Stalin] does either. I would like to see a stronger Strategic Air Command to give the country stronger bargaining power and a bigger threat against Russia. SAC is what they are afraid of, in my personal opinion. However, the decision on the size of SAC is not mine." After asking some other questions, the reporter returned to the issue of a first strike: "What do you want if not a preventive war?" LeMay's answer portrayed him as an engaged thinker on geopolitical thought and affairs and, more important, as a realist:

> We should have the strength to tell Joe what we want and to tell him to stay where he is. We need to take the offensive and we can do this without actual fighting. I use as an example—I think we should clean up Indo-China after the Korean war, and one way of doing it is to tell the Indo-Chinese who appear to want the French out, "Okay, we are removing the French in about twenty years," and for them to get ready for their independence; using as background the Philippine experience which is now history and shows clearly the non-imperialistic intention of our country.[12]

LeMay's fairly simplistic view of U.S. power spoke volumes for how he saw the world, but his response to another question was more telling of his personality and world view. When asked, "Do you think we will drop our guard after Korea?" LeMay said, "*I am a pessimist at heart* [emphasis added]. After every previous war we have dropped our guard, and I am afraid it will happen again." For LeMay, the world was not a safe place, and the United States needed protection from outside hostile forces—and he was intent upon building SAC in such a fashion as to provide that protection.[13]

———————

Protection and the Protector

The nation was not alone in needing guarding. LeMay's personal protection became an item of interest the following month. On November 1 LeMay's chief of staff, Augie Kissner, spoke via telephone with Air Force vice chief of staff Gen. Nathan Twining. Based upon this call, "a project to increase the personal security of the commanding general was initiated," though it is unclear what prompted the move. LeMay's aide-de-camp, Maj. Paul Carlton, himself later a four-star general, was put in charge of the program; Cpl. L. G. Simmons was assigned to protect LeMay.[14] A November 6 memorandum by Carlton revealed that the decision was made "in accordance with verbal directions of the Chief of Staff, United States Air Force [General Vandenberg], on 1 November 1950." The increased security ranged from "the Commanding General, Aide-de-Camp, Military Secretary, Driver and Personal Guard" being "armed at all times" to having "a perimeter guard detail . . . provided for the Commanding General's quarters," as well as other measures. Whatever the reasoning behind it, LeMay, while likely a target in any nuclear war with the Soviet Union, became a heavily guarded man in relative peace.[15] LeMay's office diary reported that he and his wife, Helen, "attended a social function in Omaha at the Pettis residence" on the evening of November 6, which tested some elements of the new security program. The diary reported it was a success and that "no unusual incidents occurred."[16] Intriguingly, LeMay's office diary from November 8 reported that there was a "meeting again today between Col Thompson [Office of Special Investigations] and the Aide to revise some of the current directives concerning the security of the CG [commanding general] . . . Believe that all will be well on the matter and a lot of heat has come off the project at present." Whatever threat had started the whole operation was not as concerning as it had been on November 1.

While LeMay may have been personally safer for the moment, events in Korea gave those at SAC headquarters cause for concern. LeMay's office diary from November 28 recorded that "the news this morning is very disturbing. The Korean battle is going badly and the Chinese have made mincemeat out of our latest attack. Gen [Douglas MacArthur] stated that conditions were out of control and the next move was up to the diplomats."[17] That same day, LeMay's head of plans phoned from Washington to tell of "a feeling of pessimism there on our progress in North Korea and a growing feeling that[t] we may have to send more units to the Far East to bolster the [Air Force] there."[18] There was a belief in the ability of SAC to influence results in Korea. To achieve those results, however, the discussion at SAC led to the subject of nuclear escalation. On December 3 LeMay's office diary reported that "the CG and deputy were in closed door sessions all day long most likely over the proper strategy for the use of the atomic bomb in the Far East."[19] Concerns over the course of the war in Korea were again an overriding issue in LeMay's daily affairs.

Even this concern was eclipsed on the morning of December 6. Nathan Twining phoned SAC to order LeMay "into Washington for an emergency meeting. Five minutes after this call came in, a special alert was sounded by ConAC [Continental Air Command]

with a radar plot at a point east of Limestone [Maine]; 40 unidentified [aircraft] flying at 40,000 Ft." In response to what undoubtedly appeared to be an incoming mass of enemy aircraft, LeMay
dispersed the SAC fleet—a measure that complicated an attacker's
ability to destroy the command's means to wage war by putting SAC
aircraft out of harm's way, as much as possible—and then departed
Offutt for the nation's capital. After a speedy trip, LeMay went into
a meeting at the Pentagon; it "was fast[,] [with] the Secretary and
Gen Van[denberg]" querying LeMay "on SAC's ability to drop the
atomic attack." The office diary noted that "no conclusions can be
drawn at this time on the action to be taken."[20] However, nothing
came of the scare in the way of an enemy attack that day. It did
demonstrate, nonetheless, how quickly LeMay was prepared to take
some sort of action and put the wheels in motion for fighting a war.

The incident put a small exclamation point on a year already
marked by the surprise of a war in Korea. The December attack
scare highlighted the need for SAC to be ready to respond to
threats in a rapid and organized fashion. It was also fodder for
LeMay's desire to not be caught on the ground and, if possible, to
preempt the enemy. To do that, however, he had to have a command sufficiently large and well equipped and properly based to
carry out such a program.

New Year, Some of the Same Problems

The first half of 1951 was busy for LeMay, his staff, and SAC.
Though the war in Korea caused LeMay immediate concern over
a proximate fight with the Soviet Union, the conflict also spelled
some good fortune for SAC and the Air Force. Historian Conrad
Crane wrote, "At the time the Korean War erupted, the new U.S.

Air Force was authorized only 416,314 officers and men, and annual appropriations were sufficient to maintain only forty-two of forty-eight authorized air wings. The war changed that considerably. . . . In November 1951 the Joint Chiefs of Staff agreed on a goal for an increased USAF of 1,210,000 military personnel and 143 wings by mid 1955, and at the end of the conflict the service mustered over 100 wings and almost 1 million officers and airmen."[21] In the meantime, however, work remained to be done to make these goals a reality.

Within the Air Force, changes had already begun taking place. In the second part of 1950 the Air Force set about "planning an expansion program, first aimed at 70 groups and later 95 wings by the end of fiscal year 1952. Under this latter program Strategic Air Command forces were to consist of six Heavy Bomb Wings, four Strategic Reconnaissance Wings (Heavy), twenty Medium Bomb Wings, four Strategic Reconnaissance Wings (Medium), seven Fighter Escort Wings, and three Strategic Support Squadrons."[22] This force came to account for roughly more than 40 percent of the Air Force's planned organizational strength. Taken as a whole, this was a generous expansion for the service, though not on the scale of what occurred during World War II. Nonetheless, SAC's enlargement marked significant growth of the Air Force and the wherewithal of the U.S. defense establishment to engage in nuclear war. As was the case through the balance of the Cold War, SAC became the unique tool within the U.S. arsenal that afforded the ability to hedge against threats not through a large conventional force as would have been otherwise required but rather through seemingly less manpower-intensive nuclear weapons. This expansion marked the rise of the relevance and importance of SAC and nuclear weapons within the U.S. defense policy community. It also spoke to the manner in which many of those making defense policy viewed SAC and the weapons the command was intended to deliver. For SAC as an entity and LeMay as an individual, this meant accepting a massive task—one that taxed the command and the service with the burden of a wartime-like growth spurt while the nation remained largely oblivious in a staid peace. Building SAC into a bulwark of Cold War defense was largely left to LeMay and the Air Force to figure out and accomplish.

LeMay, however driven, also was feeling pressure from above. During the first week of January 1951, LeMay visited Secretary Finletter in Washington, DC. LeMay's records noted that "a discussion was held with Mr. Finletter just prior to our departure, to reemphasize the need to get SAC in the best position at once and to maintain and increase our striking power as a matter of priority. He requested briefings on SAC's progress at two-week intervals. The first one will be on 17 January 1951. . . . At this time, we should also discuss major problems affecting SAC and SAC's capability."[23]

However, LeMay did not wait to get to work on the larger task at hand. That same month LeMay visited SAC bases in the western and southwestern United States. He discussed the issue of SAC expansion with the commanders of the various installations he visited; it was clear that large-scale growth was in the offing for the command. Per a memorandum from LeMay's office diary, "All Base Commanders were informed that four new wings were being organized this month and one per month starting in April. We are going to recommend an accelerated build-up." In order to achieve the expansion sought by LeMay, the memo stated that "it is anticipated that all Air Force Reserve and National Guard units will shortly be called to active duty. We will screen these people first to determine their qualifications and make assignments which will become effective immediately upon the recall of their units." Speaking to the seriousness of the growth of SAC, the memo stated, "With the exception of the Fighter Wings, present Reserve or National Guard units will be disbanded. Personnel may be shifted to take advantage of position vacancies for deserving promotions; however, the Commanding General [LeMay] warned that the primary rule to be observed in this expansion was that we would not reduce our atomic capability." The last statement was rapidly becoming LeMay's mantra. At the same time, maintenance of the effectiveness of SAC's nuclear capacities in the midst of such hurried growth was a valid concern, particularly at such an early point in the command's development; problems were certain to be encountered. Even under the tutelage of the notoriously effective LeMay, nothing was guaranteed. Simply saying there was to be no reduction in nuclear readiness and ensuring that was the case were two very different things.[24]

Getting an Answer

The question of nuclear readiness, specifically access to the actual bombs, resurfaced the next month. In a February 1951 letter to LeMay, Vandenberg referenced the June 30, 1950, letter in which the SAC commander "raised the question of initiating the atomic offensive under conditions of extreme chaos in Washington."[25] Vandenberg explained to LeMay:

Reply to your letter has been held in abeyance pending solution of problems relating to the re-designation of the alternate interim successor to the Chief of Staff, which in turn have been complicated by the recent re-organization of the Continental Air Command. The Commanding General, Tactical Air Command, is our tentative choice, pending Presidential approval. . . . It is difficult to conceive of the eventuality of the President and all his legal successors being rendered casualties in one attack. . . . It is likewise believed unlikely that communications facilities in the Washington area will be so badly damaged in a single attack as to prevent the expeditious transmittal, by some means or another, of necessary orders to field agencies. . . . It is believed that by virtue of the unique system of control over the use of the atomic bomb, we must accept as a calculated risk the remote possibility that the United States will in one attack be completely stripped of governmental leadership and suffer total loss of communications facilities in the Washington area.[26]

That this was a risk LeMay was unable to accept had been proven by his June 1950 arrangement with Gen. Robert Montague to have access to nuclear bombs in case of war. LeMay's prior arrangement for the release of nuclear weapons, apparently undertaken without preapproval from Vandenberg, is important for two reasons. First, the arrangement represented one of LeMay's early efforts toward securing custody of nuclear weapons prior to a mid-1950s decision to store such weapons on SAC bases. As a result of this agreement, LeMay had begun to chip away at the established principle of strict civilian control of the nation's nuclear arsenal. Second, it revealed a great deal about the character of the man with whom the American mantle of nuclear war had been entrusted. Specifically, he was less concerned with protocols, laws, and regulations governing the nation's nuclear weapons than he was with being able to prosecute and win a nuclear war. While LeMay's arrangement had, at least temporarily, tentatively settled the issue of weapons control for SAC, it did not resolve the problem of vulnerability and location of the weapons stockpiles. The long-term issue of weapons custody remained open.

Other elements of SAC's developing scheme of operations remained up in the air, and in typical fashion, LeMay did not keep his concerns to himself. In an April 5, 1951, letter to Vice Chief of Staff General Twining, LeMay noted that "during our meeting with the [Air Force] Secretary, 26 March, I voiced my dissatisfaction with the construction program. I stated that we have neither an adequate system of bases nor any single base within the present system adequately developed for effective and efficient operations. I stated further that where overseas bases are concerned, I am never sure whether planned development is adequate or inadequate inasmuch as the criteria can be changed and items added or deleted from budgets without my knowledge or reference to my staff."[27] LeMay's commentary highlighted his interest in pursuing centralized control—by him—in leading and managing SAC. His interest was valid; having been charged with the monumental task of propagating the command, his concern about a lack of appropriate facilities and budgets changed without notice made reasonable sense. LeMay's letter then returned to the issue of combat readiness, something that seemed to occupy much of his professional concern:

> We need, as a matter of urgency, a more adequate system of bases to permit full deployment and flexibility in operation of our current forces. We should, at the same time, be developing bases in anticipation of the forces to become

available as a result of our current expansion plans. Our bases in the forward area must be backed up by intermediate bases developed against the contingency that whole forward areas may be denied to us, either by enemy action or through the reluctance or hesitancy of our allies. The base system which I have in mind must not be limited to our minimum requirements, but should permit the execution of alternate war plans as a measure of security.[28]

LeMay was looking down the road to any eventualities that might hem in his plans for defeating the Soviet Union—particularly the conditions that threatened the fragile means by which those plans were to be executed, namely overseas deployments. Arguing against the expectation of availability of U.S. overseas bases to support SAC strikes against the Soviet Union, LeMay, either intentionally or inadvertently, also laid forth the logical imperative for the acquisition of weapons delivery systems that had the range needed to launch against Soviet targets from inside the continental United States. Overseas bases and deployments were, however, a point of friction. According to historian Phillip Meilinger:

The greatest utility of overseas bases is they are near potential crisis areas. The greatest limitation of overseas bases is they are near potential crisis areas. The issue was vulnerability. Plans called for SAC aircraft to base at forward locations in Europe, the Middle East and Asia—within un-refueled striking distance of their targets. With the detonation of the Soviet atomic bomb in August 1949, SAC realized such forward bases were increasingly vulnerable. It therefore pushed for bases in North Africa—close enough to the Soviet

Union for staging, but far enough back to allow for some protection from an enemy strike. Construction began on four bases in French Morocco, and the first was completed in 1951. Three more bases were built in Spain. These, along with airfields in England, Turkey and on Guam, would serve as bulwarks of an overseas basing system designed to outflank the Soviet Union.[29]

However, Meilinger later points out that "General LeMay recognized the vulnerability of overseas airbases and in January 1952 stated his goal as 'to launch our offensive from this continent.' That was not yet possible so forward bases were essential."[30] For LeMay, however, most impossibilities were merely temporary. Over the coming years, LeMay labored to make possible a massive strike from the continental United States, though a smaller one was already viable using the B-36. For SAC, the future lay in the ability to reside within the relative—if not temporary, in the context of nuclear war—safety of the continental United States, all the while threatening the Soviet Union. New bases and weapons systems made this possible. Receiving pressure from above, knowing the vulnerability of the command's current scheme of operations, and being a person driven to succeed, LeMay imposed more changes on SAC.

Other items drawing the attention of the SAC commander included operations involving Korea. LeMay's office diary recorded a rumor that a particular bombing unit was to return to the Pacific and that "the only reason supposed at this time is the build up of forces in the Korean theatre and the possibility that an Atomic target may present itself." LeMay's diary also noted that "a wire from Gen [Roger] Ramey this morning has us on the alert for some Atomic operations based out of Okinawa. Apparently the acft [aircraft] of the 9th [Bomb Wing] are being considered for this job. Gen LeMay has queried Gen Ramey on this matter and is expecting a call this PM as to whether or not he should go in to Washington for a conference." That call came and instructed LeMay to be in Chief of Staff Vandenberg's office at 9 a.m. to confer on the question of an atomic attack. LeMay left Nebraska for Washington, DC, that evening at 5 p.m.[31]

Atomic attacks were indeed under consideration. On April 6 President Truman directed the deployment of atomic warheads to Okinawa, along with additional aircraft from LeMay's command. The following day, LeMay met with Vandenberg to conclude dealings. Four days later, on April 11, LeMay was instructed by the Joint Chiefs "to prepare plans 'against targets listed and targets of opportunity in the Far East.'" Interestingly, Conrad Crane points out that while "the nuclear-capable SAC B-29s, and sometimes B-50s, never moved to Okinawa, the deployment to Guam continued until the end of the war." If the war on the Korean Peninsula was to escalate, some of the essential pieces, in terms of both weapons and intrinsic tensions, were moving into place.[32]

Despite the immediate attention paid to Korea, LeMay remained focused on the larger problems at hand in SAC. On the afternoon of April 17, LeMay conducted an inspection of Offutt, noting details as mundane as tire tracks on the grass and the general orderliness of the zones around storehouses. That LeMay expressed such interest in relatively minor issues was perhaps peculiar, given the other monumental issues vying for his time. However, it becomes clear in the historical refrain that LeMay's actions suggested a commander who wanted not only to have an orderly and impressive base surrounding his headquarters but also to send a message to subordinate commanders and organizations:

SAC was to be "squared away." In a sense, LeMay was communicating to those below him in the chain of command a message: if Offutt can do it, you can do it. Of course, not every base had a LeMay. But SAC did.[33]

On April 24 problems in Asia again drew LeMay's attention. That day, Gen. Thomas Power, LeMay's second in command, and a coterie of other personnel left for the Pacific to meet with Gen. Matthew Ridgway in Tokyo. Power's group was headed to the region for a specific purpose: "They will direct the efforts of the 9th Wing in Quam [Guam] should there [sic] utilization be needed." In other words, Powers and his team were headed to the Pacific to direct nuclear operations, if they were to take place. Whether SAC was a squared-away, nuclear combat–capable organization was a question nearing the fullest of tests. For his part, LeMay was busy playing a role in the larger drama. As it was in the Pacific during World War II, LeMay and Power were a team. Even in the execution of Korean-related operations, shades of what LeMay was doing to build SAC and whom he trusted in this process were seen. That same day, LeMay spoke with General Twining and "asked him to come to SAC for a visit an[d] briefing on target material and CEPs [circular errors probable]. . . . Gen Twining stated that he could not but ask[e]d the General if he could bring his people in to USAF on Friday which Gen LeMay agreed to do."[34] Based on the overall context of LeMay and Twining's discussion, the recent deployment of 9th Wing to the Pacific for possible nuclear operations, and the reference to CEPs, the planned briefing almost certainly related directly to the targets to be potentially bombed—with nuclear weapons—as part of the deployment. This, and LeMay and his staff's personal briefing of Twining on the matter, implies not only the highest levels of service-based visibility on the matter but also the level of control SAC and the Air Force exercised on the issue. This was despite the fact that other organizations and leaders had been charged with the overall execution of U.S. operations in the Korean theater. This same question of who or what entity exercised control over nuclear operations had yet to be settled.

While the biggest news for SAC appeared to have been the movement of nuclear-capable forces into the Pacific theater, something different altogether was perhaps more striking. Power had been LeMay's trusted subordinate in the Pacific during the firebombing raids against Japan that directly helped defeat the final Axis state in World War II. With Power in the region, LeMay had a reliable set of eyes and ears in the Pacific. Now that nuclear-capable forces were in the area, LeMay needed to have someone he trusted in command of the situation for several reasons. According to Conrad Crane, "LeMay was concerned about retaining control of such missions and designated Power as 'Deputy Commanding General, SAC X-RAY' with that responsibility. These arrangements were finalized in a 2 May meeting among Power, [Lt. Gen. George] Stratemeyer, and [Maj. Gen. Doyle] Hickey, which also produced a memorandum on planning for SAC 'atomic retardation operations' in the Far East. . . . SAC also remained concerned about executing war plans in the Far East. The 2 May meeting affirmed that SAC B-29s would revert to LeMay's command immediately if general war broke out."[35] SAC's retention of control of nuclear-capable strategic forces was important to LeMay. Having deployed additional bombers to the Pacific was a drain on SAC's war resources that would need to be repossessed in the event of a conflict with the Soviet Union. In retaining some SAC connection to the bombers through the X-RAY coordination center arrangement, those assets could be brought back into the fold more expeditiously if needed. In some ways, the development of SAC X-RAY was less about controlling potential nuclear operations specifically related to the Korean War than it was about being able to participate in possible nuclear operations over the Soviet Union. Power's and, as a result, LeMay's retention of command through X-RAY helped to ensure this. It was also a tangible check on LeMay's concerns and fears over a general nuclear war.

These were not the only issues entrusted to Power, as some of the most critical issues leaders face involve personnel decisions. Power began making personnel recommendations soon after his arrival in the theater and in so doing exercised the trust LeMay had in him. Per LeMay's office diary on April 30, "Power in FEAF [Far East Air Forces] requests that [Robert] Terrill replace [James] Briggs on 5 May and that Heflin remain in control of the 9th on Quam [Guam]."[36] For LeMay, it was an issue of trust; having the right people in the right place—as was the case in sending Power to the Pacific—was critical to him, whether it was related to nuclear weapons or personnel.

An International Role

Despite being at the center of multiple issues, LeMay never lost focus or let details escape his scrutiny. This ability was a defining characteristic of LeMay's leadership of SAC and allowed him to achieve results where others had failed. A record of success in essentially every leadership situation he was in kept LeMay's career on track and ensured continued investments of time, money, and trust in his efforts. LeMay's advice and accomplishments were appreciated.

One of the issues that had not escaped LeMay's focus was overseas bases. As early as autumn 1949, SAC considered the development of bases in North Africa, but desire did not automatically equal effort or achievement. Two surveys were undertaken in 1950 to assess the feasibility of SAC's use of extant capacities in the region.[37] On April 26 LeMay received a message from General Vandenberg regarding North Africa and the overall preparation of the command for a larger war. In the dispatch, Vandenberg discussed "the Moroccan base situation" and suggested that a "headquarters be sent there right away with a commander who speaks French and is capable of negotiations of the highest order. Gen Kissner is suggested [and] Gen LeMay is to comment on this in near future."[38] In the sense that the U.S. ability to fight an air war with the Soviet Union depended in part on North African bases, the negotiation regarding their operation in a country such as Morocco was critical. That LeMay's input was solicited on such a matter was not unusual. The data from the second survey were "used for a series of talks between the United States Government and the Government of France concerning the use of Moroccan bases by United States Air Force units. An agreement was reached between the participating parties by the close of 1950 and the final document was signed on 2 May 1951."[39]

Dealing in international issues while concurrently establishing a combat-worthy organization was no small order. The United States was building its presence and the scope of its power in the post–World War II order, and LeMay was at the center of it all. Concurrently, his penchant for building a strong public image was apparent. While he was almost obsessively focused on the operational mission, LeMay understood that the value of winning public approval was as critical as soundly defeating an enemy. This public relations mission was an enabler for the larger combat mission that LeMay and his command faced. To ensure a continued wellspring of public and congressional support, LeMay crafted a public relations campaign that promoted his image and that of the command and its mission.

A notable feature of this campaign unfolded in May 1951, when LeMay received approval from General Twining to accept "membership in the Board of Trustees [of the] National Geographic Society."[40] Sitting senior military commanders were not normally named to such positions, which seemed to fly in the face of the more operationally driven, mission-related chores then burdening LeMay. The nomination held the possibility, however, of serving to promote LeMay's image as the quintessential rugged individual. This certainly had some public relations value for the SAC commander. At 5 a.m. on May 18 LeMay traveled to Washington, DC, where he conducted some official business before heading to the Pentagon to "ha[ve] lunch with Generals Vandenberg and Edwards of the Air Staff." Following his meeting there, "LeMay had a private discussion with General Vandenberg in his office for approximately two hours." Later that day, "LeMay attended a meeting of the Board of Trustees of the National Geographic Society. He was unanimously elected to this Board of Trustees." In the years that followed, LeMay's campaign to propagate his image continued and grew in capacity. Even during the harried spring of 1951, LeMay kept his image, and that of the command, in mind.[41]

On the heels of the National Geographic business, on May 7, LeMay faced concerns over the central mission with which SAC was grappling during the period: nuclear war. This time trepidations surfaced in a letter from LeMay to the Air Force director of plans, Maj. Gen. Thomas D. White, who would later serve as LeMay's boss. LeMay's letter was a response to White's request to comment on a document "having to do with retardation, forward storage, the role of the Navy, etc." Retardation, or the launching of a nuclear counterattack against fielded forces, was intended to slow or stop the forward movement of an invading Soviet—or other communist—military against friendly forces or areas. Retardation was also one of LeMay's secondary concerns, as it regarded a general nuclear war with the Soviet Union. LeMay remained primarily focused on other types of targets and approaches in a general nuclear war. More immediately, LeMay opined to White that "any target which can be identified prior to hostilities, which warrants the allocation of an A-bomb, and passes the tactical suitability test, should be assigned to the Strategic Air command for destruction; further, all available forces capable of attacking the identifiable target system should be assigned to or placed under the operational control of a single strategic air commander." In this statement, portions of LeMay's effort to consolidate the U.S. nuclear mission under SAC and his purview were clearly evident. Whether this was a result of a desire to block competition from separate elements of the military was partially addressed, at least from LeMay's perspective, in the next paragraph:

> My convictions in this regard stem from the fact, among others, that a division of forces between the industrial complex and the so-called "retardation mission," if literally applied, could result in a ridiculous situation in which our force has an aiming point on one side of a city because of its industrial significance and a theater force might have an aiming point on the other side having direct effect on a particular unified or allied area commander because of its transport, storage, communications, or other facilities

which are of importance to the enemy in the deployment
or disposition of his forces.[42]

Aside from the standard interorganizational infighting that might
have motivated LeMay to some degree, his argument held some
plain truth. By 1951 the U.S. nuclear stockpile was still relatively
limited and would need to be employed wisely. To LeMay's point,
the engagement of multiple nearby targets with more than one
weapon might have resulted in a duplicative attack. To that end,
LeMay had a legitimate gripe. This was compounded by the fact
that, in a larger sense, LeMay and SAC would be held responsible for
ensuring the greater success of a U.S. nuclear assault. If he and the
command could not plan for and execute that war successfully with
the resources available, it would not reflect well on them. It could
also have left the United States in the dangerous position of having
engaged in a nuclear war without having degraded the enemy to the
point of their suing for peace or thwarting further action by them. It
created significant risk, and LeMay was not interested in risks. Until
the U.S. nuclear stockpile reached a point where such concerns were
not an issue, steps had to be taken to prevent its inefficient use.

Morocco was again a topic for conversation in early May. On
May 9 LeMay received a call from Twining, who reopened the
issue of "the North Africa business. . . . Gen McConnel[l] would
do better in North Africa and Gen Olds might get into trouble
from the Negotiation angle down there." For his part, however,
LeMay "had every confidence in Gen Olds and felt he should go
as he knew more about SAC business than did McConnel[l]. Gen
T[wining] said that t[h]e staff still felt that Gen Kis[s]ner should
go as he was a better negotiator."[43] Personally, LeMay had no such

problems; also on May 9, the head of the French air force visited with LeMay, and "a dinner party was given in his honor."[44] The visit and the entertaining of the head of the French air force were particularly important since Morocco was under French control at the time. LeMay might have disagreed with Twining on a particular issue of leadership selection for a diplomatically sensitive post, but he himself was clearly capable of working the diplomatic angle, although he did not always project such a persona. He made this aspect of his personality and skill set known only to those immediately surrounding him and those he trusted.

LeMay's and Twining's interest in seeing this issue settled did not exist in a vacuum. World affairs were a driving factor from May 7–9, as a message "went out to all Wing and [numbered] [Air Force] commanders informing them the foreign situation has worsened and that they should be ready to perform the primary mission without further warning but without creating undue alarm."[45] Being ready to fight a nuclear war and not alarming others seemed mutually exclusive. With the apparent deterioration of the international environment, the potential for this eventuality was only that much more real.

Not only Morocco was of interest for LeMay in 1951. Before SAC had a sufficient fleet of long-range bombers capable of attacking the Soviet Union from the continental United States, there was a desire for bases in Europe as well. The United Kingdom hosted a portion of SAC's bomber force from the late 1940s into the 1950s. At noon on June 23, 1951, LeMay left Offutt Air Force Base and headed to Washington, DC, an intermediate stop on a trip to the United Kingdom. That night LeMay and his wife Helen had dinner with the first chief of staff of the service, Carl Spaatz, and his wife, and then spent the night at their home. The next afternoon, June

24, LeMay's aircraft left Bolling Air Force Base in Washington, DC. After a stop in Canada that included dinner, LeMay's aircraft continued to the United Kingdom, landing in London on June 25.[46] The trip was a homecoming of sorts for LeMay, as he had served in the United Kingdom during World War II as a bomber commander. That tour of duty catapulted him to his position leading the B-29 force in the Pacific where he oversaw the firebombing of Japan and contributed to that country's ultimate surrender.

According to a SAC official history from early 1951, SAC's mission—and hence LeMay's job—held "that the Command be prepared for offensive and defensive missions against an enemy in any sector of the world." While this may have been the stated mission, reality dictated that SAC had to be prepared to fight the Soviet Union. The history continued: "The long-range bomber has been perfected to strike the enemy's homeland from bases within the relative safety of friendly territory. One element considered necessary to enable successful dispatch of Strategic Air Command's primary mission was the acquisition of bases at strategic points along the enemy's perimeter of defense." This statement implied that the planners had some particular enemy in mind. More than this, the efficacy of the bomber was also assumed, though in reality it was far from perfect if it required foreign basing and all the accompanying complications. Furthermore, the history stated: "For some time certain areas had been considered for possible use, but not until early 1951 was much accomplished toward establishing overseas bases in the European area under Strategic Air Command control." For LeMay, the issue of basing forces abroad presented another diplomatic problem with which he had to deal.

The SAC history continued: "For several years Strategic Air Command units had been gaining training experience by tours of temporary duty in the United Kingdom, but this involved no large-scale build-up of Strategic Air Command forces overseas." Prior to LeMay's trip to the United Kingdom, "on 17 March 1951 Headquarters United States Air Force authorized the activation of the 7th Air Division for operation in the United Kingdom." It was also somewhat cryptically recorded that the purpose of this organization "was to be found in the Strategic Air Command War Plans and Operations Orders, in addition to the responsibility of commanding Strategic Air Command units, personnel and equipment in the United Kingdom." In other words, by the summer of 1951 SAC and LeMay had officially established an overseas beachhead in Britain.[47] It was now partly LeMay's job to maintain that position on the ground. LeMay's position as SAC commander put him at the top of much of the U.S. military's operational nuclear hierarchy. It also left him with responsibilities not normally devolved upon a peacetime military officer, as no officer had ever been in such a position before.

At 9:45 a.m. on June 27, LeMay met with British chief of the air staff Sir John Slessor, whose support was a vital element in maintaining SAC's position in the United Kingdom. An hour later, LeMay met with the U.S. ambassador to the United Kingdom, Walter Gifford. In all, it was a morning of diplomatic engagement.[48] Keeping the United States in the good graces of the United Kingdom was important for more than one reason; SAC needed bases in Britain, but the United States also needed British support for the war in Korea. In either case, LeMay needed to walk a careful path while on his visit. The balance of June 27 and the next few days involved visits to several bases and some military operations in the United Kingdom. From there, the diplomatic tour continued; lunch on June 30 was with Sir Hugh Lloyd, commander of the Royal Air Force's bomber command, a potentially critical partner in a war against the Soviets.[49]

The importance of these events went far beyond any tactical level interest and the specific intent each of them held. In a larger sense they served as evidence of LeMay's curiosity in the breadth of issues that faced his command; they also represented his ability to subsume their entirety and subsequently make decisions that benefitted the greater good of his organization, all the while melding those outcomes with the intended practical performance of U.S. foreign policy. LeMay was more erudite in his grasp of what the policymakers in Washington wanted than some of his critics were willing to admit. At the same time, however, LeMay gave pause to some in the policy community in Washington. According to Conrad Crane, LeMay had been kept off a trip to Korea earlier in the year on the grounds that "General LeMay had become something of a 'Mr. Atom Bomb.'"[50] Whatever his reputation may have been, LeMay never became bound to it; he was a man focused on the future and results.

Between July 1 and July 3 LeMay involved himself in some parties, the review of a British bomber, and a visit to a car manufacturer: "A deal is cooking for General LeMay to furnish two Chrysler engines to the Allard Company who will then furnish General LeMay with a complete chassis and body for the SAC hobby shop." On July 2 LeMay greeted his boss, Vandenberg, at the airport in London. On July 3 LeMay attended a dinner at the Dorchester Hotel in London, where "General [Dwight] Eisenhower made the principal address." LeMay spent July 4 attending "Ceremonies at St Paul[']s at 1100; lunch with the Lord Mayor after the ceremony, at the Mansion House; and a reception at the Ambassador's in the afternoon." During this social whirl, LeMay kept his ear to the ground on operational matters: "General Sweeney arrived back from Rabat [Morocco] at 1330 and briefed General LeMay between the Lord Mayor's luncheon and reception at the Ambassador's on the situation in North Africa."[51] On July 10, following a side trip to Germany, LeMay departed the United Kingdom and began the long trip home.[52] He was about to lay aside his role as diplomat and resume more directly that of military commander. There was plenty to deal with at the command when he got back.

Back to the Command

While LeMay tended to the international role of the command and nature of his duties in early 1951, the largely internal and com- bat mission–related concerns that SAC faced remained. One prob- lem that required prompt attention was that of the B-47 bomber. In his book *The American Way of War*, Russell Weigley noted, "The instrument of the strategy of deterrence was to be an inheritance of the Eisenhower administration from the Truman administra- tion and the Korean mobilization, unquestioned American mili- tary superiority, particularly in nuclear weapons and the means to deliver them."[53]

To be certain, deterrence was the policy of the United States. Was the United States, however, prepared to execute the military action that undergirded that policy—strategic nuclear attack on the Soviet Union? According to Weigley, "Thanks to the Korean mobilization and the larger military preparations which accompa- nied it, the prospect of Soviet nuclear parity with the United States which had frightened the framers of NSC-68 seemed to have disap- peared from the horizon. . . . Instead, the United States had pushed well ahead of the Soviets in stockpiling nuclear weapons, and by the early months of the new administration the Air Force had its more than 400 [B-47] Stratojets to deliver them to the Soviet homeland from increasingly secure bases around the world."[54]

Weigley's argument concealed a major controversy behind these airplanes: although the Air Force procured Stratojets in large numbers, the readiness of those jets to go to war in 1951 was anything but concrete. As a result, in 1951 LeMay would have had a problem meeting the obligations of deterrence—or the policy of preemption he had argued for—with the B-47 alone.

The Stratojet, a Boeing product, represented some of the latest technology in aircraft design, but it was also in far from perfect shape as it came off the assembly line. Given that SAC was the U.S. nuclear command—and was intently focused on that mission—it was bound to be problematic if its new bomber aircraft was not ready for the primary job of the command. In a plain but damning fashion, the SAC history records:

> The B-47 "Stratojets," which were being produced as standard equipment for units of Strategic Air Command, had not become a combat weapon by the end of 1951. . . . Although a few early model B-47s had been assigned to the 306th Bombardment Wing, Second Air Force, it was realized that the incorporation of this jet bomber into the units of this Command had not added to the combat effectiveness of Strategic Air Command. . . . In a large part this was due to the lack of satisfactory equipment which make a plane a bomber. . . . Because of these factors a re-evaluation of the entire B-47 program was considered necessary.[55]

The SAC history goes on to report that "a shift in the B-47 program became apparent in mid-1951." Following several changes to the overall agenda, which "were primarily the nature of production and allocation of aircraft . . . some of the early problems had been successfully eliminated, others remained to plague the program, and a series of new problems arose which called for prompt action." In other words, changes had been effected, but the overall results remained far from perfect. "An analysis of the causes of the condition showed that the equipment development had not proceeded rapidly enough to meet production of the 'Stratojet.' The planes were flowing in an ever increasing volume from the production line and were sitting around waiting for the necessary modifications and equipment which were required to make the plane a combat weapon."[56] As matters stood, SAC's new bomber was of little use to the command. The B-47 was to become the mainstay of the SAC jet bomber fleet. It needed to work if the SAC bomber force was going to be able to meet its wartime mission. The preponderance of the U.S. plan for achieving and maintaining nuclear deterrence—and carrying out a nuclear war—in the coming years hinged on the flailing bomber program.

As a result, "Under such circumstances a complete review of the B-47 program was called for."[57] The decision to launch an evaluation of the program was only rational, and this was in keeping with the type of approach LeMay expected from his organization. The B-47 represented both great risk and opportunity for SAC and its bomber force. In acquiring the jet bomber, SAC and the Air Force had undertaken a project that increased the performance characteristics of its bomber fleet, giving it a meaningful edge over the Soviets. But the risk came in the form of groundbreaking technology and new processes. Whether the new technology and new aircraft would pan out in proportional results was something that only time could reveal.

The problem was bigger than LeMay and SAC. That August the Air Force inspector general "requested [SAC] to set up a

B-47 presentation on the 10th of September at which time these problems, as Strategic Air Command saw them, could be presented. . . . Following the findings made by the Inspector General . . . a conference was convened at Headquarters United States Air Force," which was supervised by Twining.[58] LeMay left the business of conveying SAC's message to his trusted deputy, Thomas Power. During the conference, Power "pointed out that Strategic Air Command had been following the B-47 program for three years and was, as a result, more familiar with the deficiencies of the bomber than most other commands"—an unsurprising situation, given that SAC was the end user of the product and that it was essential to the command's future growth in jet bombers. After he explained SAC's goal "to establish an operational engineering program in order to aid in the effort to develop an operational capability from the B-47," LeMay's deputy made a rather shocking statement. Power "stated emphatically that if aggressive action was not taken to solve some of the problems pertaining to the B-47, such as armament, radar, etc., it could develop into the biggest scandal the Air Force has known."[59] This proclamation made clear how close the project was to disaster. LeMay's office diary reported that "Power stated that we were in a hell of shape and that when we get that acft [aircraft] all hell will break lose [loose]. . . . Gen[eral] LeMay stated that he felt we were sitting on top of a national scandal with this acft and that some thing has to be done."[60] These were strong words coming from LeMay and his deputy. This was certainly a major problem for not only SAC but also the Air Force as a whole: "At the conclusion of the conference General Twining stated that the solution of the problem was up to the Air Staff and that it would be solved." This was a potential disaster that neither the relatively new service nor LeMay's command could afford. The problem needed to be fixed. The Air Force's plan for effective nuclear deterrence, the reputation of the new service, and those involved in the project depended on it.[61]

LeMay's organization was not perfect, however, and did not have a quick fix for some of the issues engulfing the B-47. According to the official SAC history, "At the end of 1951 certain major problems resulting from the readiness status of the B-47 remained to perplex this Command. It would be difficult to determine exactly the causes behind these problems but some of them were apparent. The decision to speed up production of the B-47 prior to the completion of operational suitability testing, and the delay in making available early B-47 models for these tests had been major difficulties in the program."[62] The SAC history went on to point out that "there appeared to be ample reason for both these decisions at the time. . . . Tenseness in international affairs after the outbreak of hostilities in Korea made it appear essential to build to maximum strength as quickly as possible. At the same time, making certain modifications on early B-47 models before they were released to the Air Force for suitability testing seemed a means of assuring the best possible bomber in the event that the 'Stratojet' was needed."[63]

This was a rather clear example of the fear that the initiation of the war in Korea had instilled in military leaders and how that fear had manifested itself in tangible terms. The decision to rush production of the B-47 had a major impact, at least in the mid term. As a result, "The lack of suitable B-47s for Strategic Air Command units at the end of 1951 resulted in a serious loss of striking power. The fact that operational B-47 units would not, in all probability, be trained and equipped until 1953 was a topic of concern to this Command."[64] Maximum strength and effectual strength were not the same thing, however, and this concern highlighted the very difference between them.

Eventually, changes took place. In the second half of 1951, the Air Force decided to consent to "the proposed Modification Plan. . . . This modification plan came about as a result of the gradual acceptance by all commands concerned that a number of modifications were necessary before the plane could be considered a combat bomber." But the problems were beginning to manifest themselves in operational form, which meant the larger mission and plan for the modernization of SAC were going to be impacted: "As early as September 1951 it had become necessary to alter certain conversion plans because of the expected modification program. It was obvious that no changes in the B-47 program could be worked out until this headquarters had reliable information of the effects of the modification program on aircraft deliveries." Officials convened at SAC headquarters on October 18 and conferred over what had to be accomplished on the B-47 prior to it being "considered operational. Up to 50 changes were suggested by this headquarters." The following month, at Air Force headquarters, "representatives of Directorate of Material and Directorate of Operations, Headquarters Strategic Air Command attended [a] conference which was called to acquaint all agencies and commands involved in the B-47 program with details of the modification program, referred to after this time usually as the B-47 refinement program." This program was intended to fix a majority of the problems plaguing the B-47. If these predictions held true, finally there was some hope for the massive project: "The refinement was to begin at the Grand Central Plant, Tucson, Arizona during February 1952. By October this Command was to have received its first modified aircraft, and by December 1952 it was expected that the flow of these planes into Strategic Air Command units would be at the rate of 75 a month. It was the opinion of this Command that the modifications would result in an operationally suitable aircraft."[65] That was to be in 1952, however. For 1951, it was a much different story. If the short history of the B-47 program was any indication, it was no easy task that had been set before those charged with remedying it. The SAC history concluded that "although 12 B-47s were assigned to this Command at the end of 1951 there was no immediate increase in combat effectiveness as a result. Until the bomber was considered operationally acceptable, the opinion of the Commanding General, Strategic Air Command [LeMay], was no more than 90 planes would be accepted. Limited training had commenced with the available planes at the end of the year, but the overall B-47 picture was black, and would remain that way until modified planes began flowing in quantity from the modification depot." LeMay wanted to be sure of his equipment and operations. The acceptance of B-47s into the command was another example of that thinking. It was, however, the safest path to follow, and in the exercise of nuclear war, no one could blame him for that approach.[66]

Another development in the second half of 1951 was of importance to LeMay and his career. On October 8 LeMay was travelling to Oregon for a trip with three of the Air Force's most notable leaders: Spaatz, Ira Eaker, and Twining. While en route, Twining advised LeMay that President Truman had submitted his name for promotion to the rank of four-star general. Upon hearing the news, "Naturally [LeMay] was happy and his first comment was to Gen Twining 'Did you know this all the trip out and never say anything to me[?]' Gen Twining answered yes, the President signed that last Friday. This promotion makes Gen LeMay the youngest

4 star General since [Ulysses S.] Grant." LeMay's promotion to the next higher rank was a vote of confidence in him and his efforts at SAC. In 1951 LeMay's star was on the rise, literally and figuratively. During the Cold War, the nation remained largely oblivious to the ongoing conflict in everyday life; there was no rationing or large-scale combat between the two major belligerents. In a certain sense, LeMay, SAC, and the Air Force were on their own to do the job; however, LeMay had done much to prove he was up to the task. LeMay had won the respect of his command and his superiors, and therefore he did not need a fourth star to be effective.[67]

Not Entirely Failure

Despite major problems with its new jet bomber, life at SAC did not come to a halt. Because of its size and its widely respected leader, SAC was capable of tackling more than one major concern at a time. In the early 1950s the signs of resiliency in thinking and execution that would appear in its later plans for nuclear redundancy were already evident. Much of this was a result of LeMay's leadership and the culture he instituted within the organization. In addition, SAC was an incubator for new ideas and new technology, and the result of that could be seen in palpable ways. Even as SAC was dealing with the problems presented by the B-47, another groundbreaking advance began to take shape: the development of guided missiles. The new technology was a challenge to the bomber-centric model SAC had adopted to that point and was one that started life early in the existence of the command.

The command's official history records an interesting narrative about the development of guided missiles: "Toward the end of 1950 it had become apparent that the development of strategic weapons in the form of guided missiles would eventually involve the Strategic Air Command." After some examination of the origins of the U.S. rocket program, the history states, "The progress made from the days of the 'Buzz-Bomb' to 1951 was so impressive as to open for the future an entirely new method of making war." While jet-powered strategic bombers were capable of travelling great distances at high speed to drop their nuclear payloads, thus dramatically reducing the time from decision to go to war to full-on attack from days to hours, guided missiles held the promise of diminishing that time from hours to minutes. Angry politicians and hot-headed commanders had little preventing them from nearly instantaneously translating emotion into action. If the promise of guided missiles panned out, suspicions about an adversary could, in a matter of moments, envelop the world in a nuclear war. This was not yet the case, however, as the SAC history noted that "it would be entirely inaccurate, however, to state that by 1951 we had arrived at the age of 'push-button' warfare." That time was approaching, however, and SAC would be the organization that would largely usher it in.[68]

The SAC history noted that "by the end of 1951 at least one missile had been brought near the operational stage. This missile, code-named the Matador, was designed for tactical use, but other missiles were being developed for strategic missions. Projects were well under way toward the construction of a guided missile which would be capable of traveling 5,500 nautical miles at supersonic speeds, carrying a 5,000 to 10,000 pound warhead."[69] As hinted at in the SAC history, there were missiles in the works that could fulfill the command's overarching mission. The suggestion that missiles could carry such heavy payloads at high speeds and across great distances was certainly a matter of strategic importance to the command that had been charged with said matters of security. Indeed, SAC was wise in looking down the road. Simultaneously, the same history reported that it was "obvious that America could not afford to jeopardize her strategic bombardment capability while waiting for the day that the guided missile could be perfected and produced in adequate numbers."[70] Having essentially proclaimed the broader SAC approach to the development of missiles in the second half of 1951, it was evident the command—which was an emblematic and substantial manifestation of LeMay's thinking—had placed an emphasis on a traditional, aircraft-based approach. This was a sign that the command was becoming an organization that was wholly representative of LeMay. In other words, SAC was beginning to bear signs of LeMay's efforts, a suggestion that SAC was turning a corner from its days of disorder. Simply because SAC was settling on an approach to war, however, did not mean the command was demonstratively ready for an all-out nuclear war or that massive concerns did not exist. SAC remained troubled.

Nonetheless, as had occurred with long-range, manned strategic bombers, LeMay's command ultimately translated the scientific development of guided missiles into a weapon of war. Despite the general disassociation of LeMay with the acceptance of guided missiles as the mainstay of SAC's strike force, his command recognized that they could not be avoided as an important development. LeMay was not anti-missile, but he did not fully accept the efficacy of guided missiles over the proven worthiness of the strategic bomber. In 1951, in the wake of the outbreak of the Korean War and with the general Soviet threat remaining, LeMay stuck to what he knew and what he believed would assuredly perform in the next nuclear war.

The period from mid-1950 through the end of 1951 was a tumultuous one for LeMay as an individual and SAC as an organization. For both, unresolved issues and unanswered questions about the state of the world and the well-being of the command remained. The tangible concerns to be undertaken were relatively well defined—namely the rectification of the B-47, the development of missiles, and the strengthening of a basing capability in North Africa. Alongside these ran an unanswered question—whether a nuclear war was to occur at some point in the relatively near future. LeMay's actions and arguments indicated his ongoing concerns over that issue. What made the challenges in the coming year—and those thereafter—most interesting were LeMay's proposed responses.

LeMay believed the prospect of nuclear war was very real. To appease his fear, LeMay undertook to bring under SAC's control the nuclear weapons needed to fight such a conflict, the planes and other means of delivery needed to carry the weapons to their targets, a plan for fighting the war, and the right people to do the job. At the same time, LeMay continued to advocate for a policy of nuclear preemption if a war appeared imminent. It was this last point, LeMay's support for nuclear preemption, that was most radical—and, especially in contemporary times, controversial. Though LeMay was given to action, he also understood that the right ideas and strategy were needed to undergird the means to make war.

03

Pressing Ahead

Throughout 1952 and 1953, LeMay continued his campaign of support for preemption. At the same time, the inconclusive close of the war in Korea in July 1953 did not appreciably ease his worries over a feared nuclear war. If anything, the entire experience of the Korean surprise and ensuing conflict convinced LeMay that a war with the Soviet Union was a matter of time rather than of chance. LeMay was worried that, as had been the case with Pearl Harbor, the United States could again be the victim of surprise—this time, however, as the result of a nuclear strike. If there was a next time, LeMay wanted SAC to be ready. The nation simply could not afford to lose a nuclear war with the Soviet Union.

Throughout this period, LeMay remained steadfast in his approach to building SAC. As a result, little changed in terms of how he envisioned the end product. LeMay built SAC as an institution that would live beyond him. During this period, operational realities began to meet the standards LeMay had set, but LeMay continued to push those standards further. For the first time, U.S. policy leaders had a reliable organization capable of fighting and, perhaps, winning a nuclear war—no matter how Pyrrhic such a victory might have been.

Preemption Remained a Key Topic

In early January 1953 LeMay went to the Air War College to deliver an address on his command and its mission. LeMay departed Offutt at 3:35 a.m. on January 7 for Maxwell Air Force Base via Washington, DC, New Jersey, and Virginia. LeMay made it to Maxwell, outside Montgomery, Alabama, on January 8, a day before his talk was scheduled.[1]

Like many of LeMay's addresses, the talk at Maxwell was a straightforward one, attending to subjects ranging from SAC's mission to targeting to the command structure within SAC during a conflict. The discussion offered a partial picture of LeMay and SAC's approach to war in the nuclear age. It was also a chance for LeMay to promote his command and efforts.[2]

LeMay's talk on his command and its mission followed familiar lines. He began with a discussion of his charge: "The mission assigned by the Joint Chiefs of Staff is very short and to the point. It leaves no question as to the job the Strategic Air Command must perform."[3] After discussing a Joint Chiefs of Staff directive, LeMay summarized it by stating of his command's role: "Our mission, then, is to conduct the strategic air offensive. . . . The JCS [Joint Chiefs of Staff] have further refined this mission by assigning three specific tasks to be accomplished."[4] A slide enumerating the three responsibilities was projected for the audience. He focused on a discussion of the second item on his list: "The second task is considerably more difficult to achieve. It requires the highest possible order of intelligence. . . . And equally important, it requires a freedom of initiative not likely to be provided a military commander in a democracy." Nonetheless, LeMay stated, "Within those limits, and they are severe, we are prepared to perform this task."[5] That task was the "blunting of Soviet capabilities to deliver an atomic offensive"—in other words, preemption of a Soviet assault on the United States.[6] LeMay had made clear, however, his belief that the policy authorities needed to carry out this type of mission were not likely to be granted.

Finletter Shares His Thoughts

LeMay was not the only person thinking about the notion of using nuclear weapons in a first-strike scenario, but not all agreed with LeMay's approach. One of those dissenters was a superior, Air Force Secretary Thomas K. Finletter. On April 8 Finletter offered a lecture on the "Role of Airpower in Future War" at the Air War College.[7] Finletter's remarks made clear that not everyone outside SAC had the same belief of what made the most sense in terms of the command's concept for going to war. It did not mean, per se, that Finletter disagreed with LeMay, however. Agreement, disagreement, and the realm in between were different things:

> When I look at SAC sometimes I get worried. And I'm wondering what General Kenny [Gen. George Kenney, first commander of SAC] would think about that. It seems to me that we mustn't think just in terms of the highest flying bomber going over the bomb release line, we have to move into all sorts of other kinds of thinking and we must above all recognize that these Russians are very much further ahead than we thought they were. The concentration

of the Russians on the MiG, what we know they are doing in terms of electronics and one's big worry is that they are going to get that night fighter that I referred to. All of these things mean we must constantly be impatient with where SAC is, we must be constantly worrying and worrying more than we are now about low flying and high flying attacks starting off together, all mixed up with uninhabited aircraft and also especially mixed with the air to ground business on which I don't think we are placing enough emphasis. We must not get over smug at the fact that SAC has the other capability at the present time.[8]

Finletter's statement was both concerning and foreboding. It also called into question where LeMay was guiding SAC. Finletter did not seem to have the same image of SAC's progress and eventual goals as LeMay. This dissonance proved that LeMay's ideas were not universally accepted across the top ranks of the Air Force. At the same time, what Finletter suggested directly implied that SAC—and, hence, LeMay—had missed the mark; it also foreshadowed another conflict where the focus on the large bomber and the nuclear mission led to the neglect of the close air support mission or, as Finletter had called it, "the air to ground business."[9]

Fissures in the veneer of unanimity over the question of a nuclear first strike became apparent during the question and answer session after Finletter's remarks. This was particularly interesting, given Finletter was present at the April 1950 commander's conference where LeMay had directly advocated for preemption. An audience member asked Finletter, "We have heard a great deal about this term 'retaliation.' In your mind does retaliation mean that we will not use the atomic bomb, unless the atomic bomb is used against us, or does it mean we will not use the atomic bomb unless an act of aggression is committed by Russia other than [an] atomic one?"[10] Finletter's response was mildly nuanced at the outset and drew a distinction in the question over a U.S. nuclear response to an attack: "First of all, I don't like the word retaliation. Because that is not the purpose of the atomic counter attack." After recalling the German World War II–era V-1 and V-2, which Finletter referred to as "revenge weapons," he opined, "Well, that's a pretty stupid way of approaching the problem, it seems to me that if you start thinking about revenge, you won't hit the right targets maybe. The idea of the counter atomic attack is to knock out the enemy's capacity to make war." This was a fine dissimilarity, not a grandiose difference in opinion with national policy. Finletter continued more generally, "Now, as to the question as to whether we'd use the A-bomb, as to when we use the A-bomb, you are asking me to look into a crystal ball and to interpret the sentiments of the American people, and the American government as of the time." Finletter had not directly stated any disagreement with the concept of a preemptive attack or preventive war; he left the question up to the people of the United States and their leaders. This was a point to which both Finletter and LeMay consented. Taking it a step further, Finletter noted: "But here is what I think is the answer, here is my guess as to the way they will act. I don't think that we will ever start a preventive war, I don't think we will say, they are building up this, that and the other, fission and fusion weapons, and etc., and the thing to do is to hit 'em." Though he proclaimed he had no interest in doing so, Finletter had gazed into the "crystal ball" and attempted to predict the future and the outcome of what was a partial reality; the United States was facing that very situation. In seeming disagreement with a position made by LeMay, Finletter told the questioner, "I think therefore we will not fight unless we are attacked, but I think that if we are attacked in a serious way, if this country or the NATO [North Atlantic Treaty Organization] area are attacked in a serious way, I think we will use everything we've got. It's just my guess, but I think so."[11]

There were some key takeaways from Finletter's proclamation. The first was that the secretary had not drawn a discernable gradation between preemption and prevention during his remarks; it was unclear if he felt making such a distinction was necessary. The second one was that Finletter did not directly disagree with LeMay's advocacy of preemption; he had simply made it known he did not believe a decision would be made to carry out such an attack. Finally, Finletter did not indicate whether he opposed said approach. He made clear he did not believe the United States would respond had it not been "attacked." Preemption was a first-strike scenario, not a response to an attack. Finletter's statements were not advocacy; they were assessments.

That other officials had differing views on the issue of the timing and nature of nuclear strikes was not surprising; it was both healthy for the development of good government and altogether normal that senior officials disagreed on matters of policy. This was, in fact, what made LeMay's take on the matter of preemption unique. What held LeMay's views back from the brink of extremity was the fact that others—to include Finletter—had been privy to the SAC commander's opinion on the matter and had not directly and openly reprimanded him. In a more narrow sense, when considered in the context of Air Force senior leadership, LeMay's opinions fell closer to the norm. This was an important point. LeMay advocated for a policy that differed from the declared policy of the United States, that deterrence would reign. Nonetheless, LeMay had made these overtures in the context of taking such steps only under the receipt of the proper authorities. LeMay was not a rogue nuclear commander. Similarly, Finletter's statements never specifically and wholly ran counter to LeMay's arguments. His appraisals simply contained different conclusions than those at which LeMay had arrived. At worst, it was a professional disagreement; most likely, it was honest men with differing opinions.

President Truman at Offutt

Not all of LeMay's responsibilities in Omaha were directly related to SAC operations. In the spring of 1952 President Truman planned a trip to Offutt Air Force Base to meet with the governors of midwestern states that had been impacted by flooding. On April 15 LeMay had a phone call from Maj. Gen. Robert Landry, the Air Force aide to President Truman, to notify him that the president intended to land at Offutt "on the 16th for a meeting with the 7 governors of the flood states of the Missouri Basin."[12] Planning for a presidential visit was a monumental task filled with coordination among various parties and agencies. Having only one day's notice further complicated the issue. Even in the face of a short-notice visit from the president, LeMay remained witty and seemingly calm despite the high profile of the event. The transcript of LeMay's call with the White House indicated the concerned parties were to meet and lunch at Offutt. LeMay told Landry, regarding who would lunch on base that day, "Well, OK, I think we've got enough [information]. Then the seven governors will probably be here for lunch too?" Landry replied, "Yes, the seven governors," to which LeMay quipped, "OK. Who's going to pay for lunch? Me?" Another topic of conversation was security, both for the base and the president. LeMay pointed out to Landry that "you know what our security regulations are like out here, a lot of these people are going to show up and probably can't get in the base." To this Landry replied, "I was just going to ask you about that. How about taking pictures—there will be the movie press, there will be the still press, there will be the wire service boys: the usual gang that goes with the President when he goes on a trip." It was going to be a big event. Nonetheless, LeMay retorted, with details that highlighted not only the strong security measures of the period but also the seemingly paranoid atmosphere that permeated SAC's headquarters base: "Well, what happens when an airplane lands out here is that they get a machine gun pointed at them. And when the pilot gets out of the airplane he identifies himself and he vouches for the people he's got on board. If he can't, then we take a close look at them." Being safe and feeling safe were two drastically different things; a single machine gun, however, had the power to assuage fear.[13]

LeMay had direct interaction with the president of the United States and the White House staff, though it was coincidental to their purpose for visiting. He was the senior leader and thus played the part of host. Another senior Air Force officer or civilian official could have flown to Offutt to host the president, but the duty fell to LeMay. This vignette provided clear evidence that LeMay's superiors trusted him to carry out important functions such as a presidential visit. Likewise, when the location of the president's meeting was being decided, the White House selected Offutt; the White House chose LeMay. In the end, LeMay's office diary recorded that "Truman and party arrived at 1145 16 April and was met by Gen LeMay and Gen Pick of the U.S. Engineers. After honors at the line the party moved to the Officers' club where the press was fed and the President and party had a luncheon and were briefed by the engineers on the disasterrous [*sic*] flood conditions here at Omaha. After this meeting a[nd] a short statement to the press by the President[,] he departed for the white house in the Independence."[14] The president came and went. Then LeMay went back to work.

Rumors of Movement

In his own way, LeMay had struck upon a symbiotic means to advance both his own career and the interests of the Air Force. In the spring of 1952 it seemed that his climb was about to continue. According to his records, LeMay appeared slated to leave SAC and take another indeterminate position within the Air Force. The reasoning behind the move was not clear, and the records of the potentiality of this move are themselves somewhat vague. Nonetheless, a proposed move had been considered in LeMay's case. His office diary from May 20 recorded that "yesterday the 19th Gen LeMay went to the Pentagon in Washington and had lunch with the Sec [of the] Air [Force,] Mr Finletter at his home. Results are unknow [*sic*] except that the delay in transfer of Gen LeMay and Gen Twining is confirmed pending Gen Vans [Vandenberg's] return to duty. Gen LeMay also discussed Air Force matters with Gen [Laurence] Kuter and Twining during his visit."[15] Although LeMay's potential assignment was unclear, the likelihood of it being a more senior position—possibly vice chief of staff of the Air Force, given the mention of Twining—was strong. LeMay had won great respect in the Air Force and other segments of government. He delivered what was asked of him—a guard against the nation's fears of the time—and was, by all appearances, about to be rewarded for it. As history demonstrated, however, this move did not come to pass.

Disaster and Opportunity

Late summer 1952 was marked by two notable tragedies that occurred within days of one another. On Saturday, August 30, LeMay was participating in an airshow, though his major role had him on the ground. According to his office diary, "On Sat[urday] the General opened the Air Force part of the Air Show at Wayne Major Airport. . . . The show was badly upset when one of the AF acft, a F 89, came apart as it passed over the stands and crashed, killing the two pilots and injuring several spectators as the wreckage fell."[16] Only two days later, another disaster occurred that was of greater magnitude for the Air Force. LeMay's office diary recorded events of 1 September at Carswell Air Force Base: "Disaster struck yesterday at Ft Worth when a wind storm destroyed a B-36 and injured several more. More details are still coming in but damage will be Heavy both at Carswell and the factory line."[17] From an operations perspective, this was one of the most calamitous events to befall SAC during LeMay's tenure as commander. The details continued: "More data indicates that 50 million [dollars] worth of damage done at Carswell including loss of all the B 36 docks in 11 Group and damage to 4 of those at 7 Wing. Extensive damage was done to all facilities in addition to acft and the unit will have only 9 acft flyable for a while."[18] The storm was a shocking reminder of the potential of sudden destructiveness. Unlike a nuclear attack, however, there was no radiation that poisoned the site and killed the survivors of the initial blast. A blow had been dealt to SAC's B-36 fleet and thus also to SAC's overall plan for executing a nuclear war; the B-36 was an important portion of the operational force destined to attack targets in the Soviet Union. The B-36 was also the only U.S. bomber that could carry out this mission from within the confines of the continental United States without midair refueling.

However, LeMay was a professionally resilient leader, perhaps owing to regular breaks from the home office. Whether on a sabbatical of temporary duty to another location or on a vacation—with family or colleagues (or both)—LeMay found time away from the headquarters on a steady basis. While one of his more regular temporary duty locations was Washington, DC, it was not his only destination. Plenty of other interesting stops are mentioned in his records. Just days after the incident at Carswell, LeMay's office diary recorded that "on 5 Sep 52, Gen. LeMay returned from Washington D.C. and proceeded in his private airplane to Elkhart Lake in Wisconsin where he observed the running of the Elkhart Lake Road Race, on 6 and 7 Sep. He was joined there by Col. Tilley who had recently entered the race and Mrs. LeMay who had been on leave in the East. The party stayed at the Swartz Hotel in Elkhart Lake, Wisconsin."[19] In all likelihood owing to the trust that LeMay placed in his subordinates, such as Thomas Power, he never was tethered to the office, even in the midst of a crisis like the one at Carswell. Eventually, however, LeMay always returned home.

In the case of the Elkhart Lake sojourn, there was good reason to get back; some important visitors were arriving at Offutt on September 8. Per LeMay's files: "On the evening of the 8th, a large party of VIP's headed up by Mr. [William Chapman] Foster, the Under Secretary of Defense [actually, the Deputy Secretary of Defense], and the Secretaries of the Army, Navy and Air

Force, as well as the commissioners of the AEC [Atomic Energy Commission] arrived at Offutt and were entertained by the CG at the Officers' Club on the evening of the 8th." The next day they received a briefing, and "after the briefing [the] CG took the party, in a C-97, gave them lunch, and delivered them at Carswell AFB, Texas," the site of the recent disastrous storm.[20] After they arrived at Carswell, "the party received a simulated briefing and observed various types of SAC acft on the ramps at Carswell."[21] Whether the party inspected the damage done by the storm at Carswell is unclear. The next day, the showcase of SAC was back in full swing: "The morning of the 10th, the various members of the AEC and the Defense Dept. flew in a B-36 to Eglin AFB and observed the actual drop of 9M10 Bombs from 41 thousand feet and the air burst of the bomb from the B-36. The bombing was excellent. At 1545 [3:45 p.m.] on Wednesday, the 10th of Sep, the party departed from Eglin and proceeded to Washington."[22] Taking senior members of the leadership ranks through SAC headquarters and operations meant not only that they got a sense of how the whole process came together but also that LeMay and his staff had an opportunity to shape the story in a manner that befit their narrative.

The repair of the damage done to the B-36 bombers during the storm of September 1 remained a theme of the period. On September 10 SAC headquarters received a call explaining "that AMC [Air Material Command] has given the go-ahead to begin repair on the damaged B-36's at Carswell." The next day, September 11, another call came in "to report seeing a news release to the effect that a Senate Investigating Committee headed by Senator Johnson was to inspect the Carswell storm damage."[23] While SAC was mending the immediate impact of the storm, a political one was brewing. Suddenly, one of the potential purposes of LeMay's lobbying efforts became much more apparent.

One Problem to Another

While LeMay was concerned with mission results and process outcomes, he was also cognizant of the well-being of his people, particularly as they went into battle. On September 14 LeMay left Offutt at 8 a.m. for meetings in Tokyo. Following a few days in Japan, during which LeMay met with other military leaders, the SAC commander departed for Korea. LeMay's trip to the peninsula began early on September 18 with a transport aircraft in tow to effect his return.

> Early the morning of the 19th, General LeMay attended the briefing of the 307th and 19th Bomb Gps [Groups] who were being briefed for their first day light mission of approximately one year. Gen. LeMay gave a very impressive talk to the crews and emphasized to them the importance of being able to utilize both day and night tactics in their store book of applications of the medium bomber—that the defenses they were striking at today were no worse than defenses of Germany in the last war, nor the conditions very much different. That a properly formed formation would get through as they did in the last war. The results of that day's missions proved the General's word. None of the acft were shot down, minor flak and fighters were encountered.[24]

It was evident that LeMay held a sustained interest in operational matters and his people. His interaction with aircrews on September 19 prior to their mission over Korea was also an opportunity for

LeMay to share some of his combat experience from World War II, perhaps the touchstone of his military career. Having such experience in aerial combat and being in a position that allowed him to share that experience gave LeMay credibility in the eyes of his subordinates. In any profession, experience—particularly when successful—equals respect among one's peers and subordinates. Such was especially the case in the military, where consequences were matters of life or death. When it came to understanding and leading strategic bomber crews in combat, LeMay held a record few could match—a distinctive aspect of his tenure at SAC and his role as a leader in the postwar Air Force. He could rightly claim to have been on the scene, serving in important roles and at critical junctures in the service's brief history. LeMay once again had been in the right places at the right times—and once in those places, LeMay made the right decisions.

Shortly after his talk to the flight crews, LeMay proceeded to Guam, where he inspected the facilities for about two hours and then went directly to Hickam Field in Hawaii.[25] While there, LeMay had a meeting of some note, at least from the perspective of history. Per the SAC commander's records, "On the morning of the 20th, at Hickam Field, Gen. LeMay met with Admiral [Arthur] Radford, CINCPAC [Commander in Chief, Pacific] Commander, at Pearl Harbor, and spent about 2 hours with him. . . . Meetings were unsuccessful."[26] Although his immediate task, whatever it had been, was unfulfilled, a larger result had been achieved. Although LeMay could not have been aware of it at the time, he had just spent two hours with the future chairman of the Joint Chiefs of Staff, the nation's most senior military leader. Whether the interaction between the two had been positive or negative, LeMay had made himself known to the future chairman. How that would serve LeMay and SAC in the future was yet to be seen.

September had been a busy and fraught month for LeMay. While the command was making progress toward greater effectiveness and working its way through incidents such as the destruction at Carswell, the larger issue of a strategy for fighting a nuclear war remained. The topic was again on LeMay's mind during a senior leader forum the following month.

Back to Basics

LeMay had to play many roles nearly simultaneously. He had to lead, discipline, and care for his subordinates; he also served as the manager of calamities and campaigner for research and development concerns. His most important role, perhaps, was as SAC's primary policy advocate. In this role, LeMay sponsored the concepts that guided the command in its mission—most conspicuously, the mission of carrying out a nuclear war. Given his position and SAC's central role as the country's preeminent nuclear command, LeMay was the chief nuclear policy innovator at the military-strategic and national-operational levels.

On October 15, 1952, the Air Force convened a two-day commanders conference at Eglin Air Force Base on the Florida panhandle. This event served in many ways as a bookend to an already interesting year for LeMay and SAC. On the second day of the conference, LeMay had an opportunity to lobby for his command among other senior Air Force leaders. LeMay's words also highlighted his own worries: "I'd like to re-emphasize my prediction that the present SAC force can penetrate the Russian defenses with acceptable losses due to flak and fighters. . . . Also, I am convinced that the delivery capability of SAC combined with the power of our present atomic stockpile makes it possible for us to deliver a blow against Russia of such magnitude that it will make it impossible for her to win a major war."[27] These were strong but basic comments, much in keeping with LeMay's typical approach to such discussion. If war came, LeMay wanted to be able to offer the nation's leaders the ability to destroy the Soviet Union's chances of prevailing in a war; he was prepared to again destroy a nation. What came next were more thoughtful albeit strongly worded considerations as LeMay qualified his beliefs:

> However, for this delivery potential to be realized, there are several basic vital requirements beyond SAC's control which must be fulfilled. First, we must not permit SAC to be destroyed on the ground by a surprise attack. Second, the target system must be capable of absorbing the full power of the bomb and must be within the delivery capability of her force. Moreover, the system must be selected with a view towards the overall winning of the war as opposed to influencing an individual campaign. Third, our atomic stockpile must be kept reasonably intact and ready for use wherever it is necessary to win the overall war. It can easily be rendered impotent and ineffective to diversion and multiple allocation. Last, my experience in the last four years have impressed me very much with the fact that a force in being such as SAC, geared to go off on call is a very vital thing and it can easily and quickly be destroyed through our peace time day-to-day actions.[28]

The first contingency LeMay offered was an interesting conundrum of great consequence with regard to larger defense implications: How would the Air Force achieve the end of avoiding destruction of the SAC force by a surprise attack if the attack was, by its very nature, a surprise? LeMay did not clarify this point by offering a potential answer, instead leaving the matter open for the interpretation and evaluation of the audience. He kept whatever ideas he might have had on the subject to himself during his remarks on that day.

The next two items in LeMay's discussion offered insight on his thinking about war planning and strategic decision-making. As LeMay pointed out, victory was not about winning individual battles; victory came as a result of winning wars. Although LeMay was also quite comfortable on the tactical level, as demonstrated by his advice to the bomber crews in Korea the previous month, he understood there was a bigger picture. The third exigency was vague as to LeMay's intended message. On one hand, prior to the mid-1950s, when nuclear weapons began being stored on individual SAC bases, the U.S. nuclear stockpile was kept at a few centralized sites. This arrangement left the stores of munitions vulnerable to a surprise attack that could, in a relatively limited assault, disarm the Americans of the weapons they coveted. At the same time, LeMay's suggestion that the overall cache of weapons could "easily be rendered impotent and ineffective to diversion and multiple allocation" was potentially understood as a warning against squandering the stockpile among multiple U.S. military forces and with duplication against targets. If nothing else, LeMay was protective of SAC and its mission, and through that lens the statement was more plausible. Finally, there came the question of maintaining a force at the ready despite "our peace time day-to-day actions." This was perhaps LeMay's most immediately feasible discomfort, as the challenges he faced in building the command and its combat effectiveness were plenty. Limited resources meant inter- and intra-service fights over funding, people, and equipment. As with any finite asset, their protection was a paramount role of an organizational leader. Taken on the whole, these amounted to some of LeMay's basic professional concerns. An ongoing canon of LeMay's fears fed his proposed solution: preemption.[29]

Small Reminders of Humanity

The final part of 1952 demonstrated LeMay's ability to know and understand operational details but not be obsessed with making noteworthy decisions solely upon them. Details needed to have larger implications to transcend into breakpoint motivations for action. The ability to differentiate these things was among LeMay's strong points. Also vital was his ability to discern critical matters from complicating, noisy chatter. In so doing, the SAC commander had the ability to support his narrative—even if it was not in sync with how others saw national priorities. For LeMay, the most essential element of the defense of the nation and for U.S. defense policy was SAC. At the time LeMay was making these determinations and taking these actions, he simply thought he was doing his duty. For better or for worse, LeMay did his duty well, and SAC was being built into a Cold War institution.

SAC, however, was not all business all the time. As an institution, it developed a reputation for its rigidity and unforgiving nature in discipline. However, mercy and diversion sometimes reigned within the nuclear command—notably at the most senior of levels. As tough as LeMay was purported to have been, the grizzled veteran of World War II and proponent of preemptive nuclear war occasionally showed a softer side.

An October 25, 1952, memorandum in LeMay's office diary outlined some unanswered questions related to the destruction at Carswell Air Force Base caused by the storm on September 1.

The questions resulted from a briefing given to the Air Council, an advisory body that served to inform and guide the Air Force's two most senior leaders. Based on this memorandum, it was clear that, even within SAC, the rules were not always followed. Had the devastation resulting from the storm not been so extensive, it was unlikely that the matters would have been raised by anyone within or outside SAC or the Air Force. But in this case, the details made their way into higher level records. Also seemingly outside the typical for SAC, leniency was shown. The memorandum stated that "undoubtedly there are some things that happened during the tornado episode that can be nitpicked. However, I am convinced there is no one who should be held responsible for what happened. In fact, the entire organization did a commendable job under the circumstances and we were right in so telling them." The memorandum was signed by SAC's vice commander, Thomas Power. Coming from LeMay's most trusted professional confidant, it is difficult—though not impossible—to comprehend a great deal of differentiation between the two in the handling of the issue. Nonetheless, Power was comfortable making the argument to LeMay and thereby demonstrated both a level of ease in doing so and an expectation that his petition would be fairly heard.[30] This suggested that the actual climate of the command did not reflect the reputation of a lack of mercy that preceded it.

Outside of duty hours, LeMay remained involved with one of his favorite pastimes, race cars. LeMay had a personal sports car, an Allard. LeMay's office diary reported on November 24 that "Gen LeMay stayed home most of the weekend[,] his only activity being concerned over work on his Allard."[31] On November 28 "Early Sunday morning [the] CG took off for Chicago where he discussed the racing agreement with Mr Fred Wacker of SCCA

[Sports Car Club of America]."[32] On December 15 LeMay's office diary stated that for unknown reasons LeMay reneged on an arrangement to permit the taking of "some pictures of the Allard for running in the Sunday Magazine section." As much as he found pleasure in cars and good press, there certainly must have been a serious reason for LeMay to change his mind.[33] Even LeMay, however, had a hobby.

Fighting the Good Fight

A letter from LeMay to Vandenberg on December 5 outlined some critical aspects of SAC's nuclear mission and provided further detail as to the likely scope, shape, and overall character of what a nuclear war would have looked like in the early 1950s. LeMay's letter also served as reinforcement to his interest in preemption and supports Vandenberg's knowledge of this approach. LeMay noted that "the current Strategic Air Command capability in terms of bombs that could be launched during the first six days of operations has increased to approximately 200 since July 1952. . . . Several factors prevent a more significant increase in the number of bombs which can be effectively delivered." LeMay then specified why such was the case and argued that

> specific restrictive conditions that have limited the
> assignment of an atomic mission in the EWP [Emergency
> War Plan] to newly formed bombardment wings are as
> follows:
>> a. The continual delays in the receipt of combat ready
>> B-47 aircraft have prevented our first B-47 unit
>> from becoming fully equipped and therefore it has

not yet attained an acceptable degree of training which warrants an assignment of a war plan mission. This unit is expected to be fully equipped with combat ready aircraft by the end of this month.

b. The present number of targets assigned each wing represents the optimum number of atomic targets which I consider the respective wing can effectively attack due to restrictions caused by continuing aircraft modification, retrofit and/or conversion programs.[34]

Having explained some of the problems to Vandenberg, LeMay went on to discuss other mission-related matters, and preemption found its way into the discussion in the context of being able to find and destroy Soviet bombers in the initial phase of a war. For the U.S. nuclear command, it was a high-stakes game of cat and mouse:

Certain of the major deficiencies warranting special attention are listed below:

a. *Reconnaissance*: Our BDA [Bomb Damage Assessment] capability is still severely limited, due to the lack of a suitable low level reconnaissance vehicle. This deficiency affects our blunting mission to an even greater degree. As you know, we must locate the Tu-4 [Soviet bomber] force at the outset of hostilities and maintain surveillance of its movements if Strategic Air Command is to deter the launching of an attack against the United States and United Kingdom. In February 1952 I submitted a requirement to equip some of my fighter aircraft with a low

> level reconnaissance capability. This was approved,
> but to date I have not received the required cameras
> and installation kits, nor do I have a firm estimate of
> when these items will be available.[35]

This relatively short letter provided insight into how LeMay planned on carrying out a nuclear war and preemptively striking the Soviet Union's attack force. It also demonstrated that the U.S. nuclear command was lacking in its ability to actually execute LeMay's desired mission of eradicating the Soviet Union's opposing force—assuming the U.S. and SAC knowledge thereof was even well founded. Nonetheless, the details of war were plain to see. SAC's ability to deliver two hundred nuclear bombs in six days would mean a degree of destruction that had never before been experienced in human history. It was an expression of U.S. war aims: to destroy another country or, at the very least, its ability to make strategic aerial war, although it certainly appeared that LeMay was more interested in eliminating a similar threat to the United States. Such was also an expression of U.S.—and LeMay's—fears of the Soviet Union and its intentions. LeMay had no compunction about destroying an enemy nation, but he certainly did not want it to happen to the state he represented. While LeMay believed a two-hundred-bomb war was possible, he assessed that a barrage of a scale beyond that was questionable. In truth it was doubtful much more could have been gained in the way of political or military outcomes from an even larger attack.

The specifics of LeMay's discussion of SAC's problems with reconnaissance were of the greatest importance in reference to his pursuit of and advocacy for a policy of preemption. According to LeMay's argument to Vandenberg, SAC's inability to ascertain the position of the Soviet bomber force was a major block to being able to "deter" the Soviets from carrying out aggression against the United States and, interestingly enough, U.S. ally Great Britain. Concern with Great Britain, however, was likely and largely on account of the fact that U.S. bombers were based on the island nation. Nonetheless, that the preemptive mission was LeMay's primary concern was clearly communicated through his invocation of the blunting mission. Taken at face value, this was plainly a discussion of preemptive warfare. To deter a force from launching an attack through offensive means was, in the simplest terms, basic preemption.

What was perhaps most unusual, however, was LeMay's application of the term "to deter." While deterrence was traditionally understood to mean the active threat of war to prevent conflict, in the December 5 letter, LeMay seemingly applied the term to the *execution* of a preemptive mission itself. LeMay's usage suggested an interest in correlating the concept of the prevention of war with attacking the enemy's offensive force first. Though not an exclusive possibility, it is the most likely explanation. In so doing, LeMay exhibited a gradation of political and rhetorical astuteness that had not been typically ascribed to him; he was perhaps shrewder than many realized. Nonetheless, it was clear LeMay had a plan for carrying out the preemptive mission, but he also had a critical shortcoming to bridge if he wanted to make the proposed preemptive strikes reality. LeMay's motivations for this approach were exhibited shortly thereafter.

The next day, December 6, LeMay gave a speech to the Minnesota State Convention of the American Legion in Minneapolis that was simultaneously one of his most contradictory and his most enlightening addresses.[36] His speech refuted some earlier remarks recorded in classified letters and forums. But it also generally confirmed how LeMay viewed the intentions of the Soviets in the world, thus explaining some background to the fears motivating his push for preemption. LeMay's speech on December 6 was a public touchstone to his private concerns. After introductory remarks, LeMay launched into an impassioned discussion: "It is to the everlasting credit of the American people that with our allies we fought and won World War II, and have endured with fortitude the disappointments and uncertainties that have followed it. Now we have assumed the burden of Korea and, since the Soviets finally succeeded in setting off an atomic bomb of their own, we have lived in a daily atmosphere of tension."[37] Setting up the problem for his listeners—one that was, to a limited degree, the source of LeMay's fears—the SAC commander launched into how those fears were manifest for him and, in his estimation, the American public: "It is little wonder that the American people scan the future with some fear and misgiving. One day they read in their newspapers that a third world war would mean the end of civilization. The next day they read that such a war is inevitable."[38] It was true irony that LeMay made these statements. On one hand, LeMay was responsible for the execution of such a war, at least from a U.S. perspective, and on the other, he was arguing for such a war in certain circumstances. LeMay was also prepared to employ two hundred nuclear weapons, which would likely end meaningful civilization in the Soviet Union. LeMay stated, "I myself do NOT believe another war is inevitable!" but continued by explaining, "However, if we are to avoid it, not only must we reach a successful solution to the Korean conflict, but also we must win the cold war, this global war of words and ideas in which we are now engaged." Though giving a nod to the ideological underpinnings of the conflict, LeMay added a hint of force to his recommendation as he pointed out, "We must prevent further conquests by the

Soviets and yet we would like to live in peace with them. To date we have not been wholly successful in attaining either objective. And certainly it has not been because we have failed to do everything humanly possible to get along with them."[39] LeMay's initial commentary not only explained his fears but also gave others cause to join him in similar thinking. Just as LeMay had advocated to his colleagues to prepare for war, he also argued to the Minnesota American Legion for a somewhat similar strategic end. After covering some history, namely relations with the Soviet Union and the expansion of communism in China, LeMay rhetorically asked the audience, "Well, how are you to get along with people like that?"[40] He had the answer: "Theodore Roosevelt's rule for survival was: 'Walk softly and carry a big stick.' If the only thing these people understand is power—and it seems quite obvious that this is so— then in the interest of our survival we must have power, and some to spare." LeMay took a direct approach to the problem of security in U.S.-Soviet relations and made clear that military strength was the way forward. Nor did he quibble over whether the question was one of national existence. Compromise was not an option, and having a bit of overkill to do the job was within reason in LeMay's thinking. Adding some nuance to his military-minded argument, the SAC commander made clear to his audience that "the big stick is no longer enough. Theodore Roosevelt lived in a simpler world. He didn't have the technique of the Big Lie to contend with, and the tremendous Soviet propaganda machine was not one of his problems." Seemingly inconsistent with his reputation as a simple and brutish military leader, LeMay next stated that "today's conflicts are not fought—or avoided—with power alone. They are fought with philosophy, psychology, and ideas. . . . First, we must have power. Second, we must fight fire with fire in the war of words." This was not a strange concept for LeMay, as SAC was as much a weapon in the war of ideas as it was a physical weapon. The speech continued, but the salient points were clear and the key message had been delivered: the Cold War was a conflict larger than SAC—but the military force the command provided was essential to undergirding the ideological battle paralleling the military one. LeMay's understanding of the Cold War, though typically expressed in strong military terms, was in fact nuanced. Just as there was some dissonance between the declared and actual U.S. nuclear policy, there was also friction between LeMay's public and private proclamations.[41]

For both LeMay and the United States as a whole in 1952, the Cold War was still evolving. LeMay could not predict the future and could only make decisions based on his past experiences and present circumstances. In late 1952 the Korean War was ongoing, nuclear weapons were becoming more powerful, the intentions and abilities of the Soviet Union were not fully understood, and no one knew what would happen next. For many reasons, LeMay and the United States had continued cause for fear.

A Deadly Business in a New Year

To the extent that LeMay had a healthy concern over the possibility of a coming war with the Soviet Union, he nonetheless urged a degree of restraint not of action, but of perception. On January 3, 1953, LeMay sent a letter to the deputy chief of staff for operations, Lt. Gen. Thomas White, informing him that he had "witnessed a preview of the Top Secret film 'Strategic Employment of Biological and Chemical Weapons.' . . . You may recall that on 17 June 1952 I wrote to you expressing the opinion that it would be inadvisable to produce such a film. After seeing this one, I believe even more strongly that such a film should not be in existence."[42] LeMay continued:

> This film is dangerous for several reasons. The matter of fact in which the commentary in this film depicts the results of BW [Biological Warfare]—CW [Chemical Warfare] warfare left a bad taste in my mouth. During this period of cold war propaganda, it represents an unwarranted risk. In the wrong hands, the closing punch line would certainly make good headlines. As a documentary film, by its very existence it presents a grave security risk. If the Russians were to obtain a copy of it, showing among other poor features a man in a USAF Colonel's uniform discussing a plan for killing a million people in Moscow by germ warfare, they would have a most powerful psychological weapon. I recommend that the film in its present form be withheld.[43]

LeMay's admonishment to White was revealing of a critical portion of his character and an aspect of his understanding of the implications inherent in fighting a major war with the Soviet Union. LeMay was not ignorant of the damage likely to be done by the depiction of major attacks executed on the country's notional enemy and of how horrible such a war could have been. He was aware of the consequences of what he was doing in planning for a major conflict with the Soviets, but he did not want the outside world—particularly the Soviets—to have cognition of those consequences. The truth in this instance was, in LeMay's opinion, "dangerous." Similarly, it was clear LeMay had some understanding of the morality issues that lingered about the decision to attack a major population center with weapons of mass destruction. While in this case the weapons LeMay mentioned were not nuclear—the most likely weapon to be employed by SAC's bombers—the implications were all the same. Whether biological, chemical, or nuclear weapons were used, LeMay understood the death toll would be tremendous. Based on his approach, argument, and language in this letter, LeMay understood the ethical problems with using said weapons to kill that many people—most of whom would have been civilians. He knew there was something wrong with what he and SAC were prepared to do. Perhaps this was one reason why LeMay sought a policy of preempting Soviet strategic forces, thus taking the emphasis away from destroying cities and killing masses of civilians. If anyone understood this, it was LeMay. He had done it before.

White's response several days later showed that he partially concurred with LeMay: "I share to some extent your reaction to the BW-CW film which was the subject of your 3 January letter." Giving some reason as to his thinking but also explaining away LeMay's worries, White "concur[red] that the film could be a powerful psychological weapon if it fell into the hands of the Russians. It is our intent and purpose to prevent such an occurrence by insuring the security of the film during its utilization. In this respect I have directed that all copies of the film be returned to this headquarters immediately." As was the case with his view concerning Soviet nuclear attacks, LeMay had originally argued for the preemptive avoidance of problems by not making the film in the first place; White preferred to deter problems through security measures and an after-the-fact response. It was an interesting juxtaposition. White's conclusion explained that "the closing punch line will be deleted from the film and possibly replaced by a statement re-emphasizing that the estimated effects depicted in the film are based upon very limited test data. Based upon the development of additional data from the testing programs, changes to the film may be made in the future. Your comments will be given every consideration when such revisions are undertaken." Though LeMay's initial warning had not been followed, he had influenced the subsequent process. As was apparent, LeMay did not prevail in every battle he fought.[44] The exchange between the two generals was a window into both LeMay's approach to problems and an important relationship. Though neither of the men knew it at the time, White would later serve as chief of staff of the Air Force and LeMay as his deputy as vice chief of staff. Despite later claims that the two men had differences in approach and a somewhat challenged relationship, in this instance, all seemed normal.

Other events in early 1953 were not as threatening as the topic discussed by LeMay and White. According to LeMay's office diary, in February 1953 the SAC commander made an overseas trip, which included a stop in France. While on the continent LeMay and one of his keenest companions, entertainer Arthur Godfrey, made a trip together. His office diary reported that on February 16 "In Paris, General LeMay motored, accompanied by Mr. Godfrey, to the Fontainebleau Haqq of USAFE [United States Air Forces in Europe] and had luncheon with General Norstad—made a courtesy call on General Grunther [Alfred Gruenther] and General Ridgway. Mr. Godfrey entertained the entire crew and staff at dinner at a French restaurant in the evening."[45] Nonetheless, not all was joy for LeMay, SAC, or the Air Force.

On March 26, 1953, Air Force Chief of Staff Hoyt Vandenberg wrote to LeMay on the topic of accidents in the Air Force: "The plague of accidents that has been with us since November, regardless of an overall decline in rate, is happening at the most crucial time in the history of our Air Force. . . . At a time when we are trying to expand, trying to prove our capability, and asking for the support of a new administration; we are apparently failing to demonstrate our competence to those who would like to support us." If the basic mission of the Air Force was to safely and reliably fly aircraft, then the service was not meeting expectations—at least in Vandenberg's estimation—and this was a serious flaw. He continued: "The present trend in accidents is costing more lives and more expensive equipment than ever before in our history. A continuance of this trend is sure to cost us the support necessary to our existence; and the existence *and* expansion of the USAF is now of extreme importance to the nation."[46] If LeMay had not previously understood the crux of the issue, Vandenberg had laid it out in no uncertain terms. The problem of accidents was an existential threat to the new service. He continued:

> We've made exhaustive studies to determine a common denominator or a common pattern to these accidents. A most distressing result is that the only pattern common to nearly all accidents is the lack of Command supervision. I mean by this that the immediate planners and supervisors, the Colonels and Lieutenant Colonels responsible for planning the details and emergency measures, are not doing their jobs. One very direct cause of this may be an attitude on their part that they must get an order executed to the letter[,] regardless of weather, safety consideration, or acts of God. This attitude may prevail to the extent that planning for diversion from the exact mission to comply

with safety precautions is intentionally ignored or at least neglected.[47]

Vandenberg's words must have hit close to home for LeMay and his approach to operations in SAC. The command was built on the principle of strictly adhering to orders and conducting whatever operational plan had been laid out prior to a mission. In LeMay's estimation, to successfully carry out a nuclear war, strict adherence to plans and orders was the necessary approach; the system could not work any other way. In order to have a command capable of achieving this end, SAC needed to operate in the same fashion on a daily basis. But Vandenberg saw it differently, offering LeMay a rationale for such an opinion:

> I think an example at hand is the loss of the B-36 at Fairford, England. It appears to me that a reasonable compromise between exact compliance with orders and with safety would have been to have executed a preplanned diversion to Scotland, North Ireland, or other bases in England before any aircraft reached a dangerously low fuel level at a bad weather choke point. When the weather went down at the two alternates no one did anything about other alternates before it was too late. There are almost as many other examples as there have been accidents.[48]

While the chief of staff recited only one instance of the problem, his claim about other examples was very likely grounded in truth. In any case, LeMay certainly would have taken Vandenberg at his word. It also meant LeMay had a problem on his hands. Vandenberg, however, had more to say:

It is my belief, Curt, that over-emphasis on competition for jobs or between units or crews could cause a prevalence of this do or die attitude; and, in turn an intentional ignoring of safety standards. I realize the responsibility we both have to maintain a combat ready force; but I am most serious in my belief that at this time in our development and expansion that factor weighs less in overall long time benefit to the nation and to the Air Force than an easing up on training requirements in favor of a safety first standard. It may be that a seasonal pressure period and a corresponding relaxation of intensive realistic training during the worst weather months would accomplish the desired result. This, of course, would force some readjustment to our normal parts supply flow and might result in a too stringent effect on our all-weather ability. In any event[,] I believe we should achieve some relaxation of pressure at least to the extent that immediate planners and commanders normally feel that where reasonable the mission should be adjusted to meet highest safety standards and that they should preplan for such exigencies. I feel that the future of the Air Force hangs in the balance at a time when our country needs an expanded Air Force more than ever before.[49]

This was a strong critique of LeMay, if not an outright rebuke of his approach to adherence to orders and the SAC way of doing business. Operations in SAC were conducted with rigidity. Per the chief of staff's evaluation, the cost of upholding this standard was too high.

Several days later, on April 6, LeMay replied to Vandenberg on the matter of safety and accidents. Whereas Vandenberg had addressed LeMay and the problem from a general, strategic perspective, LeMay's response was rather tactical and formulaic—at least in explanation. LeMay and Vandenberg, in a sense, were speaking different languages, but the verity of one frame of reference over the other was a moot point. Both men had a clear respect for each other, and, as LeMay's memo reflected, an honest appreciation for the other's point of view. LeMay could have simply replied with a "yes, sir!" and moved on, but he instead responded with a well-reasoned, cogent, and serious letter: "I have given much thought to your letter of 26 March on the subject of aircraft accidents and have taken certain actions outlined below. First, let me say that I fully appreciate the points raised in your letter and I share your concern regarding the possible impact of accidents on the Air Force Program."[50] LeMay explained some of the steps he had taken to resolve the problem: "I have had my [numbered] Air Force Commanders in for a conference on the subject of accident prevention and have re-examined our training and development programs. I have done the same thing with my key staff officers. Additionally, all Wing and numbered Air Force Flying Safety Officers have been brought in for a conference and have been given definite instructions concerning their future duties."[51] While tactical in nature, LeMay's actions were also typically decisive. The SAC commander took actions he believed would resolve the particular set of issues at hand; there was no need to expose the organization or the mission to liability. It was this same thinking, however, that had precipitated the issue. LeMay was not perfect. After specifying what he had done and discussing the issue of supervision, LeMay told Vandenberg:

> Neither I nor my commanders feel that crews are over-trained or that overemphasis has been placed on competition

between units and crews. Neither do we believe that there has been an intentional ignoring of safety standards anywhere in the command. The very pronounced emphasis we have placed on accident prevention makes this unlikely. I want to assure you that we have never exerted pressure to accomplish operational commitments to the extent that planners and commanders were obliged to sacrifice safety. It is necessary, of course, to engage in realistic training to a reasonable degree[,] but we have always attempted to strike a sound balance between close simulation of the EWP requirements and safety considerations.[52]

In other words, LeMay had respectfully disagreed with his boss. This was an important inflection point in the relationship between LeMay and Vandenberg. While the men were always professional in their regard, they were not particularly warm. Nor were they in absolute agreement on matters relating to operations. The efficacy of the Air Force system of administration was not always an "old boy" network that promoted close personal friends. Nonetheless, LeMay excelled at getting his job done—as did his command. LeMay concluded his letter by assuring Vandenberg that "everything within reason will be done to prevent future accidents within Strategic Air Command." Just as LeMay had likely taken Vandenberg at his word, the chief of staff likely took the SAC commander at his; with LeMay's record at SAC, Vandenberg had good reason to do so.[53]

In early May 1953 LeMay received some interesting news. The SAC commander had made a trip to Nevada to witness a nuclear test that had been delayed due to conditions. When LeMay arrived at his headquarters, he found out that Nathan Twining was named the new Air Force chief of staff and Thomas White vice chief of staff.

In response, "Gen LeMay called to offer his congratulations and help."[54] The office of chief of staff of the Air Force was an important one, and its holder played a critical role in the service's operation. General Nathan Twining, like LeMay, was a pilot and longtime veteran of the Air Force and its predecessors and had served in leadership roles during World War II. In late 1950 Twining became the Air Force's vice chief of staff. Dealings between LeMay and Twining were typically pleasant. By certain appearances, LeMay and Twining had a generally warmer relationship than the SAC commander had enjoyed with Vandenberg. LeMay did not dislike Vandenberg, nor did he not respect him. LeMay and Twining, however, simply seemed to have a similar world view, which their interactions over the coming years reflected. LeMay's relationship with Twining became an increasingly important one as time passed.

LeMay tangled with White on one issue, however, that remained important to him: the question of a war with the Soviet Union and the ability to successfully fight it—at least in the manner LeMay wanted to be able. On May 8 "General White phoned General LeMay at 1445 this date regarding the recce [reconnaissance] tech labs SAC has requested. He said he thought there was a good chance of getting them approved if General LeMay would agree to delete the three for the [numbered] Air Force Headquarters. General LeMay said he wouldn't sign a paper saying he didn't need those three; that if he can't have them, it's up to the Defense Department to say so." These were sharp words and a strong disagreement, not necessarily with White, but at least with the situation. White replied that "they have already said how much money we will have to spend and it's a case of deleting the things that will hurt least and that they are taking care to see that SAC is taking the smallest share of the cut." The memo explained, "He [White] asked General LeMay to call him tomorrow and let him know what he wants to do—cut out the three at the AF Hq or three somewhere else." Rather than dig his heels in any further at that moment, "General LeMay agreed to let him know tomorrow." This was a minor but interesting twist in the story of LeMay. For a man known for his unyielding will, it was clear from this incident that LeMay also knew how to remember the big picture and when to back down. Even LeMay had limits.[55]

Similar Yet Different Ideas

Though the Korean War dragged on, the end was near. An armistice in 1953 resolved the fighting, and not a single nuclear weapon had been used. It was an interesting conclusion to a war that created more questions than it answered. Perhaps the most prominent unanswered question was whether a nuclear war was still in the offing and if the war in Korea had made this more or less likely. LeMay, however, continued to believe he had some answers to the larger questions of the security problem the Cold War presented the United States.

On July 15 LeMay offered remarks to the annual meeting of the Institute of the Aeronautical Sciences in Los Angeles.[56] LeMay opened with the historically charged statement that "it is difficult to pin down the exact origin of the doctrine of directing airpower against the sustaining resources of an enemy nation. It must have been sometime in World War I. Certainly it persisted in the Twenties as a strong belief, and in the Thirties there emerged from this belief a firm concept which has profoundly influenced not only the nature of our military forces, but also the outcome of a great war and the course of world history."[57] This statement was a fascinating contrast to LeMay's thinking about preemptive warfare and the targets he associated with such warfare. LeMay did not, however, engage in a debate over whether the bombing campaign brought about an end to the war. Rather, he astutely applied the term "influence." Though giving an essentially public address in an unclassified forum, LeMay skirted the issue of preemption in his statements. He stated that "at the outset of a major war, SAC's medium and heavy bombers, operating from the U.S. and prepared advance bases in other parts of the world, would immediately mount simultaneous atomic attacks against a great many selected targets located over a wide geographical area of an enemy's homeland. These coordinated, nation-wide attacks would be directed against selected objectives including bases, industrial complexes, communications centers, sources of power, stockpiles of material and other targets in support of area commanders"—which certainly sounded like a strategic bombing campaign. However, the real punch came next: "The attacks would be designed to cause serious damage to enemy offensive air capability and to destroy the vital elements of his war-making capacity." More simply said, LeMay and SAC intended to destroy the Soviets' ability to attack the United States. This was preemption in a rather basic form.[58] But whether for political purposes, public relations, security classification of the topic, or other reasons, LeMay carefully veiled his statements in mildly vague terms. He was usually imprecise when discussing preemption in public venues. Nonetheless, it was clear what LeMay communicated to his audience.

Preemption, however, was not the only salient issue that night. LeMay later told the audience that "we have learned from history that the offensive weapon comes first. Then the defense against it is developed through necessity. Each new weapon affects the balance temporarily until the defense can work out a solution to bring the situation into balance. During the last war we saw a number of examples. Perhaps the German submarine campaign is a good one.

It began, as you will recall, with the subs sinking ships faster than we could build them—and ended with the subs being driven from the sea by a complex variety of sub killing weapons."[59] For LeMay, it was clear that many lessons could be drawn from World War II. He then pointed out that "the struggle of one technology against another—the offense against the defense—is a part of a never ending battle. Our job in SAC is to constantly evaluate the picture with respect to air defenses, to plan ahead, to anticipate and to be ready for the contingencies." Though LeMay may have been discussing air defenses in this instance, he might as well have been talking about the overall manner in which he saw warfare in the nuclear era.[60]

In closing, LeMay explained that "the long-range bomber and the atomic bomb with its terrible destructive capacity, turns the factor of time again against the defender. Every important target in even the world's largest nation can be reached at the most within two hours after bombers cross their frontier. Time is of utmost value. There may not be enough of it once an atomic attack is launched. Hence, the reason for the existence and the constant poised readiness of the Strategic Air Command."[61] There it was: LeMay's thinking on preemption and the need for an immediate capacity to attack an enemy. If there would not be enough time to respond after an enemy attack was launched, then when should it happen? The answer was simple: before one was fully under way. From LeMay's perspective, an enemy attack surely meant the loss of the war—and it needed to be preempted. There was no other option.

In No Uncertain Terms

With a new chief of staff came new thinking, some of which generally mirrored LeMay's outlook on national security. Like

LeMay, Twining wanted to sound the warning of inaction and lack of readiness. "The Coming National Crisis," a top-secret "Memorandum for the Chief of Staff, U.S. Air Force" dated August 21, 1953, and signed by Gen. Robert M. Lee, articulated some of Twining's thoughts to his colleagues, the Joint Chiefs of Staff, while confirming the unanimity between LeMay's thinking and that of his new boss.[62] Beginning in summer 1951, General Lee served as "the deputy director of plans under the deputy chief of staff for operations, Headquarters U.S. Air Force, Washington, D.C., with a simultaneous duty as the Air Force member of the Joint Strategic Plans Committee. Shortly thereafter he became the director of plans."[63] Lee's memo to Twining recounted some background, to include a few recent and seminal events concerning U.S. national security—one of which was the advancement of the Soviet nuclear program. Under that heading, the first item listed stated that the "National Security Act of 1947" made "the Joint Chiefs of Staff (JCS) responsible for providing military advice to the President, the National Security Council, and the Secretary of Defense." As the memo went on, it pointed out that it was "considered mandatory to move the present planning situation off of top-dead-center. The necessity for formulating the FY [fiscal year] 1955 budget in the near future, and the possibility that fundamental and far reaching decisions will be made without there being an opportunity for adequate expression of Service views, creates a requirement that positive action be taken to establish the fundamental basis for national security planning. This basis is recognition of the threat and realization that it will soon assume unmanageable proportions."[64] Given this assessment, it was clear that at least part of the Air Force held a view that certain ideas— namely a belief in a lack of a military voice in the decision-making process—needed a more proactive declaration. Just as LeMay had made a case for a policy of preemption, Lee made a broader case for defense policy writ large. With Project Solarium, the development of President Dwight D. Eisenhower's "New Look" defense policy, under way, there was no better time than the present for Lee to make the point. He eventually noted that "the attached memorandum is proposed as a vehicle whereby the Chief of Staff, U.S. Air Force, may go on written record as having recognized the problem and fulfilled his responsibility. It is considered particularly appropriate that the Air Force take the leadership in facing this problem."[65]

That document included statements that amounted to the underpinnings of a policy of preemption and was crafted by senior Air Force leadership. It provided historical context to LeMay's statements on the same topic. It afforded evidence that suggested LeMay was not outside the norm in his arguments and was part of a larger movement in making his declarations on the topic. Per the document, and after having laid groundwork, the memo stated:

> I can remember no general American or press attitude before World Wars I and II which branded as immoral the actions of a nation which were necessary to the defense of that nation. Yet, we have now become so publicly conscious of the morality aspects of self defense, that we have convinced ourselves that it is contrary to the American way of life to take timely action for our survival. . . . In the past we have always reacted to the threat after it had been exposed, and have been able to mobilize and take military action that eventually resulted in a successful conclusion.

Delays resulting from indecision and hesitation on the part of our government have not assumed vital significance because, prior to the presently-developing situation, no enemy of the U.S. has had the means to exploit such delays to deal a mortal blow to our nation.[66]

In a different sense and per the memorandum author's narrative, the historical U.S. reply to a security concern had been forbearance. The United States did not take an unjustified offensive posture. At the same time, according to the memo, no U.S. adversary to that point had been able to take an action that could have destroyed the country. The memo stated that "now, however, for the first time in our history we are confronted with a threat of such nature and magnitude that it can literally destroy the nation, and, ironically, we have philosophised ourselves into a passive and inactive frame of mind." This was not enough, however. "When all logic will support the view that to 'accept the first blow' in atomic and thermo-nuclear warfare is to accept national suicide, we have been tolerating the pseudo-moralist who insists that we must accept this catastrophe." These were strong words that left little room for dissention in the pursuit of American foreign and defense policy.[67] They also sought to redefine them. The memo made some curt conclusions: "Our security situation may be broken down into two periods of time. During the first period we can retain the ability to achieve our security objectives by military action if war eventuates; during the second period our security objectives *cannot* be attained through military actions because the problem will have become militarily unmanageable. Postwar survival of remnants of the population, at a low standard of living, might be possible during this second period of time, but this eventuality is not accepted as meeting the requirements of our security objectives." The problem was laid out. The United States had a critical national security decision to make. In the eyes of the chief of staff, there was going to be a tight window in which to make said decision. Building upon this argument, the memo pointed out that before

> entering the second period of time, if our objectives have not been achieved by means short of general war, it will be necessary to adopt other measures. We must recognize the time of decision, or, we will continue blindly down a suicidal path and arrive at a situation in which we will have entrusted our survival to the whims of a small group of proven barbarians. If we believe it unsafe, unwise, or immoral to gamble that the enemy will tolerate our existence under this circumstance, we must be militarily prepared to support such decisions as might involve general war.[68]

These were striking words, particularly given their source. The chief of staff—or at least his staff—had argued for unspecified "other measures" to be taken. Such vagueness was—in most instances—uncharacteristic of the military policy process, but it may have resulted from a genuine lack of understanding of the problem. This was certainly the case in the perception of the strength of the Soviet threat at that time. The Soviets were not about to launch a major surprise assault on the United States, but that did not matter. The defense establishment generally and genuinely believed the contrary—and saw it as its job to assess and counter the threat.

What came next in the memo was revealing of this misconception and fear—one echoed by LeMay. The memo noted that predicting "the Time of Decision is a military responsibility which, however unpleasant, we cannot avoid. The Chief Executive, the NSC, and the American people have a right to know when we will enter a period of time in which we will be unable to provide for their security under current policies." Twining's trepidation was evident in his laying out of the logic of his argument and in almost justifying bringing up the issue. This was an interesting contrast to LeMay, who exhibited greater confidence in his beliefs and statements. When he spoke on a controversial matter, LeMay gave less indication of having to explain himself and justify his beliefs to others—though it did occasionally happen. For the two men to have worked so closely and on the same issues, it was surprising that a greater continuity in approach did not exist. The section concluded: "If, in possession of the essential facts, the American people choose to live in a world in which their survival is dependent upon the pleasure of a sworn enemy—if they knowingly support a national policy which leads to a condition of military impotence, we will not be responsible for the consequences. However, it would be morally wrong for the nation to be led to destruction with no voice in the matter."[69]

Twining then made some suggestions:

I therefore recommend that as a matter of urgency, the Joint Chiefs of Staff prepare and forward to the Secretary of Defense, the National Security Council, and the President a statement which: a. Provides an assessment, time-wise, of the nature of the threat and an estimate as to when the problem can no longer be managed by military means. b. Vigorously supports a decision on Project Solarium which provides for a maximum effort cold war program designed to achieve decision before the problem becomes militarily unmanageable. c. Emphasizes that such an intensified cold war program will require preparedness for general war. d. Recommends a Fiscal 1955 force composition based on military requirements, rather than fiscal policy.[70]

In part, Twining was well within his right as a military service chief to make these arguments. It was the chief of staff's responsibility to ensure the service was able to function in its wartime capacities and to share with the nation's civilian leaders his best military advice. In another sense, Twining was doing so in terms that seemed to be apologizing for a retreat in advance of the battle.

Although LeMay did not sign the document, it had more to do with him and SAC than it did with Twining or the rest of the Air Force. The mission of defeating the Soviet Union and preventing the nation's feared reverse that was asserted by the memo largely fell to LeMay and his command. If anything, the memo made clear just how Twining had prioritized LeMay's mission in terms of national-level interests. The document also demonstrated that Twining was at least as concerned as LeMay over the issue of U.S. security in the Cold War environment. To some extent, Twining was simply expressing the tensions of the era. These tensions, however, were based less on the facts of the day and more on an unknown future. Twining, like LeMay, did not want to face a situation that was beyond his control. But in foreign policy and defense matters, there were no guarantees of safety. LeMay now had a boss who was similarly tempered and as concerned as he was about the matter. Whereas Vandenberg had been a foil to some of LeMay's concerns and moderated his anxiety, Twining's words were expressions of a man who was also troubled by the matter.

Whether each man fed the other's worries or simply verified the other's independently held beliefs (based on international ideological inconsistency, a scarring memory of World War II, and the means to do it all again), such feelings were not easily dispelled. Twining and LeMay were afraid.

The Drumbeat Continues

Even if it was distress over the future that animated LeMay and Twining, current problems vied for LeMay's attention in ways that directly related to SAC's primary mission—as well as LeMay's cherished policy of preemption. Haywood Hansell, who preceded LeMay as the B-29 commander in the Pacific during World War II, sent a letter to LeMay on October 9. Though LeMay outranked Hansell, the salutation "Dear Curt" reflected the comfortable familiarity the two men had. This letter, however, had more than friendly purposes. After summarizing plans for an upcoming trip to see LeMay, Hansell stated, "WSEG [Weapons System Evaluation Group] has just completed the evaluation of the effects of the SAC offensive as described in the SATTS [Summary of Air Targets and Target Systems] target list. That is on its way to the Joint Chiefs of Staff and should be delivered sometime next week." The WSEG was the military organization responsible for evaluating weapons and their effects; during the Cold War, this also meant evaluating nuclear weapons. Hansell explained to LeMay that

> our next assignment is the analysis of the deliverability of the weapons. The first study assumed that the bombs would reach the bomb release line in the numbers proposed and with an average circular probable error of 3000

feet. I should like to have the opportunity to discuss the findings of this study with you and one or two others of your staff in private, and to this end I would like to come out either on Saturday or Sunday, the 17th or 18th, before Dr. [George I.] Welch arrives on the night of the 18th or the morning of the 19th.[71]

In other words, there was something that Hansell wanted to tell LeMay that he did not want Welch, the acting director of research in WSEG, to know about. This became more apparent in Hansell's next words: "I am not sure that I am actually authorized to discuss this study prior to its acceptance by the JCS, which is one reason I would prefer to confine the discussion to the minimum number of people at this time." Whatever the issue was, Hansell had his concerns. The next paragraph exposed not only more of Hansell's purpose but also his service parochialism to LeMay. Hansell pointed out that "the second phase of the study, the SAC capability to deliver, is one in which we will need all the help we can get. I feel that in the past WSEG has been heavily stacked against us. There have been far too many Army and Navy members and civilians with Army and Navy training." In Hansell's estimation, these were not friendly forces. He next discussed the specifics of WSEG's service-affiliation makeup and pointed out that

Tommy White and Pat Partridge [Air Force deputy chief of staff for operations] are well aware of this situation, and we hope ultimately to have it corrected. . . . In the meantime, I am making every effort to see that the group which undertakes this particular study should be as well balanced and as well informed as possible. . . . Although my efforts

to get additional personnel assigned on a permanent basis
to WSEG have met with rebuff by the present Director, I do
have some opportunity to obtain personnel on a loan basis,
temporary duty, for this particular project. . . . However,
here again my numbers are limited.[72]

After further discussion of the personnel issue, Hansell explained
that he felt "the two fields that are apt to be most sensitive are that
of airbases and the fighter versus the bomber duel. I hope to get
some help in the latter category from RAND, although I believe
our greatest assistance from your Command probably would lie
in the field of a competent analyst who is especially well qualified
on the question or [of] air bases and their influence on operations." This was a sage observation. Even LeMay had recognized
the vulnerability of aircraft parked at their bases to enemy attack.
Hansell told LeMay, "I am bringing Dr. Welch with me who is the
Acting Director of Research. I think perhaps you know him. He is,
I believe, the most fair-minded and the most air-minded member
of the WSEG and is obviously in a position to exercise considerable influence in so far as this study is concerned." Hansell divulged
that he was "trying to get him [Welch] the plush treatment in an
effort to encourage his Air Force inclinations. I will greatly appreciate any special courtesies in an official manner that he may be
shown." Though Hansell was partly known for his attempts to
adhere to some moral principle during the strategic bombing of
Japan during World War II, in this instance he clearly just wanted
to win. Hansell cautioned LeMay that "for obvious reasons, I prefer not to discuss this with Dr. Welch. So would you please address
any communications to me through General Partridge. . . . I shall
be looking forward to seeing you and the other members of your

Command with whom I have served in the past. Please give my best to Mrs. LeMay."[73]

Hansell's note to LeMay was important for what it did and did not say. Though LeMay and Hansell had encountered some challenges together in the past (for example, LeMay's dramatic shift in strategy after assumption of command of the B-29 operations against Japan), the relationship did not appear poisoned. LeMay intentionally burned few bridges. He and Hansell certainly understood what was at stake. SAC, like the Air Force as a whole, was a relatively new organization. Despite the efforts made and results shown by the service's predecessor during World War II, the new service still needed its own coterie of boosters. It was also clear that Hansell understood (even if LeMay perhaps did not) that there were holes in the plan for fighting a nuclear war. If he needed to preempt the Soviets, LeMay wanted to bomb Soviet aircraft as they sat on the tarmac—but U.S. aircraft similarly configured presented an equally valid target.

Despite the outlook Hansell assessed in his letter to LeMay, service rivalries did not always dictate the execution of operations. For LeMay and others in the chain of command within the organization, the question of being ready for a Soviet attack—or, perhaps more appropriately, being ready to attack the Soviet Union—was an issue of immediate importance. Senior military officers were equally aware of LeMay's efforts. At times, others offered to provide their own forms of assistance. On November 14, 1953, the commander of Seventh Air Division in England, the organization responsible for SAC forces posted there, sent a message to LeMay or Power. It stated that "during discussion of SAC capabilities with Admiral [Arthur] Radford, the question of time required for capsule delivery came up. He suggested that perhaps you might wish to make arrangements with the Navy for utilization of capsules they are holding. He stated the capsules the Navy is currently storing are not allocated to the Navy but are available to any JCS force that may need them."[74] The capsules referred to were almost certainly nuclear capsules, the component of a nuclear weapon that contained the nuclear material. Prior to the development of on-base storage for completed weapons, these components were stored separately from a high-explosive shell that surrounded and, in the event of their use, detonated the nuclear package. Stored separately, the nuclear capsule was essentially inert. Once it was mated with the high-explosive shell, a completed nuclear weapon was formed. Most of the nuclear capsules were kept under the custody of the civilian AEC, the inheritor organization to the Manhattan Project of World War II, for more than safety reasons, however. The civilian government thought it inappropriate for the military to possess the completed weapons prior to receiving approval from civilian authorities to employ them. As a result, the military was unable to use nuclear weapons without explicit civilian approval; at the same time, the separate storage of high-explosive shells and nuclear capsules was designed to prevent a mistaken or unauthorized detonation. The program was a robust check on these new types of weap-ons. These checks, however, also meant that if a nuclear war came, LeMay would be unable to immediately initiate SAC's response. The command might have had the aircraft, crews, and plans for striking the Soviet Union—preemptively or otherwise—but it did not have the completed bombs it needed. Though LeMay did not have a particularly high opinion of the Navy, Radford's offer could have provided at least some relief for his lack of weapons. Despite the funding battles between the Air Force and Navy, there was no available evidence to suggest it was not a genuine offer. If anything, the offer further contributed to the argument that others outside the Air Force and SAC sensed the necessity and centrality of SAC to the U.S. defense program.

On December 7, 1953, LeMay spoke before the Pittsburgh post of the American Ordnance Association. As with previous remarks made by LeMay, his speech was an opportunity not only to win supporters for his efforts at SAC but also to engage the issue of preemption. LeMay explained to the audience that he wanted to "devote my discussion to what I think airpower can contribute to the defense of the United States. I should also like to give you my views on how the military application of atomic energy has affected the importance of airpower."[75] After some discussion of other commands within the Air Force, LeMay came to the topic of SAC: "This is the force with which I am most intimately concerned and which I would like to discuss with you in some detail." Following a brief recounting of the basic composition of the force, LeMay affirmed that SAC's job was "to destroy the war potential of an enemy to the point where he no longer retains the will or the capability to continue military operations." The statement was plain in intent. The general went on to say

> that this force must constitute the principal offensive striking power in our military arsenal. I further believe that the combination of the long-range bomber and new air weapons can give us the most powerful force for peace that the world has ever seen. If we build the right kind of a strategic air force and keep it ready to go at a moment's notice to any target in the world, and if [a] potential enemy knows that his works of man face certain destruction if he starts a war, I do not believe he will start it.[76]

LeMay had laid out the ostensible imperative for the existence of SAC. In no uncertain terms, at least at this point in his discourse, LeMay was arguing that SAC was designed to prevent a war. As LeMay continued, the other purpose of SAC became clearer. To that point, he had "concentrated my discussion on the Strategic Air Command and its importance; the power of the Soviet Union and its vulnerability, and the kind of force we need to exploit this vulnerability. I will outline now the principal task[s] the Strategic Air Command must be able to perform." What came next was a carefully worded expression of the essence of LeMay's argument for preemption, but his meaning, nonetheless, remained clear throughout: "We [SAC] must be able to destroy the Soviet long-range air force, wherever this force may be based. This must be done in the minimum possible time period after a war starts. Obviously we cannot afford to let this force hammer at our cities and those of our allies while we attempt a piecemeal destruction." LeMay's intent in this statement was obvious. To extinguish the Soviet bomber force "wherever this force may be based" was to eliminate it on the ground, before it had been sortied. In LeMay's estimation, such was the optimal way to prevent attacks on Western states and metropolises.[77]

Turning the Corner

SAC and the United States had turned a corner because of LeMay. No longer was the country or its primary nuclear command in the wary position of uncertainty that had dominated the security environment of the late 1940s and early 1950s. Much of the impetus behind this was LeMay's trepidation about a repeat of a surprise war. Given the experiences of Pearl Harbor and World

War II, the Soviet detonation of a nuclear weapon in 1949, and the Korean War shortly thereafter, one could hardly blame LeMay for his continued concern over the future.

LeMay's solution to the security problem facing the United States was not a surprising one. He was a realist who believed that threat and power needed to be met with the same. What was different about the realism that defined LeMay was that he did not seek to out-of-hand eliminate what he perceived as the danger. LeMay and SAC had a desire to remove the problem, but that desire did not involve a blind preventive war. Certain conditions needed to be met, most notably an imminent threat of war. LeMay held strong to convention.

Preemptive attack, unlike preventive war, afforded LeMay—and the enemy—a moment of pause that could help avoid war for years, if necessary. For as much as LeMay was prepared to launch an attack against the Soviet Union, he was equally charged with avoiding a war, and he took this responsibility seriously. Nonetheless, LeMay remained wedded to the concept of preemption, which prevailed as the overarching theme from 1952 to 1953.

04

Clarity in Expression

L eMay's fear of a nuclear conflict with the Soviet Union did not cease with the end of fighting in Korea. He came to grips with his concerns through continued vocal championing of his desired solution to a possible nuclear war. Between January 1954 and July 1955, the SAC commander's advocacy for a policy of justified nuclear preemption entered a phase of clarity and forcefulness. This tone matched that of the Eisenhower administration's recently inaugurated "New Look" policy, formally known as National Security Council resolution 162/2. This policy shifted the U.S. approach toward the Cold War from one of general disagreement bounded by arms to one that prized nuclear weapons and the threat of using them as a critical tool of deterrence. SAC provided this deterrence.

Whether the result of coincidence or recognition of the efficacy of his command—or both—the decision to vest much of the nation's security fortunes in the hands of SAC and LeMay came to define not only LeMay's legacy but also the nature of the Cold War. Further definition was wrought by the fielding of new weapons. Though the B-47 made up the bulk of the mid-1950s' SAC jet bomber force, the emergence of the Boeing B-52 Stratofortress was a notable development. The new bomber gave SAC the range, speed, altitude, and carrying capacity LeMay sought as a replacement for the increasingly vulnerable Convair B-36. The B-52 also gave the public an iconic image that represented the extreme nature of the conflict. The new bomber reflected LeMay's fears and a potential resolution to the problem—as the SAC commander saw it. The B-52 made a successful preemptive attack on the Soviet Union all the more possible. The golden age of the military experience in the early Cold War had arrived.

National War College Remarks

The National War College in Washington, DC, was the institution to which the military services and certain government agencies sent their most promising officers and civilian employees. On January 28, 1954, LeMay spoke to an audience at the college. In addition to the institution's prominence as a pulpit for military leaders and civilian officials alike, it was able to serve as a classified environment—a fact that adds to the importance of LeMay's remarks.[1] The top-secret classification of the briefing suggested that his comments were likely to reflect his true feelings on the subject. Unlike many of his previous statements on the topic of preemption, LeMay did not orate with ambiguity in his remarks before at the National War College. The speech LeMay made gave a window into his thinking and fears.[2]

LeMay opened by telling his audience that "I have three hours to tell you about the Strategic Air Command," which included a treatment of "the present force and its capabilities, as opposed to future trends and requirements," as LeMay felt "that too many people are dealing with the future without having an accurate understanding or appreciation of the present forces and the problems that face us today. . . . I will cover my part of the story in the first two hours, and then answer your questions during the third hour. When I am through, I hope you will have a better understanding of strategic bombing and its relationship to our national objectives."[3] As was typical of LeMay, with his engineer's mind and training, he intended to focus on practical matters. He simply wanted to make things work. Alongside that mentality went LeMay's tendency toward feasible plans, something reflected in SAC's preparations for war. His remarks were clear and concise. This was a small story that taught a larger lesson—one that was essential to a more nuanced understanding of the Cold War.[4]

LeMay arrived at the issue of SAC's charge: "The Strategic Air Command's mission and targets are designated by the Joint Chiefs of Staff. Briefly stated, the mission is to conduct the strategic air offensive utilizing atomic weapons." He next addressed the manner in which the attack was to be carried out: "The mission embraces three principle tasks: the blunting or Bravo task, which is to destroy the Soviet atomic force on the ground; the retardation task, to prevent the massing and launching of Soviet military forces; the destruction task, to systematically destroy the Soviet war-sustaining resources." While their naming conventions straightforwardly described the second two tasks, the first task was a veiled reference to a preemptive attack. It was hardly possible to see it any other way, given that the purpose of the mission was to catch Soviet nuclear entities "on the ground." LeMay then engaged in a brief discussion of the mission sets: "The Joint Chiefs of Staff have assigned the blunting task the highest priority. . . . I might add this is our most difficult task." As LeMay pointed out, the important blunting task presented some difficulty in successful achievement. What he left unsaid on this occasion was that preemption of an enemy attack was a challenging task from both an operational and an intelligence perspective. For a preemptive attack to be successful, it was necessary not only to know the enemy's intentions and the location of its forces but also to destroy those forces before they could be committed to military action. As for the other two mission areas, "Retardation targets have not been designated as yet. These targets are being nominated for destruction by other JCS commanders. The bulk of the targets are in the destruction category. Although blunting has the first priority in point of time, we are prepared and capable to carry out operations against all three categories of targets simultaneously."[5] The formula LeMay discussed constituted a meaningful portion of U.S. nuclear operations in the event of such a war. What LeMay had laid out was the principal means by which the military planned to defend—albeit through offensive means—the United States against a Soviet attack. This point had been made clearly during World War II: the security of the United States depended upon an offensive, not a defensive, scheme. As had been exhibited against Germany and Japan, the United States did not intend to repel invaders but rather attack and eliminate threats on foreign territory. The U.S. approach during the Cold War was little more than a replication of the successful model employed during much of World War II.

LeMay made a worthwhile distinction that suggested a war with the Soviet Union was not his first choice—at least from the perspective of the Soviet Union initiating one: "This is SAC's mission as previously defined. However, I feel our real mission goes far beyond the mere delineation of this wartime task. We think we must remain sufficiently strong to convince any enemy it will not be to his advantage to start a universal war. As things stand now, with our present capability I think there is certainly a question as to whether there is any profit in anybody starting a war."[6] These were striking words coming from the SAC commander. From one perspective, LeMay's comments were a betrayal of his position as the nation's preeminent nuclear authority; if it was LeMay's job to make nuclear war, then he needed to have the nominal capability to do so successfully. LeMay's comment to the contrary cast aspersions on the entire enterprise. It also suggested that the stalemate of arms that characterized the later decades of the Cold War was in place well before the advent of ballistic missiles. If LeMay was right, nuclear war was an exercise in futility by early 1954. Perhaps this is why LeMay persevered in his advocacy for nuclear preemption; it was a way to escape the reflective fate of a nuclear war with the Soviet Union—if national leaders chose to enter into a conflict. Had the United States been able to eliminate the Soviet nuclear threat early in a war, a nuclear exchange would have been one-sided. The United States would have potentially been saved from attack. But that was no simple task.

Audience members wasted no time in getting to the issue of preemption after LeMay's comments. The first questioner asked LeMay, "You said your first task was to destroy the enemy's atomic capabilities on the ground. Can you discuss a little more in detail your possible success in that line?" The inquiry got to the heart of the issue of preemption: Was such an approach a realistic operational possibility? LeMay replied:

I also said that was our most difficult task. Some five years ago when I first took over the Strategic Air Command, we had a very small capability compared with what we have now, and we could ignore in our plans some of the rules in the rule book. . . . One of the rules is you must fight and win the air battle first before you can go on with your operations. Russia at that time had no atomic bomb and not much in the way of delivery capability even if they had one. So we weren't worried about a tremendous attack falling on us. We were free to go about the business of putting down one on Russia. Since that time they have developed atomic weapons and they have a means of delivering them. And as their stockpile increases, the danger to this country increases. Therefore, something has to be done about going back to the rule book and fighting the air battle first.[7]

LeMay provided some background that was important to the overall discourse and to the larger question of his advocacy for preemption. The critical concept of air battle related directly to the issue of preemption. While not immediately defined by LeMay, the concept of the air or airpower battle was the view that combat between enemy air forces represented the preeminent fight between nations, and such forces were the first and most important target to be attacked and defeated. In practical terms this meant the application of first strikes against an adversary—as LeMay saw it, preemption. LeMay continued:

We think the best chance of preventing attacks on this country is to get those airplanes on the ground before they take off, rather than depending on the Air Defense Command to shoot them down after they get here. A specific answer to your question is impossible. I don't know how we are going to do it. Our intelligence system is pretty sorry in telling us or answering some of the questions we particularly want to know. We hope it will get better as time goes on, and I believe it will. I think however—and this is my personal opinion—that it will never be good enough to tell us that so many airplanes are coming off this field at such a time to attack the United States. I think we are going to have to make up our mind at some time or other to launch our attacks, and that may well be any time from when the bomb actually falls on the United States back to where our intelligence reports they have an intention of doing it. What that time will be, I don't know. I move when I am told. I think, however, the time will come when most of our effort, at least in the first attacks, will be a counter air force effort against the Russian air force. I believe the public will demand it. I think that is the most efficient way of stopping an attack. I see no other way of doing it. The airplanes that are already airborne when the attack is laid down, of course, will not be stopped by this method. We will have to depend on the air defense system for them. But as I see it now, that is the only way we can do it. I think a large portion or percentage of the stockpile of weapons we have at our disposal will be expended on this task.[8]

This approach showed LeMay's pragmatism at work. If there was to be a war, it made no sense to wait to be attacked once clear indications of a threat were apparent to U.S. leaders. But a successful attack on Soviet air forces required the foe's aircraft to be still at their bases, and that meant a first strike. The purpose of such an attack would not be conquest but simply self-protection. LeMay was forthright in his admission that he was at a loss for making such a plan an operational reality and in his ambiguity about the likely outcome. LeMay was being honest in his belief in preemption; it was the best option in a bad situation.

LeMay Continues His Clarion Call

On March 4 LeMay made one of his most important speeches to date in terms of his advocacy for preemption to the Society of Automotive Engineers in Detroit. After thanking his audience, LeMay remarked in self-deprecation, "You will note that in his generous introduction Mr. Biggers very wisely did not list public speaking among the many accomplishments he attributed to me. I have not won much of a reputation for speeches, especially long speeches." He continued:

> I am sure that most of you are aware that in their new assessment of our military requirements for the years ahead the Joint Chiefs of Staff, the National Security Council and the administration have placed increased emphasis on airpower as the principal element of our military strength. Further, in January of this year, Mr. [John Foster] Dulles, the Secretary of State, called attention to the fact that 'basic policy decisions had been made to depend primarily upon a great capacity to retaliate, instantly, by means and at places of our choosing' as our answer to aggression. . . . Tonight, I would like to devote my discussion to a review of some of the fundamental military considerations underlying the present emphasis on airpower and the promise of instant retaliation so that, if you will, you may take away with you the conviction that we must not falter

in our determination to maintain an air strength superior to that of any other nation. Also, I would like to tell you of some of the programs and problems of the Strategic Air Command, which is the hard core of U.S. power for peace.[9]

LeMay was describing a critical linkage between policy and action. The SAC commander's comments also provided insight as to how he understood his role in the larger enterprise of national security. Technology, too, played a part in policy: "One immediate consideration necessary to any assessment of the weight and balance of our defense preparations today must include an appreciation of the rapid and revolutionary advances that have been made in aviation in recent years. It is important for all of us to recognize that over the past ten years the performance of aircraft, in speed and range and altitude, has improved more than 100 percent."[10] LeMay was not exaggerating; given the development of jet propulsion, swept wings, and the proliferation of aircraft pressurization, the ability of bombers to reach more distant targets at higher altitudes and speeds also expanded. The implications were reciprocal; with the right technology and production, the Soviets could do the same. In a preemptive scenario, it did not matter how fast, far, or high enemy bombers could fly; LeMay did not want them to leave the ground. He continued: "The high performance aircraft of today, such as our B-36 intercontinental bomber and the B-52 heavy jet bomber now in production, can range over any part of the globe. Dispersed, coming from many directions, flying in any weather and at extreme altitudes or in optimum tactical dispositions, their interception would be improbable or at least most unlikely." LeMay's argument was a central one concerning the efficacy of strategic bombing based on the belief that at least a portion of the attacking bombers would make it to their targets. No study, operational test, or exercise could conclusively prove or disprove this point; only actual warfare could do that. LeMay had experienced warfare in World War II, but the Cold War was a new type of conflict. International political realities and military technology had changed. Nonetheless, the United States and SAC were investing in the belief that the bombers could make it through Soviet defenses to their targets. A key consideration in terms of technology was the type of weapon the U.S. military intended to employ in a strategic bombardment attack. LeMay addressed this issue next: "Another consideration affecting the present emphasis toward airpower is the remarkable development of nuclear weapons in size, variety and quantity. The atomic bomb makes it possible now to accomplish in a few days the destruction that required years during the last war. Hiroshima, you will recall, was destroyed by a single bomb delivered by one airplane. Today, as President Eisenhower has announced, atomic bombs are more than 25 times as powerful as the weapons with which the atomic age dawned, while hydrogen weapons are in the ranges of millions of tons of TNT equivalent."[11]

The issues of more powerful bombs and far-ranging aircraft played into LeMay's thinking. Many in the mid-1950s had witnessed similar technology at use in war a decade earlier. Perhaps not the singular cause for Japan's collapse during World War II, the use of heavy bombardment and the eventual dropping of nuclear weapons did play a critical role in the U.S. defeat of that nation. The use of heavy firebombing raids was of LeMay's doing. He also had a hand in the nuclear raids against the cities of Hiroshima and Nagasaki. In the span of roughly six months, forces commanded by LeMay destroyed much of Japan's urban base. LeMay believed his actions had been a core reason for U.S. success in that theater—he

An early image of Curtis LeMay as commander of SAC. Note the original SAC patch on his left shoulder, which predated the fisted glove and lightning bolt crest that later came to represent the command.

Courtesy the Air Force Historical Research Agency, in the Air Force Collection

LeMay (*second from right*) visiting with, from left to right, an unidentified individual, Nathan Twining, and Ira Eaker during a moment of leisure. This may have been the "rustic" trip the group took in 1951 during which LeMay learned that he would receive his fourth star. LeMay was an avid outdoorsman.

Courtesy the Air Force Historical Research Agency, in the Air Force Collection

LeMay talks with a young racer. LeMay was a keen car enthusiast and opened SAC runways for use as tracks during special events. With the proceeds he raised from such races, LeMay was able to fund quality-of-life improvements for his airmen.

Courtesy the Air Force Historical Research Agency, in the Air Force Collection

This 1950s photo depicts the flight line at Castle Air Force Base during an open house or ceremony. The aircraft in the foreground is a B-50, a design based largely on the B-29 airframe but with a stronger set of engines.

Courtesy Joe Pruzzo and the Castle Air Museum

A mobility test on 23 May 1951 at Castle Air Force Base, California. LeMay's primary concern as SAC commander was ensuring readiness to carry out a nuclear war. These exercises were conducted to prepare the command and evaluate operations. The aircraft shown here is either a KB-50 or KB-29.

Courtesy Joe Pruzzo and the Castle Air Museum

Brig. Gen. William Eubank inspects a formation of SAC personnel at Castle Air Force Base during the 1950s. Despite Eubank's smile, SAC was known for a serious atmosphere and stringent discipline.

Courtesy Joe Pruzzo and the Castle Air Museum

LeMay (*center*) at Castle Air Force Base with William Eubank (*left*) and an unidentified officer.

Courtesy the Air Force Historical Research Agency

William Eubank (*left*), wearing a flight suit and standing next to a B-47, greets his family on the Castle Air Force Base flight line. Though SAC was serious in its approach to operations, one of LeMay's primary quality-of-life interests was creating an environment conducive to a stable home life.

Courtesy Joe Pruzzo and the Castle Air Museum

LeMay visited Castle Air Force Base, the hub for B-52 training, in 1955. He made great use of such visits, getting a feel for what was going on in the command while also passing along things he believed to be important.

Courtesy the Air Force Historical Research Agency, in the Air Force Collection

LeMay in discussion with an unidentified master sergeant during his base visit to Castle. Note the rank worn by the noncommissioned officer has all stripes facing one direction, as opposed to today's version worn by master sergeants.

Courtesy the Air Force Historical Research Agency, in the Air Force Collection

LeMay examining flight equipment worn by SAC crews. The painted helmets, which spoke to the character of the era, differ from those worn by contemporary crews.

Courtesy the Air Force Historical Research Agency, in the Air Force Collection

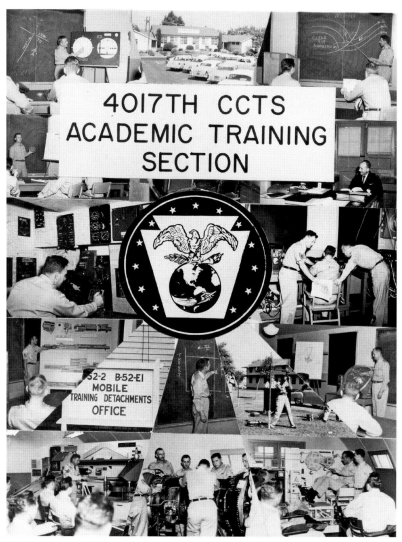

A collage of photos from academic training operations at Castle Air Force Base's 4017th Combat Crew Training Squadron (CCTS). The squadron's purpose was to train B-52 bomber crews.

Courtesy the Air Force Historical Research Agency, in the Air Force Collection

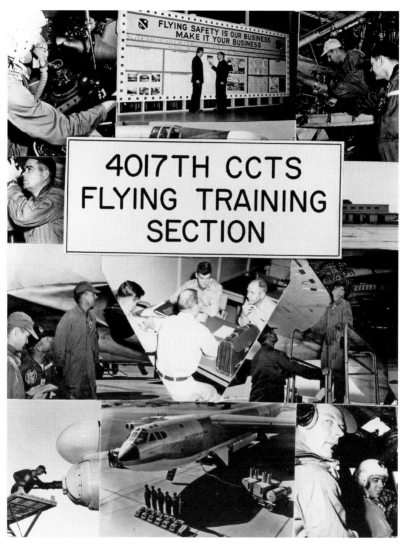

One of the core experiences in learning to operate the B-52 was flying training.

Courtesy the Air Force Historical Research Agency, in the Air Force Collection

A B-52 and personnel in and among the hangars at Castle Air Force Base in 1956. This was early in the B-52 program and not long after the initial aircraft were being delivered to the Air Force, a time during which "bugs" were still being worked out. Nonetheless, the new jet offered LeMay and SAC a long-range, high-speed alternative to the B-36 in an intercontinental attack scenario.

Courtesy Joe Pruzzo and the Castle Air Museum

also knew that future conflict would be different. In a war that involved nuclear weapons and strategic bombers, there was a distinct possibility that defeat could come quickly. LeMay's words in Detroit spoke to that belief: "The obvious implication is that the fury of several years of war as we once knew it could now be compressed into the space of several days or weeks at the most. The long-range airplane with atomic weapons, now considered almost conventional, can bring destruction to vast areas in an incredibly short period of time." Although LeMay's targets in Japan had primarily been urban, industrial, and military ones in the central and southern part of the country, he believed that "in an all-out atomic war, battlefields will no longer be restricted to small areas where surface forces come together. The potential battlefield will at once encompass the length and breadth of a nation."[12]

If an analogous—though largely conventional in nature and less destructive in extent—campaign had been successful against Japan, why would that not be the case if the United States employed even more powerful thermonuclear weapons in 1954 against the Soviet Union? But the question of destroying an enemy's cities and population in order to force Soviet defeat and see the United States prevail was not the initial purpose in a preemptive approach for LeMay. His concern was the protection of U.S. cities and people. Despite a reputation of favoring offensive action, LeMay's primary conclusions about national security during the Cold War centered equally around the achievement of an effective defense. Offense was simply a means by which to achieve a more effective defense.

LeMay's remarks to the Society of Automotive Engineers clearly reflected this belief: "These are modern technological truths towards which we must reorient our thinking in any consideration of the military measures necessary to preserve peace. From this starting point, we must then go on to assess the balance between development in air defensive and air offensive capabilities." LeMay set the stage for an argument in favor of a first strike against the Soviet Union that was enabled by an offensive bomber force. The greatest defense the United States could possess was not a force that drove enemies from its home skies but rather one that prevented them from getting there in the first place. According to LeMay, "These are the hard realities of Soviet military might that we should not try or hope to contest, in building a force within our economic reach, equal to the task of providing national security." In other words, conventional forces were not the appropriate choice, fiscally or militarily, for success in defeating the Soviet Union in a military conflict during the Cold War. In both the Eisenhower administration's and LeMay's thinking, the proper choice to meet the challenge was a nuclear-enabled force—that is, SAC.[13]

In LeMay's estimation, the real threat to the United States came from the skies: "The Soviet Union has a powerful Air Force. The Red Air Force, larger than our own and growing more powerful month by month, has the capability of launching aerial atomic attacks against this country." For the SAC commander, the most prominent concern was another air force and its nuclear payload, but he offered a solution: "There is every reason to believe that our airpower and air weapons are superior to those of the Red Air Force. And, certainly we have in this nation the scientific and technical production genius to maintain this edge in air superiority." The term air superiority was associated with fighter aircraft and engagements that are typified by air-to-air actions and was not an effort normally attributed to bombers. But how was air superiority to ensure victory in a nuclear war? LeMay went on: "This continuing qualitative superiority in modern airpower and air weapons offers the only real prospect of neutralizing the massive manpower and geographical advantages held by the Communists. At the same time, this superiority in airpower opens up to us a Soviet weakness through which we might achieve victory, if war should come. Before identifying this singular Soviet weakness, exposed by airpower, please permit me to pass on my views concerning the relative balance between the offensive and defensive in terms of air capabilities." The SAC commander also warned the audience: "Add to this the reasonable assumption that they [the Soviets] have made hurried progress in nuclear weapons development since first exploding an atomic device four years ago." In doing this, LeMay brought to the fore his belief in the need for a long-range American strategic bomber force. He told the audience:

> The first and most obvious answer to this frightening knowledge of Soviet air-atomic capabilities might be to increase the weight of our air defense preparations. This is one answer, but only a partial answer. The problem of air defense of our cities and our factories becomes more and more difficult as the speed and range of strategic bombers improves. . . . We must remember that there has never been a target which air defense, no matter how concentrated, could prevent a determined bombardment force from attacking. Even under conditions most favorable to the defense, a sizeable portion of the bombers—atomic bombers—will always get through.[14]

It was an old argument that was alive and well in 1954. In support, LeMay offered evidence based on the experience of U.S. strategic bombers in World War II and Korea. LeMay returned to his primary path of logical development and explained that

> continental defense is extremely important, of course, and must be improved as much as is economically feasible within the resources allotted to the Air Force. If our air defense measures ward off only two percent or twenty percent of an attacking force, the effort and the expenditure would be worthwhile. But in this connection we must not accept the comfortable delusion that the threat of sudden aggression can be met by home defense alone. The pages of history are filled with grim lessons and one that sticks out most sharply is that a true defense requires both a shield and a sword.[15]

The rhetorical punch line of LeMay's argument for preemptive nuclear attacks came next. He explained to his audience:

> The principal offensive force in warfare today is the long-range bomber armed with nuclear weapons. The uncomfortable knowledge that this country could come under enemy attack means also that the potential enemy's homeland is well within range of our qualitatively superior airpower. And our ability to strike [back], hard and sure, is in practice, the best and most dependable defense of our extensive borders. The long-range bomber enables us to carry the greatest destructive power the world has ever known to an enemy's doorstep, in event of war. It can reach over and beyond the masses of manpower the Communist World has mobilized around the Iron Curtain. It is the

only means by which we could bring our full power to bear directly against his muscle and heartland. As the extended arm of our air defense, the strategic offensive would enable us to hit the enemy's air bases and atomic installations, destroying his striking power at its source rather than at its destination. An English leader, recalling World War II, pointed out recently that it took the bombers to push the air war away from British skies, back over German territory, and that the only method of stopping the V-2 missiles was to bomb the launching sites.[16]

Although LeMay's remarks were nuanced, his argument for preemption was clear: elimination of the threat "at its source rather than at its destination" meant striking before those attacks had departed for the United States. To make this happen, SAC's attacks had to precede those of the enemy. By advocating a preemptive approach, LeMay's words also suggested that the nation's early Cold War nuclear targeting philosophy was not entirely focused on the destruction of enemy cities. It also called into question a core understanding of the basic nature of the U.S. approach to strategic defense at the time. If LeMay's primary concern was the preemption of nuclear attacks on the United States, then was the United States a wholly inhumane actor? Destroying an enemy's attack force before it could be launched was potentially more humane than primary attacks on belligerent cities. Such an avenue of approach was intended not to retaliate but to protect. In this narrow question, LeMay's words left significant room for healthy debate. It was also worth some consideration that he made such assured statements in public. LeMay laid out the logic for such an approach in a manner that suggested long thought and critical insight on the topic.[17]

In many ways, the SAC commander's remarks in this venue were conclusive. Recurring statements represented proclaimed policy and clear advocacy for such a policy. By 1954 this was the direction of LeMay's comments. Throughout the late spring and summer of that year, LeMay reinforced the record of his public statements. One address clearly engaged the issue of preemption, another hinted at the question, and the final one offered insight into how LeMay saw the role of SAC in the Cold War. The context came first.

A Time of Clarity

On May 12 LeMay was at the Waldorf-Astoria Hotel in New York to accept the Billy Mitchell Award. It was unclear whether the SAC commander accepted the award for himself or on the behalf of his organization, but his remarks suggested the latter. His address at the event gave more perspective on preemption: "Recent Governmental announcements of national policy have tended to emphasize the importance of a modern and an adequate Air Force to our own defense and that of our allies. Eventually we may have a United States Air Force in being which will be able to achieve the almost legendary visions Billy Mitchell propounded some 25 years ago. I feel sure that if he were around today he would approve the present directions our national policy is taking."[18] LeMay's analysis of recent defense policy was accurate. Under the New Look, the U.S. Air Force rose to a prominent—if not dominant—position in the U.S. defense structure. In large part, the responsibility for the transformation of this policy decision into reality had fallen to LeMay and SAC. In some ways, LeMay had become more important to the U.S. Air Force and the United States than the award namesake had ever been, and the SAC commander was certainly Mitchell's equal from the perspective of transformational airpower thought. LeMay had developed into a meaningful force in his own right.

Rather than broadcasting his belief in preemption, LeMay's speech on May 12 concerned deterrence and provided context to how SAC fit into the larger Cold War security complex: "The ultimate goal of all our efforts in the Air Force is to prevent war by confronting would-be aggressors with the threat of massive retaliation should they succumb to their hostile tendencies." In more private venues, preemption was the enabling watchword of SAC and LeMay's advocacy, but in the instance of the Mitchell award, LeMay avoided the topic of first strikes. He did tell the audience that "if we maintain a true capability to execute our policy of massive retaliation immediately upon the outbreak of hostilities, I submit that we have taken a long step toward taking the profit out of war for potential aggressors. When an aggressor realizes beyond any shadow of a doubt that there can be no profit for him in a war, I believe the odds are in our favor that he will not start one."[19] This was deterrence in a straightforward formula. As had been the case in instances of his clear advocacy for preemption, what mattered most to LeMay was the protection of the United States.

At the same time, LeMay's words rallied support on the home front. His public speeches related the story of the threat as LeMay saw it and also explained what was being done to rectify the situation. This was in keeping with diplomat George Kennan's edicts concerning the general nature of the conflict as an ideological fight as much as it was a potentially kinetic one. LeMay knew where the true power rested: with the general populace. Taxpayer money funded his command's endeavors. For LeMay, public speaking, while not a favorite pastime, was a necessary evil in a representative democracy.

On May 21 LeMay was speaking in Washington, DC, to the Armed Forces Chemical Association. The SAC commander's remarks regarding attacks on the Soviet Union's bomber force resembled those made in previous public speeches. They also served as a vehicle for the discussion of questions surrounding preemption. LeMay told the group that "if the world should be plunged into total war, one of our primary objectives would be to win the air battle. . . . While air defense units here at home hammered at the enemy attack, the long-range bomber force would bring our major weapons to bear directly against his muscle and heartland. This strategic offensive would enable us to hit the enemy's air bases and atomic installations, destroying his striking power at its source in the earliest phase of the war. This long-range offensive would be an important means of stopping aerial attacks against this country."[20]

LeMay's suggestion that the nameless enemy's airborne attack could be eliminated at its source left little room for interpretation. If the force could have been eliminated there—on the ground— then what was under way? Although they were not as overt as other statements in their support for a preemptive approach to nuclear war, they also did not notably contradict previous utterances.

LeMay continued to build the case. Accompanying a letter to Air Force Chief of Staff Nathan Twining on May 28 was a "draft of a JCS paper concerning planning responsibilities for the defeat of Communist airpower at the earliest possible time after the initiation of hostilities. . . . It is believed that the urgent necessity for a comprehensive plan for the defeat of enemy airpower is apparent and that the various JCS Commanders concur that this objective is most important. However, a review of the atomic annexes proposed in the plans of the various JCS Commanders indicates a reluctance to undertake concrete tasks designed to achieve this objective."[21] While the letter did not specify details for a plan to engage Soviet forces before their commitment to battle, LeMay's words hinted at the topic. The point was an important one: the decisive target was enemy air forces, and cities and civilians were not directly mentioned.

LeMay addressed the subject again the following month, in a June 11 letter to the Air Force deputy chief of staff for operations, Lt. Gen. Frank Everest. LeMay attached "a staff study [entitled "USAF FORCE COMPOSITION 1958, 1965"] prepared by our people out here. I had them prepare this study to help me get a better feel for the proper balance of SAC forces in the overall USAF force structure. . . . While I realize that my staff faced many limitations in assessing the political, interservice, and international pressures which affect the strength and composition of the Air Force, I consider this study as fairly representative of our thinking on what the combat structure of the Air Force should be in 1958 and 1965."[22]

Asserting that the study in question reflected the opinion of the command implied that whatever it said amounted to the official SAC position, and preemption was among the topics discussed. According to the document, "In any war in the period 1958–1965, the overriding task which the Air Force must be capable of accomplishing in the shortest possible time after the outbreak of hostilities is the destruction of enemy airpower. This requirement should determine the size and composition of the force."[23] In the mid-1950s the U.S. targets of first choice were, ostensibly, enemy airfields, but population centers were not necessarily beyond consideration, as the study implied: "A force which possesses the capability to destroy enemy airpower in the early days of the war will have a residual capacity to discharge the other responsibilities of the Air Force."[24] Simply put, once the most dangerous threat had been eliminated, other types of targets could be attacked. The document continued: "Only those units which can be effective in the destruction of enemy airpower in the early days of the war will be able to participate in the decisive phase of the war. Conventional deployments of forces by surface means will not be possible during the decisive phase of the war. Those units which cannot be brought into action during the decisive phase should be relegated to second priority."[25] The ability to destroy Soviet air assets seemed to determine the hierarchy of SAC assets. This was a militarily wise and efficient approach to waging a nuclear war, but it also was more humane than a "cities first" strategy. In attacking Soviet air forces first, LeMay and SAC could avoid the deaths of not only possibly millions of Americans through preemption of Soviet military action but also conceivably millions of Soviets. This did not mean civilian casualties would have been avoided completely; collateral damage would have been significant.

The study went on to provide one of the clearest, most methodical explanations of overall SAC philosophy in the mid-1950s: "International tensions are not expected to lessen materially during the next ten years. The security of this country must not be compromised. The Air Force will be our first line of defense. The goal of the Air Force during the next ten years is to prevent a war if possible and if in spite of our efforts, war does eventuate, the Air Force must be prepared to deliver a massive strategic offensive."[26] This was also a reinforcement of long-held Air Force thinking that considered strategic bombardment the most effective way to defeat an enemy. In the nuclear era, this thinking took on new meaning. It was only natural for a study that SAC drafted to present itself as the primary way to protect the United States. But a pragmatic realism also drove the argument: "Maintaining the combat capability and the security of our offensive Air Forces are of overriding importance. Insofar as possible our offensive forces should be based in this country and our effectiveness in delivering offensive blows should not be dependent on political decisions of other nations." In other words, overseas bases were a liability.[27]

When and how a nuclear war was to be initiated depended on policy decisions by the United States. Though the United States had foresworn preventive war via NSC-68, there was not an official U.S. policy regarding preemptive attack.[28] A decision to launch a preemptive attack required policy-level approval. In a publicly declared sense, the decision for or against this had not been made. The void left room for the military to advocate its position. This was the policy space SAC, and, by extension, LeMay, was prepared to fill. The study pointedly stated, "Attempting to create an air defense with a capability of destroying anything approaching 100% of possible enemy attacking airplanes is futile. The best objective we can hope to accomplish with air defense during this era is to force the enemy to take cognizance of our defensive posture, employ tactics which are less than optimum to him, and strive to cause him to waste a significant portion of his bombs. Any attacking enemy force can be severely harassed, but a determined force can only be stopped by destruction on the ground before it is launched."[29] If the abolition of enemy air forces was SAC's primary objective and the optimal time to do so was prior to their employment, then either a preemptive attack or a preventive war had to be undertaken. LeMay intended this statement to be noticed. What remained was a decision as to the conditions under which such an attack would have been carried out.

Offense before Defense

On August 30–31 LeMay visited Plattsburgh, New York, which was to be home to a new SAC base. The location of Plattsburgh and other new bases in the northeastern United States would allow some SAC bombers to make direct strikes against the Soviet Union, partially reducing the need for overseas bases. This contributed to a more secure and reliable intercontinental capability for SAC because the bases were not subject to the political decisions of other nations, and the threat of sabotage that existed in foreign nations was eliminated. Remarks that LeMay made at Plattsburgh had bearing on the question of his advocacy for preemption: "If the Kremlin should plunge the world into war, our offensive airpower would be one means of stopping aerial attacks against this country. It would be the *only* means by which we could come to grips with the enemy, and it would be our primary means of achieving decisive victory."[30] Here was LeMay's tactical imperative for preemption: if enemy bombing attacks against the United States were to be more readily prevented, they needed to be stopped before they took to the air. In other words, U.S. bombardment of the enemy was more about the immediate protection of the nation's skies than it was about degradation of an enemy's will to fight or ability to destroy their economy. LeMay explained that "our air defense system, of course, would reduce the weight of an attack if enemy bombers were overhead," which was something LeMay had no intention of allowing. He continued: "But in this connection we must not accept the comfortable delusion that attacks against this country can be met by home defense alone. It must be remembered that there has never been a target which air defense, no matter how concentrated, could prevent a determined bombardment force from attacking. Even under conditions most favorable to the defense, a sizeable portion of the bombers will always get through."[31]

LeMay next tackled the issue of offensive strikes against the Soviet Union: "However, the uncomfortable knowledge that this country could come under attack means also that the enemy's homeland is well within reach of our superior airpower." Whether with intercontinental B-36 Peacemakers or aerial-refueled B-47 Stratojets, SAC possessed the ability to launch attacks on the Soviet Union from bases within the United States and, with approval from the host nations, from overseas locations. There were, however, limits to this power. If SAC did not attack Soviet aircraft at their bases before they departed, the possibility of an attack against the United States remained. LeMay asserted that "while our defenses at home hammered at the fingers of an enemy's attack, our long-range striking force would bring our major weapons to bear directly against his heartland. As the extended arm of our air defense, the strategic offensive enables us to hit the enemy's air bases and atomic installations, destroying his striking power at its source." This was the logic behind LeMay's support for pre-emption. He noted that "an English leader, recalling World War II, pointed out recently that it was the bombers which pushed the air war away from British skies, back over German territory, and that the only method of stopping the V-2 missiles was to bomb the launching sites." LeMay's anecdotal citation of operations against German V-2s during World War II offered perspective on the logical basis of his thoughts behind the imperative of offense.[32]

The SAC commander next came to an important attendant factor: limited Air Force resources and uncertainty in the ability of air defense forces to effect successful protection of the United States against Soviet attack. LeMay argued that "air defense of our cities and our factories, which becomes more and more difficult as the speed and range of bombers improves, is extremely important, of course, and must be emphasized as much as is economically feasible within the resources allotted to the Air Force for all purposes." Air defense was vital, but resources needed to be prioritized: "If our air defense measures ward off only a small percentage of an attacking force, the effort and the expenditure would be worthwhile. But we cannot build a fence around America." This was a simplistic appraisal of the situation. It was also an accurate assessment from the perspective of the Air Force's ability to prevent—through defensive action alone—an attack on the United States. In LeMay's thinking, there was another answer: "The ability to strike back, hard and sure, is still the best and most dependable defense of all forty-eight states. We must depend upon our long-range force to overwhelm the enemy before his atomic attacks overwhelm us."[33]

There was no way to prove the verity of LeMay's remarks concerning the effectiveness of strategic bombing versus air defense in the protection a nation. What did make sense was the concept of destroying a threat at its source before it was sent into combat. A vulnerability was created when equipment such as aircraft was kept in collective locations such as airbases. If the targeted country could attack an enemy airbase after receiving knowledge of the impending use of its aircraft but before they had been launched, then the attack could be successful in eliminating a nascent threat.

In this line of thought, that was likely to be more effective than an attempt to pick off attacking bombers one by one with air defense forces. Preemption made sense if it worked.

However, LeMay's argument was not a full-throated case for preemption. The SAC commander hinted at the issue and then offered a statement that suggested his interest in retaliation. He may not have wanted to make statements contrary to the declared national policy of deterrence and retaliation. What was clear was that LeMay also made statements that suggested he was interested in something else. This was where LeMay excelled; he had a knack for adaptation based upon the situation at hand.

A similar risk-benefit calculation was present in LeMay's approach to the Cold War and his advocacy for preemption. Preemptive strikes could start an unnecessary war if LeMay was wrong in his assessment of an impending enemy attack. If an attack was in fact imminent—and the preemptive strike was successful— the effort could instead carry the United States relatively safely through such a conflict. LeMay clearly believed this was the right policy choice, and elements of the argument for it were present in his remarks on August 31: "The Strategic Air Command, with its massive air-atomic capability for instant retaliation, is more than just another military organization—it is a force for peace. As long as this hard core of our military strength remains strong enough, and ready enough, the danger of a surprise attack against America is diminished. The penalty for such aggression would be too great." The point at which enemy actions would have been considered aggression—either by him or the country's leaders—was not clear, however. Was en masse fueling of bombers and loading of weapons enough to elicit a response from the United States? Or did the

United States need to first receive an attack before responding? LeMay did not state where the line was drawn. He continued in his remarks:

> This is the purpose guiding our preparations. In this uneasy age, the promise of prompt and overwhelming retaliation is as indispensable in preventing a war, as it is to winning one. This is the reason for the construction of the jet bomber base here at Plattsburgh. . . . It is easily understandable that a force capable of deterring war must be a force *in being*. Bombers on production lines and bases on paper would be of little value. The force must be ready to go when the bell rings. This striking force must be maintained at such a high degree of strength and readiness that its ability to carry out its mission, if suddenly called upon to do so, will not be questioned. It must be trained to peak efficiency and maintained constantly in a state of instant readiness.[34]

The question remained, however: How prompt of a response would the United States have been willing to undertake? There was no clear answer in LeMay's words on August 31; his argument that the force had to be ready "when the bell rings" left some uncertainty. But the shape of the organization LeMay described matched what came later in the form of the SAC Alert Force—bombers, aerial refueling tankers, and their crews ready for immediate departure for their targets.

LeMay's inexactitude over when SAC would be given the launch order during a nuclear crisis suggested several things. There may have been something he did not want to say with regard to preemption in the Plattsburgh forum. Perhaps it was concern over publicly expressing an opinion that exposed some conflict with declared national policy. LeMay only touched upon the concept with his words at Plattsburgh, but greater clarity was coming.

Back in Omaha

On September 2 Brig. Gen. Richard M. Montgomery, SAC Chief of Staff, outlined some issues that needed the SAC commander's attention upon his return from Plattsburgh. One of those items spoke to the pragmatism and detail with which matters were handled within the command—as well as the political awareness of its leadership. According to the document, "General Sweeney is sending a Major Herron in for a short interview with General LeMay on Friday, 3 September. Although I have been unable to locate anyone in the staff familiar with this individual, I did locate a recording of a conversation in October 1953 between General Power and Terrill concerning a study Major Herron of the 15th AF [Air Force] Comptroller shop had made on the 43 (Maintenance) career field." Someone on the staff took the time to research a matter as seemingly minor as a field grade officer who was to have a "short interview" with LeMay. The document went on: "His [Major Herron's] conclusion was that maintenance people were overworked and that something should be done about it. From the conversation I judged that General Power discussed the matter with you and you further discussed it after arriving at March AFB that same day." The document offered "a brief run-down on Major Herron. . . . He is a wealthy Californian who is influential in politics and apparently close to the Governor." From the perspective of the SAC military mission, these points had no bearing, but from the larger outlook of continued political support for SAC and its mission—an essential element of military success in both fiscal and strategic terms—Montgomery's information was germane. The inclusion of such material as the issues of a major's political associations showed the command leaders' appreciation of the role of politics and politicians. However, LeMay and his staff were not foolish with respect to outside influences on the command. This was the case when it came to those with connections in politics. Montgomery's next comment revealed the true purpose of the document:

> [Herron] is eligible for promotion to [Lieutenant] Colonel but due to administrative tie-up (his records were en route from one location to another) his name was not considered during the last go-round. . . . Herron is somewhat unhappy about the promotion and has been to see General Sweeney recently about it. General Sweeney pointed out that he had no objection to recommending Herron for promotion for apparently he is qualified; however, having created the stir he did and having come to General LeMay's attention personally, General Sweeney thought that Herron should talk to General LeMay at this time. . . . Apparently Herron is desirous of talking with General LeMay for the purpose of straightening the whole matter out. Major Herron appears to be a rather intense individual but somewhat misguided at the time he came to the Commander's attention.[35]

Montgomery concluded his discussion with the details of his visit: "Major Herron plans to arrive here about 1000, Friday morning and Colonel Doan will see that he is brought directly to the Command Section. General Sweeney recommends that the Commander see him." For LeMay's chief of staff to recommend he take the time to see a single field grade officer from among the entire command was intriguing counsel. That Montgomery spent the time he did on research related to the matter, among all the issues that pressed against LeMay and SAC, was itself noteworthy. What came next from LeMay's chief of staff only reinforced the point. Immediately following the discussion of Herron, Montgomery engaged in another matter that regarded an individual with political connections: "Assistant Secretary of Defense (Properties and Installations), Franklin G. Floete, called from South Dakota to say that he would arrive in Omaha at 1028, 3 September, aboard Braniff airplane from Sioux Falls. He wishes to spend 2–3 hours visiting with . . . people looking over [fiscal year] 56 Public Works program, see the base, and have a short visit with General LeMay. He cannot [remain overnight] but plans to go West from here later in the day." Montgomery concluded by stating that Floete had asked to be transported from the local airport; a hand-written note on the document pointed out that a colonel was to take Floete to LeMay's office.[36]

Hosting a senior government official was not unusual for LeMay or SAC. Military commands depended upon the support of their policy-level overseers. LeMay and his subordinates were particularly cognizant of the importance of such interactions and were effective at building relationships in that regard. The instances with Herron and Floete were more evidence of the effort at SAC.

The Killian Committee

On February 14 nuclear war and surprise attack were among the topics in a report made to President Dwight Eisenhower by the Technological Capabilities Panel of the Science Advisory Committee.[37] Known as the Killian committee, after its chairman

James Killian, the group was established to craft a report regarding the question of "U.S. technological capability to reduce the threat of surprise attack." The result was that

> the committee set as its objective an examination of the current vulnerability of the United States to surprise attack and an investigation of how science and technology could be used to reduce that vulnerability by contributing to the following five developments: An increase in U.S. nuclear retaliatory power to deter or at least defeat a surprise attack; an increase in U.S. intelligence capabilities to enhance the ability to predict and give adequate warning of an intended surprise attack; a strengthening of U.S. defenses to deter or blunt a surprise attack; the achievement of a secure and reliable communications network; and an understanding of the effect of advanced technology on the manpower requirements of the armed forces.[38]

The stated mission of the group alluded to the same issue at the core of LeMay's advocacy for preemption—to stop, or blunt, an imminent nuclear attack—and established a linkage between policy-level considerations and what LeMay had been advocating for during the same period. Clearly, LeMay was not alone in his thinking about nuclear war; those who influenced policy at the national level were using the same terminology as he was using at the operational level. Given LeMay's later relegation by some to the ranks of extremists, this indicated that he was—in a limited sense—inside the norm of defense thinking at that time.[39]

The report did not directly mention or endorse a first strike. It did, however, skirt one of the issues that motivated LeMay to consider preemption as a viable option. This was encapsulated in the first part of the document, which foreshadowed remarks LeMay made in July of that year during the Quantico conference. The title of the report, "Surprise: Its New Importance and Meaning," implied that the concept of surprise had changed—which spoke to the concerns LeMay had about a future war being unlike any of its predecessors. Given the topic and time period of the document, there was little doubt that nuclear weapons were the underlying issue that the title referenced. Both the idea and reality of nuclear bombs had changed the dynamic of surprise in war and the timeframe that a nation had to respond to a present or building threat. Nuclear arms afforded an attacker the ability to potentially disarm and destroy a nation in one blow. Something different needed to be done to resolve a different type of problem. At the time the document was written, "Because of our air-atomic power we [the United States] have an offensive advantage but are vulnerable to surprise attack." The report's reference to the benefit of an aggressive approach offered a potential solution to the issue. For LeMay, the resolution meant a first strike to preempt an enemy attack that could substantially harm the United States—an approach that stood the possibility of eliminating a majority of the nuclear threat posed by an enemy. Per LeMay's thinking, to reap the benefits of that head start in power, the United States had to use it before it had been bombed by enemy air forces and potentially deprived of its nuclear delivery capability. This approach was typical LeMay.[40]

In Like a Lion

A March 21 memorandum from LeMay to Air Force Chief of Staff Twining contained key details of LeMay's thinking about nuclear war. With the subject line of "USAF Force Structure and Program Objectives 1957–1965," the top-secret document was also an advocacy piece. LeMay explained that "the revised study 'USAF Force Structure and Program Objectives 1957–1965' has been reviewed and my specific comments and recommendations for a revised force structure are attached. In addition, I wish to reiterate certain comments I made on this subject at the January Commanders' Conference at Ramey."[41] LeMay then laid out several items, telling Twining that "there are certain guiding principles under which the Air Force is operating at the present time. . . . The intercontinental concept—the establishment and maintenance of an intercontinental force as the first priority task. b. Emphasis will be primarily on the offensive force, with as good a defense as can be procured after the needs of the offensive force are provided for. c. The first requirement is to win the battle against Soviet Airpower."[42] It was clear what LeMay lobbied for in his letter. Aside from the motivation of self-preservation and command interest, LeMay's argument reflected the general direction of U.S. defense policy. Given the priorities of the New Look, LeMay had placed himself on a solid footing.

LeMay went on to explain that "the policies and principles under which we have been operating I believe to be sound and will continue to be sound in the future. Accepting these principles, we should develop a force composition best capable of carrying out these principles." LeMay next set the stage for his well-known argument. At the same time, the SAC commander opened the path by which "Airpower Battle," or "Air Battle"—a concept related to a preemptive attack that had been enshrined in Air Force philosophy—was defined. He contended that "the primary objective of such a force therefore should be to win the battle against Soviet Airpower." LeMay made clear his desires for what, in description, amounted to SAC: "A force capable of winning this air battle would also be capable of performing any other tasks required of it after the air battle had been won; whereas the development of a force based upon the achievement of specialized tasks would not, on the other hand, be of optimum composition to win the air battle."[43] This was a tall order for SAC to fill.

LeMay sustained his discussion and gave further explanation: "The proposed composition of SAC in 1965 would not give us the capability of destroying the presently accepted target system much less the expanded target system which undoubtedly will require destruction during that time period. The composition of SAC or an air offensive force during any time period must be of such a nature as to assure without doubt the destruction of the accepted target system." This warning from LeMay was not unique; he routinely offered his concerns and admonitions about the future to those in his professional sphere—including his audiences—as they related to national defense. While LeMay was an effective commander and logical thinker, he was also given to worry concerning issues of what he regarded as military necessity: "We desire to commence the employment of intercontinental missile systems at the earliest possible date, but we cannot accept such systems as a substitute for manned bombers until their performance, reliability, and tactical usage have been thoroughly demonstrated. Even if we had the B-65 [missile] today, and it completely met the designed objectives laid down for its performance characteristics, it could not be depended upon to any acceptable degree in winning the air battle and could play only a minor role in achieving destruction of the target system as a whole." LeMay's concern over the efficacy of intercontinental missile systems, commonly known today as intercontinental ballistic missiles, was equal confirmation of his larger apprehension about trusting unproven new military hardware. This was a curious turn given LeMay's maverick willingness to adopt risky means and methods, such as the low-level night firebombing of Japan during World War II. The risk LeMay took in the Pacific was a big one that paid off well, but that was in 1945. It was not clear what had changed inside LeMay by 1955 that led to his angst. Jet bombers had never been flown en masse in combat by U.S. crews, but LeMay did not demonstrate the same unease over that platform. To the contrary, LeMay actively pursued the acquisition of jets. Perhaps the attacks against Japan during the war were the anomaly. Whatever the reason, his feelings about missiles were typical of his nervousness about being ready for war in general.[44]

LeMay continued by offering succinct definition to the concept of the air/airpower battle: "I would like to see the present TAC [Tactical Air Command] force equipped with better weapons with which to fight the air battle. The place to win the air battle is on the ground, not in the air, and the bomber airplane is the best delivery vehicle to do this." This simple and conclusive statement made a linkage between the airpower battle and preemption. "Therefore, I question the validity of such a large number of fighter-bombers and day fighters as proposed in the force composition for TAC. I don't know of any task a fighter-bomber can be called upon to perform that cannot be accomplished better by either a light bomber or a medium bomber." Whether he advocated for his command, given the composition of its fleet, or for the approach in general, LeMay maintained his status as a supporter of bombers. TAC was a counterpart to SAC and was responsible for missions typically assigned to fighters. It was also a challenge to LeMay and to SAC supremacy within the Air Force.[45]

LeMay next offered some fodder for the logic he applied in support of his argument for preemptive attacks. In a nominal discussion of the shape of "the Air Defense Force," LeMay turned to what was arguably his favorite topic, telling Twining that "even the force programmed for Air Defense will not be able to stop the enemy from inflicting prohibitive damage on us." LeMay did not believe there would be a strong return on the resources put into air defense, and he felt there were greater priorities to be supported before air defense. He argued to Twining that "the best defense force is that one so equipped and so organized as to most effectively destroy enemy airpower on the ground"—in other words, a first strike.[46]

LeMay's persistent arguments for first strikes were the result of fear, as was his anxiety over the inclusion of missiles in the SAC force and war plan. Fear, however, was not always unfounded. In LeMay's mind, the Soviet Union constituted an authentic security concern for the United States. Whether the Soviet Union could have mounted an effective aerial nuclear attack against the United States in 1955 was debatable, but the general American perception of the Soviet threat was unquestionable.

In remarks at the Commercial Club of Chicago on March 23, LeMay clearly advocated for preemption as well as directly addressing the changing nature of time in conflict, given the introduction of nuclear weapons and strategic bombers into warfare. Those remarks were a continuation of arguments he had made since taking charge of SAC. Some of the issues LeMay raised had manifested themselves prior to his arrival—most notably, the question of whether warfare had intrinsically changed after the introduction of long-range strategic bombing and nuclear weapons during World War II. Early in his remarks, LeMay stated that "war has an entirely new identity, a new meaning now—and it is essential that we recognize this. Few of the guidelines and concepts that shaped other wars have any validity today." LeMay pointed out that the 1945 nuclear attack on Hiroshima "altered the scope and tempo—and the entire time scale—of war."[47] What LeMay identified was an argument regarding the efficacy of strategic bombing and nuclear weapons. The conflation of the two into a fervent belief among many U.S. military and political leaders (and eventually the public) held that one employed with the other could succinctly defeat an enemy. Whatever led LeMay to such a conclusion, the outcome remained unchanged: in his mind, the character of war had shifted.

The most prominent question was not, however, whether warfare had changed, but rather whether targets should change. During World War II, LeMay targeted civilian population centers in his firebombing campaign against Japan. Given that precision bombing had not produced the results expected or demanded in the European theater, LeMay made a change in the Pacific theater that resulted in a dramatic—but ethically questionable—shift in outcome. The reasons for that outcome have also been deliberated: Were the firebombing raids effective in the capitulation of Japan, or did the Soviet declaration of war against Japan on August 8 drive the Japanese decision to quit? The firebombing raids against Japan's cities were the most obvious visual representation of defeat to Japan's military and civilian leaders. There simply was no conclusive single reason why Japan decided to surrender. However, what was more important to know: how the war ended, or simply that it had ended?

In the postwar years, LeMay and many others in the military and politics believed—rightly or wrongly—that strategic bombing had been decisive. Nuclear weapons and long-range strategic bombers became the panacea for the defeat of major adversaries—and apparently the Soviets agreed, as they pursued their own strategic bombing capability in the years after World War II. Eventually the theory of nuclear deterrence emerged, with the conviction that an adversary could be prevented from attacking by holding the adversary military or cities at risk via a counterattack.

In his remarks in Chicago, LeMay told his audience that "years of war, as we once knew it, can now be capsuled into hours. All of the firepower of four World War II years can now be laid down between sunup and sundown from bomb-bays already in existence."[48] To an audience that likely well remembered World War II and understood the weight of LeMay's words, this was a dramatic statement. Subsequent generations came to take overwhelming firepower for granted, but for the generations that lived through World War II, a major war was not always push-button or nuclear in nature.

Just as the character of war had changed, at least in LeMay's mind, so had the priority of targets. By 1955 he was no longer as ardent an advocate of cities as primary targets. He told his audience: "With bombs of enormous radius of destruction, why insist on pinpoint accuracy[?] I can best answer that by stating that wars are won by destroying military targets, not people [populations]. We want to put as much destructive force on targets as we can in order to get the job done quickly. . . . We do not want to intentionally harm civil populations for practical as well as humane reasons."[49] At its most basic level, LeMay seemed to have had a change of heart.

He soon alluded to the impetus for that change, arguing that "first, it is obvious that the only way any enemy nation can seriously damage our country is through air attack." Whether he genuinely believed in what he said, the statement was based in a degree of doctrine. LeMay and perhaps others may have seen airpower as a panacea to the problem of protracted war and as a potential tool to end conflict with less struggle, loss of life, and expenditure of funds. LeMay's statement also reflected a common belief that the United States was insulated from invasion and sudden attack by oceans and distances from potential foes. In his estimation, strategic bombing changed the dynamic of what was possible and what outcomes were to be had in the application of air forces. LeMay introduced some specifics: "It is true that the coastal areas are open to attack from naval forces, but the depth of such attack would be extremely limited compared with the expanse of our heartland. Perimeter attack could not be decisive, but mass air action could be."[50] LeMay's corollary ruled out an entire category of military action—as well as his competitors for defense dollars. What followed, however, was one of the most direct public arguments LeMay ever made on the topic of preemption. In the belief that an aerial strike could do substantial harm to the United States, LeMay stated that "the first-priority action of SAC would be to attack bases of the enemy's strategic air force. We must first win the air battle, catching his bomber force on the ground wherever possible, and in any event, denying his bombers a base to return to." This statement also made clear LeMay's perception of preemption's relationship to the concept of the air battle.[51]

Next came a brief discussion of how, in practical terms, such an attack would come together. LeMay laid out the general parameters for his audience: "Let's assume that we have reason to believe an enemy attack is in the making. This intelligence would be passed to every strategic air commander here and overseas within a matter of minutes. The alert would be on. The commanders would be ready, on order, to put their bombers in the air. When enemy intentions were clearly hostile, we would receive our orders from the Joint Chiefs of Staff and be on our way."[52] LeMay's remarks gave his audience the impression that the decision for war was entirely outside SAC's purview. Instead, his words suggested the responsibility to direct his force to war rested with the Joint Chiefs of Staff. Excluded from his account, however, was further explanation of exactly whose intelligence drove the process. If the SAC intelligence directorate's data—and interpretation of those data—were used, LeMay and his command would have had more control over the process than he suggested. LeMay and SAC would have influenced both the when and how of the U.S. approach to nuclear war.

Eventually, LeMay gave a more direct account of the question of the attacks themselves. The importance of airpower was the centerpiece in LeMay's explanation of what was to come first in the strikes on the notional enemy. He described an approach to aerial warfare that was novel in that it valued a type of conflict that was similar in description to limited war. Simultaneously, what LeMay spelled out—without regard to the degree of mass applied—was at its core strategic in its basic nature: "Our initial attacks on the enemy's air installations would aim to deprive him of his effective air strength." What LeMay proposed was an approach to conflict that valued the deprivation of capability rather than the imposition of national pain to achieve one's military and political objectives. This suggested a caricature of the U.S. approach to nuclear war that did not match the one that was popularly understood throughout much of the Cold War: that cities were at the top of the list. LeMay explained the logic behind his method: "It could well be that our offensive would never have to go beyond this point, because the remainder of his military forces would be at the mercy of our airpower."[53] This approach was simple in theory: eliminate the enemy's ability to attack the homeland and create the conditions for the termination of conflict. Not one to rely solely on theory, LeMay told his audience:

> But if the crippling of his air strength were not enough to bring about capitulation, attacks may be required against his war-sustaining industries. The ruin of Germany and Japan in the last months of World War II—when we had finally brought our air force off the drawing boards and into the air—parallels what could now be done in a few hours. In concert with attacks on vital industrial targets, we would hit troop concentrations and supply dumps as well as transportation and communications networks. The result of such an air offensive must inevitably bring the enemy war machine to a halt.[54]

This was the fundamental center of LeMay's thinking about targeting during the Cold War. It was as much about the efficient elimination of a threat as it was about the all-out destruction of a foe. It did not require an "all or nothing" commitment from U.S. leadership when deciding whether to launch a nuclear strike. Rather, it had escalatory options built into the scheme of operations: if the war did not end with the purge of the enemy's air force, further steps could be taken. Understanding LeMay's argument as it regarded nuclear targeting also meant seeing another side of the SAC commander that suggested he was not just a warmonger. He reinforced his purpose before the audience and also paid credence to the role of deterrence, offering that "a nation disarmed—without the means to continue the fight—will quickly lose its will to fight. We have the power to so disarm any enemy nation. And it is the very existence of this power that will probably make it unnecessary for us to apply it."[55]

LeMay's remarks before the Commercial Club offered a public glimpse into thinking that he had previously expressed mainly in classified venues. That LeMay was willing to share his thoughts and advocate for preemption in public spoke to his confidence in the approach he supported. It was also an indicator of his willingness to weather criticism he might have drawn for supporting nuclear first strikes. His remarks on preemption were certain. LeMay left nothing to ambiguity in Chicago; the SAC commander knew what he wanted, and he wanted his audience to know it. Given the clarity of his words and the accompanying explanation, there was little doubt that LeMay supported justified preemptive war.

On May 10 Lt. Gen. Harold George, who had been returned to active duty from retirement, presumably to advise the chief of staff of the Air Force, wrote to the SAC commander. The letter offered a plain view of the contemporary concerns of senior leadership. The ostensible role of George's message was to inform LeMay of a planned visit by the "George Committee" to SAC headquarters.[56] The larger purpose of the committee, formally known as the "Net Evaluation Subcommittee [of the National Security Council]," however, was to deliver "integrated evaluations of the net capabilities of the USSR, in the event of general war, to inflict direct injury upon the continental U.S. and key U.S. installations overseas, and to provide continual watch for changes which would significantly alter those net capabilities." This was a broad charter that, in theory, gave the committee significant ability to influence defense policy and operations—based on its observations.[57]

Further background as to the committee's intent was gleaned from George's letter. The letter explained the leadership and staffing of the committee and informed LeMay that the body had received briefings from three of the military services as well as "various other activities and agencies of the Government." George's correspondence suggested the importance of the SAC mission within the U.S. defense equation and the centrality of LeMay's position in it. In the letter, George told LeMay that the committee would arrive at Offutt "on May 23 for a two-day visit to your Command. I understand you have already been advised as to those dates." The fact that LeMay's command would support two days' worth of briefings suggested the importance of the group's work. Taking staff at a major headquarters away from their jobs was no small diversion. George recognized the degree of exertion required to carry out the task, but he felt "sure that the job that my Committee has been given to do will justify it."[58]

George sought information on specific topics that mattered to the most senior ranks of the defense establishment:

I would appreciate if you could have discussed with this Committee the following subjects:

a. Initial and continuing SAC offensive capabilities, considering loss of overseas bomber and tanker staging bases.

b. Specific alert planning now, and transition to, programmed position for mid-1958, considering only tactical warning [of an incoming attack].

c. Weight of SAC effort that could be airborne and estimated effective, under these three condition, as of mid-1958:

(1) An initial surprise attack, based on a USSR decision to give first priority to damage to the Continental U.S., with no strategic warning, but with tactical warning intervals appropriate to target location and type of attack.

(2) An initial attack, based on a USSR decision to balance all factors involved in initiating general war, preceded by the amount of strategic warning estimated to be most likely under those circumstances.

(3) An initial attack preceded by sufficient strategic warning to place U.S. military and non-military defenses in a condition of full alert and to initiate U.S. retaliatory action.

d. SAC estimate of Soviet Long-Range Air Army capabilities as of 1958, to include Air Crew radar bombing, long range high speed navigation, and air refueling proficiency.

e. Estimated B-47 and B-52 attrition in offensive action against Soviet Union, as of mid-1958, considering Soviet Air Defenses and USAF programmed bomber defensive improvements.

f. Base dispersal planning, with estimate of mid-1958 status of SAC forces as to locations within ZI [zone of the interior] and overseas.[59]

A central question could be distilled from the list George presented: In the event of war, would SAC be able to get off the ground and get to its targets? This was the same question that concerned LeMay for several years. His response was to argue for preemption to ensure the effectiveness of the bomber force in the face of an impending confrontation. In LeMay's estimation, preemption also offered an opportunity to avoid the homeland being damaged by nuclear strikes.

Quantico

The George letter demonstrated that LeMay was not alone in harboring anxieties about the ability of airpower to successfully realize U.S. national security goals. Toward the same end, LeMay wanted to build a more effective approach to achievement of defense goals through the application of airpower. LeMay's position as the head of SAC gave him extraordinary access to and influence with the most senior military and policy leaders in government. While not alone in his efforts, he had an important stage from which to make his case as it regarded preemption in the face of an imminent attack. In July 1955 LeMay used that stage.

On July 14 the SAC commander met with General Twining at Air Force headquarters in Washington, DC, in advance of the 1955 Secretaries' Conference being held at Quantico, Virginia. LeMay arrived at Twining's office at 9:15, only fifteen minutes after Twining's arrival, and the two men were together there into the noon hour. At least part of that time was spent laboring over the SAC commander's presentation for the upcoming conference. With Twining's help, LeMay's presentation became one of his most direct messages in support of preemption.[60] In addition to senior officers of each of the military services and the various service secretaries, attendees included Director of Central Intelligence Allen Dulles; Treasury Secretary George Humphrey; Defense Secretary Charles Wilson; AEC chairman Lewis Strauss; Assistant to the

President Fred Seaton; Special Assistant to the President Nelson Rockefeller; and the vice president of the United States, Richard M. Nixon.[61]

The presence of these officials provided direct contact between the ideas LeMay espoused and those who made the policy—and likewise indicated the level of importance of LeMay's role and words as the SAC commander. The continued passive support for LeMay also suggested a degree of reflexive acceptance by some at the conference of what the SAC commander said. He was in command of perhaps the most critical element of the nation's Cold War military defenses, and everything he said or did was worthy of evaluation. His superiors in attendance that day had the ability to remove him from his position if he said anything beyond the realm of reasonable acceptability. LeMay would in fact remain in command of SAC for nearly two more years and then be elevated to the position of vice chief of staff of the Air Force in 1957 (and eventually to chief of staff in 1961, where he led the entire service). These moves spoke to the seeming confidence LeMay's superiors had in him—as well as his ideas.

LeMay told the audience that "the Strategic Air Command, representing much of the offensive power of the nation, is growing in size, in skill, and in effectiveness. I consider it to be fully capable of inflicting decisive damage to an aggressor nation during the present time period if its force is properly utilized. Proper utilization of this force involves preserving it until it is airborne." The comment related directly to an issue that had animated LeMay throughout his SAC term: how and when to employ his command in a nuclear war. The timing of a decision to launch strikes against an enemy had a great deal to do with which, if either, side might prevail. It was the final sentence, however, that most clearly invoked the issue of preemption. This became all the more evident by the end of LeMay's discourse that day.[62]

One topic LeMay addressed was the essential capability of the command to carry out nuclear raids. LeMay's account of these events offered a fascinating look into an aspect of nuclear war that was closely held and formerly classified. It also offered a pragmatic example of what LeMay meant when he proposed preemption as a solution to what he viewed as the nation's security quandary. LeMay offered that, during the period in question, his command had the "potential to launch a predominantly intercontinental attack of 180 atomic and thermonuclear strike aircraft within 12 hours of alert and to launch additional strikes each 12 hours until at the end of 48 hours a total of 880 strike aircraft will have been dispatched. With 36 hours' alert time, 400 strike aircraft can be dispatched in the first wave and two subsequent waves at 12-hour intervals will total 1,000 aircraft which have been dispatched."[63] In the event he was "given three to four days' alert time, over 1,000 aircraft can participate in the first simultaneous strike against Soviet objectives. This, of course, emphasizes the importance of having the maximum possible alert time before dispatch of initial strike aircraft." What came next, however, was the most important detail as it related to the question of preemption: "Most of these sorties would be directed against Soviet airpower targets. The air battle must be won first, and as quickly and as decisively as possible." The air battle concept had reappeared and was applied in the context of the destruction of Soviet air forces. This was more evident based upon LeMay's next comments: "The massive effect achieved by adequate alert time not only hastens the decision in the air battle which minimizes damage at home; it also affords the maximum immunity for the SAC force by confusing, saturating, and diluting the enemy defense. Thus the force can be preserved to continue its air battle, retardation and enemy war potential objectives."[64]

There was another side to the equation LeMay presented: a shorter timeline for SAC to prepare to launch attacks. The SAC commander told the group, "On the other hand, in the event of a surprise attack against the United States by Soviet forces that were not detected until they entered our early warning radar screens, the SAC force would have the capability of evacuating bases and subsequently delivering a reduced attack. This retaliatory effort by the strategic force might be decisive; however, by giving the Soviets the initiative it is probable that the outcome of the war would not be favorable to the United States." LeMay had drawn a clear line between attack and retaliation. The obvious implication was that one situation involved SAC undertaking a preemptive strike—as LeMay had called for in his previous speeches and communiqués—and the other was a reciprocal attack. Although he framed the issue differently, the problem LeMay had posed was one of time and decision. These two dependencies drove LeMay's push for preemption, and they fundamentally resided outside of LeMay's control; it was not up to him as to when to initiate a conflict. That choice belonged to the nation's civilian leadership— and a good portion of it was the audience before whom LeMay appeared. Nonetheless, it was something that LeMay could influence. Having posed the problem of decision to those gathered, LeMay prepared to make a full-throated call for a change in policy or a shift in approach as to how, in a practical sense, that policy was carried out.[65]

As he approached the end of his presentation, LeMay came to what were arguably some of the most consequential words he ever spoke on the issue of a first strike, owing largely to his audience that day and the clarity of his comments:

> Finally, I would like to mention a thought introduced by Ambassador Henry Cabot Lodge on a visit to my headquarters last January. He suggested that the word "aggression" be redefined and accepted by the United Nations. The new definition should, in my opinion, recognize that we are now living in an age when it can no longer be an issue of morality that a nation must receive the first physical blow before it can respond with force; in fact, the first blow can now signal the end of a conflict rather than the beginning. Therefore certain enemy actions short of war should constitute sufficient threat to the non-aggressor nation that it would be justified in launching direct attack at least on enemy strategic airpower to forestall its own disaster.[66]

It was an unquestionable call for a policy of preemption. It was not an unqualified one, however. Although he did not minutely specify the conditions under which a preemptive strike should be initiated, LeMay did make clear his belief that the decision to go to war should be predicated on an opponent's undertakings that did not amount to acts of war themselves. This concept diverged from a longstanding accepted norm of war. The context of LeMay's reasoning was left partially unstated, but it was obvious: nuclear weapons had been developed, and strategic long-range bombers had been made operational. As a result, LeMay proposed airpower assets as the logical target for preemptive strikes. He did not call for the immediate and initial bombardment of factories, cities, or civilians. He wanted to stop a war before it could consume his own nation, and doing so primarily meant the destruction of strategic airpower. In conclusion, he stated: "I share the philosophy contained in an article entitled 'Courage or Perdition?' published in the *Review of Politics* by the University of Notre Dame; and I quote: 'Only one thing is worse than nuclear war—defeat in such a war,' and 'We are forced to look hard at the 14th fact of the atomic age which, perhaps, is the most ominous of all: That in an atomic conflict the force which plans to strike second may never strike at all.'"[67]

The meaning of LeMay's comments before the audience at the Secretaries' Conference was plain: times had changed, and the United States needed to rethink its approach to defense if it wanted to survive in the nuclear era. LeMay saw during World War II what a strategic air force armed with nuclear weapons could do. The combined application of both weapons could either lead to the destruction of cities and the deaths of many people or deprive an enemy of the ability to incur that damage upon the homeland. To achieve that end, however, in LeMay's mind, required undertaking a first strike—that meant the preemption of a would-be attacker. In a methodical and cogent manner, he shared with his audience a message designed to influence and educate. He was a collected, thoughtful, and calm nuclear commander who sought a better way to fight a war and avoid a national catastrophe. That was LeMay's purpose in his argument for preemption.

Heart of the Argument

From January 1954 to mid-July 1955, SAC continued to mature into an organization able to fulfill its intended mission, and the command was on the cusp of achieving even more. As the increasingly capable B-52 bomber prepared to enter SAC in meaningful numbers, it became clear that LeMay had a firm hold on the development of nuclear warfare within the U.S. arsenal—as well as the ability to do that for which he had argued.

But LeMay's legacy at SAC was typically that of an extremist bent on the execution of a nuclear war as a catchall solution for the ills that troubled the U.S. relationship with the Soviet Union. The evidence from his period at SAC, however, revealed that such a portrayal was not accurate. What LeMay argued for both publicly and in classified settings differed from that image. He saw a limited nuclear campaign as a tool for undercutting the need for a broader series of nuclear strikes. LeMay did not lack the will to go further; he simply wanted to localize a nuclear war to certain enemy forces, rather than launch a campaign that made its initial aim the destruction of an adversary's civilian population. His aim was to preempt the enemy's strategic air forces and thereby prevent attacks against his country. If the enemy was unwilling to surrender following attacks against its strategic air forces, LeMay sought to strike targets of a wider scope. In the two years he had left in his service at SAC, LeMay continued to believe in and advocate for this approach.

Strong until the End

In the mid to late 1950s the tensions between the Soviet Union and the United States grew more intense. At the same time, nuclear weapons had become more powerful, the means by which to deliver them became more capable, and the strategy and tactics for their employment were more refined. LeMay—presiding over SAC, where most of those weapons and delivery systems resided and the strategy and tactics associated with their use were developed—was at the juncture of policy thinking on nuclear war and defense operations during a time when there were serious questions over whether such a war was about to take place.

Expressing Concern

LeMay's comments at Quantico were delivered to one of the groups he wanted to influence with his words, but LeMay understood he had multiple constituencies to persuade—among them, his military colleagues. Though LeMay held a position of great importance and influence, his power and ability to get things done at and with SAC depended considerably on the assistance of others. A good collegial relationship required honesty and communication to endure and thrive. That was how LeMay approached his relationship with not only his peers but also his subordinates—and that was how they reciprocated. Despite occasional disagreements, professionalism and a focus on the mission before them prevailed. LeMay's correspondence, however, carried a seriousness that reflected the gravity of the larger issue at hand: nuclear war and national survival. This was reflected in LeMay's response to a July 18, 1955, letter from Maj. Gen. Frank Armstrong, commander of Second Air Force—an organization responsible for roughly one-third of SAC's forces.

Armstrong opened his letter to LeMay with an attention-getting statement: "I am certain you are aware of this most important matter; however, I am going on the record by writing this letter to you. . . . At the outset I want you to know that I have given this subject many hours of thought. Now that my staff and I are convinced that I am logically correct in my thinking, I shall pass this on to you. I shall deal with Second Air Force and its capabilities."[1] Armstrong explained to LeMay some things his boss would have already known but that he sought to reinforce. He exposed what he saw as a critical problem with SAC's approach to a potential war with the Soviet Union:

> We have B-47s and KC-97s [aerial refueling tankers] around which our EWP [Emergency War Plan] is constructed. We will have those aircraft for a long time and it is imperative that we have the capability of fighting them. The B-52 will come along and take its place in the EWP and, even then, we must be able to operate the B-47. I shall

deal with the capability of the B-47 and the KC-97. We now have sufficient B-47s to do the job, provided they can be flown to the target and back to an operational base. We have tankers to service the bombers, but not in sufficient numbers. We are going for the B-52 as an inter-continental bomber which proves my point beyond a doubt. Before the USSR came up with the capability of destroying our ocean stepping-stones—islands—we had the capability of going to and from the target. We built, and are continuing to build, our strategy around refueling. As of today, the "tail is wagging the dog." In other words, our bombing capability depends not on the bomber but on the tanker. That theory was excellent a year or so ago. It is not sound today; however, I must admit it is our only hope. We have developed refueling, night and day, to a high degree. In September, I will fly four to six wings on an overseas maneuver. The route will be the same we have flown many times because it is the only one available. The Russians know the route well. Personally, I do not expect that route to be available during hostilities. If it is, we win. If it is not we do not go any place—period. Once again, I point out that the complexion has changed and we are absolutely dependent on tankers and tanker bases.[2]

Armstrong laid out for LeMay what he saw as a seminal problem in SAC's plan for war with the Soviets: getting to the targets. And if Armstrong was correct, it would have been a crippling problem for LeMay. The implications were obvious and far-reaching—perhaps SAC was not as capable as LeMay had purported the command to be. LeMay had a major impediment to the achievement of the mission with which he had been charged to carry out, and Armstrong was in as good a position as anyone to understand the situation.

Armstrong told LeMay that he believed the Soviets were aware of SAC's "routes across the Atlantic" and that "[the Soviets] understand that we must use islands for our tankers to support our bombers." Portions of LeMay's plan for war seemed to have fallen apart. Armstrong pointed out that a plan for an attack on the Soviet Union directly from bases within the United States was "a costly, as well as doubtful, operation." All in all, the Second Air Force commander had a negative outlook on SAC's prospects.[3]

Armstrong's next statements cut to the core of LeMay's argument for preemption: "To mount a strike from this country and reach the target requires hours. Even if we were going to make a surprise attack it is doubtful that we could do it from the ZI [Zone of the Interior (continental United States)]."[4] This was an important statement reflecting Armstrong's doubts about the likely efficacy of such an approach, and it implied that others beside LeMay had the notion of a first strike in mind when thinking about a war with the Soviet Union. Armstrong's statement of concern also indicated a specific problem associated with a surprise attack—the time it took the bombers to get to their targets. It was that liability, perhaps more than any other, that threatened the success of a first strike. Armstrong's appeal cut to the core of the issue and gave cause for the invalidation of LeMay's concept. In any case, it was another problem that Armstrong had laid at the SAC commander's feet in his letter.

Without the ability to refuel the bombers mid-air, SAC would not be able to carry out its mission against the Soviet Union. According to Armstrong, this would have been the case even if the

United States had bombed the Soviet Union under conditions of surprise. But Armstrong was not finished: "Should we mount a strike and reach the North African complex to find it denied—no tankers available—we could not reach the primary targets and that bomber force would be a complete loss. We could never retrieve them because of the lack of fuel and crashes. The same thing would occur along the northern route if bases in England were denied."[5] The problem was clear; SAC had a potential roadblock to getting where it needed to go during a war. Armstrong suggested a way forward to LeMay: "Our first and main efforts must be mounted from those bases where refueling is not required. Time and distance will be the essence. . . . We must be in position to get to the target immediately if we hope to pin the Russian down by knocking out his bomber fields, thereby preventing the Russian Air Force from denying ocean islands to us."[6] In Armstrong's eyes, promptness was simply the enabler for a solution, not the answer. The desired end state was the elimination of the enemy bomber force. Armstrong's thoughts mirrored LeMay's approach: catch the bombers on the ground and prevent their employment in a conflict. Armstrong's thoughts indicated that LeMay was not alone in his response to the larger problem of the prevention of attacks. In the two men's minds, preemption was the best answer to what seemed an existential threat.

Armstrong next moved to the relationship between SAC's plans and foreign policy. In doing so, he exposed possible dissonance between the United States and the United Kingdom but did so with a sense of sympathy:

Where our initial striking force will be located and who will command it is of no importance to me. I do know that they must be in place and ready to strike. . . . England, our largest stepping-stone, is in my mind between a rock and a hard place—be damned if you do and be damned if you don't. If England goes with us, operational bases used by SAC will certainly be hit. If England is neutral, our ZI first strike bomber will not be allowed to make the return flight. . . . If England decides to think the matter over a couple of days, our plans will be of no avail. The same is true of Iceland. To lose Goose Bay [Canada] would be disastrous.[7]

From Armstrong's perspective, the picture for possible success in the execution of a war—or at least the type of strikes discussed in his letter—was bleak. But the same could have been said about nuclear war as a whole.

Per Armstrong, it was as though the chances for things to go well with SAC's plan for war were almost nonexistent. But another aspect to what Armstrong had written was connected to the question of preemption—and whether LeMay was alone in his contemplation of such an approach. In his reference to "our ZI first strike bombers" from the United States, it was unclear what type of first strike Armstrong had in mind. The possibilities ran the gamut from a preemptive strike to simply a reference to the first wave of SAC bombers en route to their targets. Given the broader context of the letter and a mention of a possibility of a first strike— though Armstrong had cast aspersions on the success of such an approach—his reference most likely was to a preemptive attack. What was unambiguous in Armstrong's message was that there was a need to eliminate the Soviet bombers first.[8]

Armstrong also addressed the perceived Soviet threat to SAC's forward bases, proposing a possible improvement to the situation by adjusting where aircraft were based. But what mattered more than a potential remedy was the grander point Armstrong made in his conclusion:

> Curt, the whole thing boils down to this. B-47s are dependent upon tankers. Tankers are dependent upon forward bases or islands from which to operate. If either is denied the bombers cannot carry out their mission completely. They might do the job half-way and then become lost for further operations. We must have a force capable of destroying USSR medium bomber bases immediately when hostilities begin. That can only be done by having a force, in being, within striking distance of the targets. If we lose our refueling bases, SAC cannot strike. It is just that simple, or complex, depending upon the way one looks at it. We "go" provided we can refuel. We "stay home" if we cannot.[9]

Armstrong's entreaty to LeMay highlighted the problem of aircraft. SAC's mission as a military force was entirely dependent upon equipment, without which it could not perform its assigned task. As had been the case with the B-47 and its problems, SAC needed a fix. The command already had the B-36 bomber, which could have flown nonstop from the United States to strike the Soviet Union. However, its slow speed made it vulnerable to some enemy defenses such as high-performance jet fighters. Another advance that increased SAC's capabilities—particularly to counter enemy air defenses—was the B-52 bomber, which was faster than the B-36 and had the range to strike targets in the Soviet Union from the United States. The new bomber also possessed electronic countermeasures to defend it from emergent threats.

The SAC commander's measured response on July 26 flew in the face of a LeMay caricatured by smoldering anger and being ready to start a war: "Your letter of 18 July represents a lot of searching thought and is appreciated. . . . I and my top staff have taken several days to give it the thorough consideration I feel it deserves. I will comment in some detail to demonstrate the background for my decisions and present point of view." Given the magnitude of the issue laid before him, it was no surprise LeMay afforded the problem some contemplation.[10]

The SAC commander agreed at least in part with Armstrong's conclusion in his letter of July 18, telling the Second Air Force commander that "I consider victory in the air battle will determine the decision in any future war. All offensive air power must be effectively employed against the air battle objectives to win this victory as quickly and decisively as possible." Which targets qualified as air battle objectives became an important reference as LeMay proceeded: "I am concerned about the low level of the theaters' offensive air force potential for contributing to our major task of destroying the enemy capability to deliver high yield weapons against the United States and her allies. The forces in the advanced areas are also extremely vulnerable to Soviet attack. I consider SAC to be a backup force for the limited theater capability with the probability SAC will conduct a great majority of the active operations in winning the air battle."[11]

In support of his point, LeMay explained that the bases and forces in question were indeed necessary but that Armstrong's concerns were not: "Assuming the loss of the island bases and a major portion of our prepared bases in the North African–Spanish–Mediterranean area, the late production models of the B-47 will still have the capability of taking off from or staging through

Hunter Air Force Base [near Savannah, Georgia] or several bases in the northeast areas, and fly non-stop to such bases as may be available in Spain or North Africa." From LeMay's perspective, all prospects of success were not lost. He added: "Employing a 'full-house' type staging operating through these advanced bases, it seems probable we could strike the Soviet target system." Despite LeMay's prediction, it was impossible to tell whether a prospective attack would have been successful. Nonetheless, LeMay's discussion exposed further details of what a nuclear war might have looked like and how more than one option for its execution existed—even as early as mid-1955. It also explained much about LeMay's nature—and his approach to adversity. It was as if LeMay left himself options or was able to find them among the chaos of a hypothetically imminent war.[12]

With regard to an attack on the previously mentioned "Soviet target system," he noted without optimism that "this type of operation, of course, requires bases with a minimum support capability in Spain, North Africa, and the Mediterranean area. . . . The present total number of programmed bases in this area we both recognize as being inadequate."[13] The letter's final paragraph, however, echoed comments LeMay made just days earlier at Quantico, reinforcing that what he told senior leaders there was indeed his true thinking on the topic:

> I am hopeful that the word "aggression" will be redefined and accepted by the United Nations. The new definition, in my opinion, must recognize that we are now living in an age when it can no longer be an issue of morality that a nation must receive the first physical blow before it can respond with force; in fact, the first blow can now signal

the end of a conflict rather than a beginning. Therefore, certain enemy actions short of war should constitute sufficient threat to the non-aggressor nation that it would be justified in launching direct attack, at least on enemy strategic air power, to forestall its own disaster. If this new philosophy can be accepted, it might well give us the solution to many of our current problems.[14]

LeMay's advocated approach to nuclear war raised questions that went beyond pure advocacy into the realm of national intent and societal outlook. In those regards, LeMay was both a reflection of that intent and a driver of concern. He represented the fears of an anxious American society, but he also was a source for disquiet through his remarks and efforts to shape SAC into an organization capable of global nuclear war. Nuclear war was an altogether new concept during LeMay's time at SAC and carried repercussions with which humanity had just begun to wrestle.

Continued Vulnerabilities

In a November letter to Air Force Chief of Staff Nathan Twining, LeMay shared that "one Soviet advancement intensifies my concern about the tenability of our overseas bases. National intelligence estimates indicate that by 1960 the Soviets will have 1,000 ballistic medium range missiles (1,300 NM [nautical miles]) which will give them adequate weapon coverage of all our UK, Spain, and Mediterranean bases, as well as Thule, Keflavik, and the Alaskan complex. Furthermore, these missiles will have a 3 mile CEP [circular error probable] with 3 MT [Megaton] yield." In other words, in the near future, SAC's advanced positions would no longer be defensible. LeMay explained that "little, if any, warning will be available, thus tankers and bombers within missile range will probably be lost and the bases rendered untenable. . . . This, in addition to a large proportion of their medium jet bomber force which has the capability of destroying our forward bases, causes me to question our dependence on these bases to support the strike force." LeMay ended with an indication of the need for a massive shift in how SAC undertook its operations: "Certainly from 1960 onward we must plan to launch our alert forces from the relatively more secure ZI and Canadian bases."[15]

To LeMay, such locations in the zone of the interior enhanced SAC's ability to respond to a Soviet attack. At the same time, the risk inherent in an attack on the continental United States was greater than with overseas locations; an attack on SAC bases abroad may not have resulted in an assured nuclear response, but one launched against bases in the continental United States almost guaranteed a reply in kind. Given that, forces posted to the zone of the interior also provided an inherent deterrent.

There too, however, a problem presented itself. Though some SAC bombers had the ability to take off from the United States and strike their targets, most could not—which meant the need for either bases on foreign territory or aerial refueling to support the bombers returning from their targets. LeMay directly addressed this point: "In order to launch from ZI bases and still have the range capability to get the bombers back to the forward base complexes for recovery, we must alleviate the serious tanker limitations." By this account, the ability to refuel midair was the critical apex of bombardment efforts planned as part of a nuclear war. The SAC commander explained that "by 1960 we will have 11 B-52 wings (45 UE [Unit Equipped]) and only

16 KC-135 squadrons (20 UE). This means that the remaining 30% of our heavy force will be dependent upon refueling support from the seriously inadequate KC-97s." LeMay provided a possible solution: "In our studies to determine means of maintaining an effective 1/3 alert force, we have concluded that B-52s and B-47s combined with KC-135s offer the most flexibility, timing, and security. One KC-135 provides the equivalent support of 3 KC-97s and has the advantage of not requiring forward positioning. With this combination it is possible to maintain an effective 1/3 alert force within relatively more secure areas." The mismatch of tankers to bombers meant that SAC could not employ its forces in an optimal fashion, which potentially brought into question the efficacy of SAC's entire approach to nuclear war. Certainly the need for foreign posts did, as Armstrong's letter had posited. Now LeMay had reached a similar conclusion. In the final paragraph of his letter to Twining, LeMay explained that "as was pointed out to the Joint Chiefs of Staff recently, the Soviets, by 1958, may have a superior long range bombardment capability. We must counter this threat with the largest and most effective alert force that can be sustained. Moreover, we must recover a high percentage of the bombers if we are to preserve the capability to deliver all the weapons in our stockpile. The KC-135 is the only tanker available that gives us that capability." LeMay's argument was straightforward and blunt, but as he noted, the real issue at hand was the ability to drop bombs on their targets—all of them. Bombers and tankers were simply the tools of the trade. As SAC commander, LeMay represented just one of the Air Force's competitive internal constituencies. Ultimately, and as was often the case, LeMay got his way. The Air Force eventually purchased several hundred KC-135s

for the SAC fleet, many of which continued their service past the disestablishment of SAC in 1992.[16]

The "alert" concept and the SAC commander's emphasis on new aircraft had a bearing upon the matter of nuclear first strikes. SAC had to get its planes in the air and en route to their targets as fast as possible to make first strikes a success in the event of war. Bombers and tankers placed on alert gave the command a more effective means to launch a preemptive attack.

Preparations for War

LeMay wanted SAC to be prepared for a war that might arrive at any time. While LeMay did not write off the future—his efforts to procure more modern aircraft countered any notion of that—he was more concerned about what could be the immediate problem that faced his command and the United States: the possibility of nuclear war and the general tension between the Soviet Union and the Western powers allied against it. This strain was reflected in the discourse of diplomacy earlier in 1955. The Geneva Conference held in July did not broadly produce the desired outcome of a reduction in tension between the Soviet Union and the West. During remarks delivered to the Harvard Advanced Management Association on December 15, LeMay noted optimistically that "although the outcome of the Geneva Conference was considered by many to be a disappointment, the fact that the Communists even agreed to sit and discuss the prospects of world peace was perhaps highly significant."[17] Later in his remarks, however, LeMay added a dose of more typical pessimism: "Undoubtedly, there are lessons of the present age that we have yet to learn, but I think we must now know beyond any doubt the most important lesson of all—superior long-range, nuclear air power is the key to peace if continuing peace is possible—and it is the only means of victory if a major war is inevitable."[18] LeMay then set forth in further discussion of the question of peace and, if war took place, how the United States might achieve victory. His comment resembled other public statements he had previously delivered and also became an initial touchstone for a soft proclamation of advocacy for preemption: "Until it is clear that lasting peace is a reality beyond any doubt we must continue to build the United States Air Force's power, both offensive and defensive, and maintain it ready at all times to strike instantly and decisively at the first sign of aggression." Whether an enduring peace was ever a feasible reality was not a question that LeMay or anyone else in the room could have answered. What was more certain was what LeMay argued for in its place, which obliquely hinted at a first strike. What he meant by "strik[ing] instantly and decisively at the first sign of aggression" went unanswered in that sentence, as did a clarification of what constituted "the first sign of aggression." At the very least, the statement opened the door of support for an attack against an enemy before one had been levied against the United States.[19]

LeMay further pushed open the door of support for preemption as he continued, telling the audience, "We must recognize that the most serious threat today to the survival of our nation—in the event no workable inspection and arms control program can be agreed upon—is an attack by a substantial long-range nuclear air force with the capability of inflicting nation-wide damage to our own United States."[20] The threat of large-scale damage to the country was the core to LeMay's logic behind—and the argument for—preemptive military attacks. The crux of

LeMay's argument came next: "Such a force can be deterred or— in event of aggression—destroyed, only by superior air power, both medium and long range, backed up by adequate defensive air power." Stating that medium- and long-range aircraft backed by defensive airpower could have destroyed an enemy's air forces implied that such efforts had been carried out by offensive power. For offensive forces to be eliminated by offensive platforms, they almost certainly had to destroy them on the ground. By its very nature, this implied preemption.[21] After reviewing the missions of two other Air Force commands, LeMay moved on to an examination of SAC, stating that his command was "responsible for extremely long-range missions designed to knock out the source of enemy air power, such as his fuel supplies, weapons stockpiles, airdromes and the bombers and fighters they support."[22] What LeMay described was an effort that deprived an enemy of the capabilities to make war, not a deterrent response. He later stated that "our combat operations are based on the premise that the fastest way to end any war is to deprive an enemy of the means—as well as the *will*—to continue the fight." This meant the destruction of the opposition's force; for SAC, the way to accomplish such an end was through bombardment, which meant destruction of enemy forces on the ground. That was the heart of what LeMay was prepared to do.[23]

Preparation for nuclear war was an evident theme in a letter written to LeMay by Air Force Lt. Gen. Samuel E. Anderson on December 21, 1955. At the time, Anderson served as the director of the Weapons Systems Evaluation Group, the agency responsible for the assessment of armaments, which included nuclear weapons. Anderson's letter had two goals: the first was to set up an introductory meeting for the organization's director of research with LeMay, and the second was "to request that your staff do some work in connection with next year's 'Net Evaluation' study. This is the study made this year under the chairmanship of Hal George." This was the same George who had requested to visit SAC in May. Anderson continued, "At this time I have not been told the precise role WSEG would play in next year's study. However, it has been suggested to Admiral Radford that WSEG coordinate the gaming of the air battle or battles." Anderson then relayed a third-party discussion he had regarding "the desirability of utilizing high speed computational techniques in running such an exercise." Anderson told LeMay that "if this should prove to be feasible the greatest advantage would be that of being able to rerun strikes many times, thereby arriving at a more realistic answer than one obtains from one run of one strike." This was an early application of computers in an effort to make war more successful and efficient; it took some of the responsibility out of human hands and automated it. It was a trend toward push-button warfare that typified SAC and the nuclear age.[24]

Looking to the Future

In January 1956 LeMay attended a commander's conference at Wright-Patterson Air Force Base in Ohio. The event gave LeMay an opportunity to share his opinion on several matters, including his take on the most effective way to defeat an enemy air threat. The topic of preemption came up.

LeMay's remarks at Wright-Patterson had a starkness that reflected the serious nature of nuclear war. He first contended that "the decision made in 1946 to provide the United States Air Force with an atomic striking force probably stands as one of the most prudent military decisions in American history." While history had yet to validate such wisdom, the choice LeMay lauded was a substantial one that indicated the direction of postwar U.S. foreign and defense policy. If those indications were any guidepost, LeMay's argument held some water. The SAC commander then turned to more specific analysis: "This was a wise decision because it resulted in the United States going to the offense and building a potent military deterrent to war." With this statement, LeMay dispelled any notions that SAC was a typical defensive force—though this did not preclude its deterrent mission. SAC was not intended to, per se, defend the U.S. homeland, but it was intended for the nuclear command to eliminate threats through deterrence and attack. LeMay hinted at this point as he stated, "Our capability to lay down a devastating atomic offensive has been recognized by the World as the force that has prevented general war for the past decade." Whether LeMay's edict was correct was debatable.[25]

To that assertion LeMay appended a statement that highlighted his persistent trepidation over what he perceived as foreign threats. He made a prediction that, while not perfectly accurate, was not wildly off the mark of what was to occur. He told his audience that "first, by 1958 or certainly by 1960, according to Intelligence estimates, Russia will for the first time possess the capability of causing unacceptable damage to the United States. Of course I am referring to her long range atomic striking capability." LeMay then explained an issue with direct impact on SAC: "Second, it appears that in this time period Russia can effectively deny us the use of forward areas. Here I am thinking of the large numbers of intermediate range ballistic missiles which she is forecasted to have by 1960." He next argued that "during the period 1960–65, both USSR and the United States will be in a position to integrate intercontinental ballistic missiles into their striking force." Regarding LeMay's final prediction, even in light of what could be termed an ominous outlook, he made no call for preventive war to eliminate the threat. LeMay had shown restraint where other leaders had not done so. Although preventive war was not among LeMay's preferred approaches, other ends outside the national policy of deterrence and response were not foreign to his past arguments.[26]

LeMay next made a rare foray into the domestic arena, from which he had largely shied away during his military career: "There is still another situation which has developed that should cause us some concern. It is that the Russians will continue to talk peace, and there are too many people that believe them. This could seriously affect the forces we are given. We must keep this in mind when making our decisions." LeMay did not specify whose beliefs were of concern, but his take on the matter was clear: the SAC commander had no faith in trusting the enemy. From there LeMay began to transition to another theme: "Before we talk about the decisions to be made, I would like to review with you some basic points on which we all have agreed."[27] Whether the audience actually agreed with what he was about to say was unknown, but it did not matter. LeMay was saying what he believed and what he interpreted as national policy: "The United States is committed to a policy of peace. That is, our military power will be utilized primarily to prevent aggression. However, if war cannot be prevented on terms acceptable to the United States, the Air Force must insure that we win—no matter how it starts or how hollow the victory might be." The gravity of LeMay's statement could not be downplayed; his arguments were ones in which the notions of deterrence and aggression were subject to unique definitions. In other words, while LeMay did not explicitly argue that the mission of SAC was to deter an attack, he implied that such was the case. At the same time, the point to which an enemy needed to be deterred, and the marker of when deterrence failed and force needed to be applied, suggested a nonstandard interpretation.[28]

LeMay began by telling those assembled that "the first requirement or objective of our Air Force is to win both phases of the Air Power Battle—the deterrent phase and the combat phase. The deterrent phase of the Air Power Battle is being fought now. The deterrent phase that I am talking about is the day to day appraisal both sides must make to determine relative military strengths." In this sense, LeMay was repeating generally accepted standards of a deterrent philosophy and the practical process by which deterrence operated. Thus, LeMay reinforced the fact that he understood what deterrence was during the Cold War and that preemption was a deviation from the traditional understanding of deterrence— the publicly declared policy of the United States toward the Soviet Union. He continued: "There can be no doubt—at such time as Russian forces have the ascendancy over our forces, and it is to her advantage to attack us, she will attack. We must have such a force in being that for Russia to attack the United States would mean committing national suicide." But LeMay had a desire to take action that took the danger out of a potential failure of deterrence. He explained that "we all know that the best way to destroy an enemy air offensive force is to attack it in its most vulnerable situation—on the ground before it is launched." In so doing, LeMay reiterated one of his clearer statements on preemption—so clear that he saw no need to explore the subject further or to qualify his statement. When the nation's primary nuclear commander argued a preference for such an approach, it was hard to differentiate between his preference and the most likely course of action. Said another way, while the declared policy was deterrence, the SAC commander's proclivity was for preemption.[29] The incongruence between what LeMay advocated and what was called for in national policy was dramatic. Whereas the national policy was to deter and, if deterrence failed, respond, LeMay saw it otherwise: his organization—and the nation as a whole—needed to be prepared to launch a first strike.

LeMay did not shy from the big issues enshrined in national policy and used senior officers as a sounding board for ideas related to those concerns. This was the case with regard to his service supervisor, Twining. An exchange between LeMay and Twining in early 1956 carried with it a simultaneous sense of seriousness and familiarity. Letters on February 4 and February 8 demonstrated the collegiality of their relationship. The two letters also engaged the issue of preemption head on, revealing that LeMay understood that his advocacy for preemption could create problems for him and the Air Force at large—and that steps were taken to lessen the negative impact of LeMay's advocacy.

Twining wrote to LeMay on February 4 concerning an article in *Time* magazine: "Through somewhat devious channels, involving no great reliability or accuracy, word has reached me that *Time* magazine is in the process of reopening the subject of 'A Definition of Aggression.' This rang a bell in my mind and, on thinking it over, I recalled that last February during your briefing for Secretary [John Foster] Dulles and Ambassador [Henry Cabot] Lodge this subject was discussed. On the off-chance that you may be contacted on this subject by *Time* it occurred to me that it might be helpful for you to have my thoughts in advance." The mention of "A Definition of Aggression" was probably a reference to the discussion with Lodge that LeMay had recalled in his remarks at Quantico in July 1955. That discussion included, at least tangentially, the topic of preemption in the presence of both Lodge and the secretary of state, Dulles. Twining's disclosure established that LeMay had direct contact on the issue of preemption with one of the most senior policymakers in the U.S. government.[30]

The February 4 letter from Twining stated that "as I see it, the only useful end which a discussion of the definition of aggression could serve would of necessity include the adoption of a specific definition by the United Nations."[31] This was an argument akin to the one LeMay made during his 1955 Quantico speech, when he supported Lodge's call for the United Nations to adopt a new characterization of the term.[32] Twining told LeMay: "Discussions for any other purpose, such as possible U.S. unilateral adoption of a definition, do not appear to me to be particularly promising." Twining's assessment was an interesting turn, particularly given LeMay's fervent advocacy for a new understanding of the concept. Nonetheless, LeMay himself had put the onus for a new characterization of the term on the United Nations during his remarks at Quantico. Twining continued: "I leave to your imagination the problem of arriving at a workable definition of aggression, which would protect our interests, and then securing United Nations agreement on this specific wording. To take this a step further and assume that we had achieved this task, I then ask myself what the results would be." In Twining's final estimation, the likely outcome of the matter would be unacceptable for the U.S. defense apparatus, as he told LeMay: "I cannot but conclude that the logical course of events would result in a requirement to punish or otherwise act against aggression as determined by the United Nations. I believe this would require our making forces available for this purpose. The end result then would be to have U.S. force directly responsive to the demands of an international organization. This is a position which the Joint Chiefs of Staff strenuously objected to in 1950 and would object to today."[33] Twining painted a picture of a military chain of command that eventually led outside U.S. authority. The concept of having Air Force bombers outside the span of national authority put at risk SAC's ability to respond when the nation's interests dictated. In so doing, this approach could have entirely negated a reliance on preemption if the United Nations chose not to act at the right time. Such a possibility almost certainly would have been unacceptable to LeMay.

Twining then turned to the follow-up to LeMay's meeting with the secretary of state and ambassador to the United Nations in early 1955: "In addition and immediately subsequent to your discussion with Dulles and Lodge, we developed a proposed definition of aggression and assessed it to determine our readiness and vulnerability in peace and war in the event of its adoption." The most significant unanswered question of Twining's statement was the identity of the "we" referred to in the passage. That the chief of staff and unnamed others were under the impression that the creation of a new characterization of "aggression" was called for suggested that one result of the Dulles-Lodge meeting was the perception—at least on Twining's part—that such was possibly acceptable to even more senior leaders. Twining questioned the ultimate wisdom of having done so, however, as he told LeMay that "we came to the conclusion that while the specific definition we had in mind could possibly improve our position to some degree, its obvious potential for harmful consequences was much more significant." It did not mean the issue was dead.

What followed in Twining's letter held the potential answer to LeMay's advocacy for a policy of preemption. If that was the case, the letter to LeMay had the ability to color the common perception of the U.S. approach to the potential for nuclear war. Twining explained: "This whole subject area is, as you know, closely allied with the disarmament problem particularly as this problem relates to inspection and surprise attack. This area is particularly sensitive at the present time and the Joint Chiefs of Staff have recently, by a very narrow margin, succeeded in influencing the Commander-in-Chief in the right direction in this area. Any disturbance of this delicate balance at this time could be harmful." Twining's indication that President Eisenhower had been swayed with regard to the topic was meaningful news and suggested that the president had considered the possibility of a new definition of aggression, an argument interwoven with that for preemption. It was a major revelation that suggested that two nuclear use policies were developing within U.S. policy and defense circles: one publicly proclaimed and one for actual application. Twining advised LeMay that "I pass these thoughts on to you in the belief that you are a logical candidate for *Time* to question on this problem. I believe any military contribution to this discussion would be fruitless and could be extremely harmful." In Twining's estimation, *Time* was likely to contact LeMay on the topic, and the SAC commander needed to keep his opinion to himself if he desired a redefinition of aggression. Twining reinforced the issue: "I feel strongly enough about this to say that if you find the pressure on you is extreme, we should attempt to get the State Department to exercise a moderating influence on *Time* in the light of the U.S. position in the United Nations." Twining's concern was palpable, and his recommendation that LeMay turn to another government body—the State Department—indicated how seriously LeMay's boss took the entire matter. Twining did not want the situation to become fouled in the tangle of the press. Twining's willingness to further discuss the matter, telling LeMay, "In the event you feel any further discussion on this would be helpful I suggest that you come in and talk it over with me," denoted the importance he assigned the situation as well as the fact that he wanted LeMay to clearly understand his guidance.[34]

LeMay replied to Twining on the matter roughly four days later: "Reference your letter of 4 February, *Time* Magazine did contact PIO [Public Information Officer] here last week about the possibility of a story based on 'A Definition of Aggression.' Their interest apparently was aroused by a piece in one Chicago paper which quoted a statement of mine out of context." Even if it was not a citation of LeMay's Quantico remarks, the title in question was incriminating enough; by that point in 1956, and given the content of Twining's February 4 letter, the topic clearly was preemption. Although the SAC commander had called for a new definition on at least one occasion, LeMay told Twining, "*Time* was advised that any story of this nature would be above the military level." This was an effort to snow *Time*, and LeMay admitted as much in the next line. He told Twining, "Every effort was made to duck this one and when they continued to press, a tenth anniversary story was offered as a red herring to draw them off the scent." This was a stunning admission that either he or his staff distracted the press to cover his tracks on what was almost certainly his advocacy for a policy of preemption. This revelation exposed much about both how far LeMay was willing to go to get what he wanted and the military's dealing with the press during the early Cold War era. The way SAC handled the media in this regard was, at the least, devious. Though LeMay had an interest in not seeing an article published on his advocacy for preemption, he also had an obligation to be forthright. However, the *Time* magazine correspondent was also clever. LeMay described to Twining the situation: "*Time* expressed considerable interest in this [the tenth anniversary story] and sent a correspondent to discuss further details with Reade Tilley. This man shrewdly avoided any mention of the 'Definition of Aggression' angle but after several hours of discussion, Tilley was of the opinion that he had that angle very much in mind and was playing his cards carefully knowing we intended to avoid it. PIO then offered full cooperation on an air power story, but advised them no comment on 'A Definition of Aggression' would be forthcoming. . . . When the *Time* correspondent left, details of his visit here and our position were telephoned to Casey in your Information Office. I agree with you that a *Time* story with military comment on 'A Definition of Aggression' could be harmful and we have done our best to forestall it." LeMay wanted his superior to know what had transpired and that they were on the same page. LeMay concluded by reporting that "the way matters stand the *Time* New York office has not yet notified their correspondent they will proceed with the story. If they should, I also agree with you that we might best refer the matter to the State Department. I appreciate your guidance, Nate, and will see you Monday when we can discuss the matter in further detail." LeMay rarely expressed the type of concern he did in this instance; his desire to review the problem with Twining made clear this was a real problem in the SAC commander's eyes. The greatest implication of the episode was the reason why LeMay and Twining handled the issue of preemption so carefully—they did not want to risk the loss of senior-level support. For his part,

LeMay wanted to see a change in policy that met his desires. A negative public reaction to military advocacy for any type of nuclear first strike might have tipped the president into banning the concept from consideration or denying the military's pursuit of such authority. It would have been a disaster for LeMay's efforts. What was patently evident was the lack of any directive from Twining or commitment from LeMay to forsake support for a policy of preemption.[35] The SAC commander's advocacy did not dissipate, and subsequent statements in closed settings reflected his continued promotion of it. No evidence suggested that LeMay changed his beliefs because of what Twining said, but he chose his words more carefully in the wake of Twining's letter.

On February 22 LeMay appeared at the University of Notre Dame to make remarks upon receiving an award, and he used the opportunity to discuss some of his favorite topics, including preemption. LeMay's opening was typical of his approach to his stewardship of his subordinates: "It is good to come here tonight to acknowledge your most generous recognition. But the Award for Patriotism is not mine alone. I can only accept it on behalf of the nearly 200,000 men and women of the Strategic Air Command." After making numerous statements on patriotism and covering his take on the U.S. security situation, LeMay came to an area more closely related to his day-to-day responsibilities: "This is the air age, and in the air age an entirely new military concept obtains. Through the air, no part of the world is safe from attack by long-range aircraft. As we meet here tonight, we are just a few hours from potentially hostile bomber bases. Any part of our own country can be reached through the air—and through the air any part of the world is accessible to us." LeMay's take on the defense situation amid what he perceived as a new threat was fairly dark but not atypical in the Cold War era. The world's strongest nations were preparing for a war for reasons that were only partially understood by each party. What was even less well understood at the time were the opposing parties' intentions. In any case, LeMay wanted to be ready for the worst: "In the air age, continents and oceans no longer are barriers to attack. Land masses and traditional land defense in depth offer no protection against the space-consuming ten-mile-a-minute speed of the jet bomber. Only the coordinates of latitude and longitude are significant . . . and these can be read from the stars to find targets on the earth below." The world was different, even if not to the extent LeMay's words suggested, but his perception mattered a great deal because he based his responsive actions—especially his advocacy for preemption—on it. The SAC commander now hinted at that issue, recommending to his audience a scholarly article that he had referred to in the past: "We are also in the age of nuclear power, the age of nuclear weapons. In a recent paper published here at Notre Dame, there was an article entitled 'Courage or Perdition' which lists 14 points of the nuclear age. The author recognizes clearly the fact that there is no turning back from this age. We have either to master the atom and learn to live with it, or we might easily die by it. I suggest to those of you who have not read this paper that you would find it very interesting and certainly worthwhile." LeMay's reference to the same article that he cited during his remarks at Quantico in July 1955 was an indication that his advocacy for preemption had not halted as a result of Twining's letter from February 4, 1956. The SAC commander simply became more subtle in his approach.[36]

In classified forums, LeMay remained as vocally committed to preemption as ever. The dissonance between what LeMay said behind closed doors and what he said in public was noticeable. On

April 25, 1956, LeMay and key members of his staff testified before the Subcommittee on the Air Force of the Senate Committee on Armed Services.[37] The SAC commander's testimony was part of the "airpower hearings," the result of an incorrect belief that the United States had fallen behind the Soviet Union in the number of strategic bombers it possessed—the so-called bomber gap. The airpower hearings were as much spectacle as they were a substantive solution to a falsely conceived problem. The bomber gap was a misnomer that reinforced SAC's position on the need for further resources.

LeMay's appearance before the committee gave deeper insight into his thinking than was typically exhibited in public. The testimony before the Senate was critical to the story of LeMay's advocacy for first strikes in another way; everything he and his staff said was on the record, and they were obligated to follow through on what they told the Senate lest there be negative consequences. Therefore, there was an incentive for LeMay and his staff to be honest in their remarks.

The chair of the subcommittee was Stuart Symington, who had served as the first secretary of the Air Force from 1947 to 1950. After he was sworn in, Symington asked LeMay who else would be testifying. LeMay responded: "This is my testimony, and I am responsible for it. I am just using them [the staff] to present the charts." LeMay was clear that his testimony represented only his thoughts. Nonetheless, Symington played by the book regarding witnesses, directing that "every man who may talk this morning should be sworn at this time." The larger point was an important one: though others spoke that day, the ideas that the SAC staff relayed actually belonged to LeMay. [38]

One of the more important briefers that day was Col. Edward M. Nichols, chief of the control division within the command's operations directorate.[39] After he discussed strategic airpower during World War II, Nichols began detailing SAC's present mission: "Our mission, as defined by the Joint Chiefs of Staff, is to conduct a strategic air offensive, utilizing atomic and other available weapons. . . . Now, they [the Joint Chiefs of Staff] have broken this mission down into three tasks. . . . The first task is the BRAVO or blunting task. The blunting task is to destroy the Soviet atomic forces on the ground. Here we are going after their airpower to prevent them from dropping atomic weapons on this country or our allies." Nichols' description of the mission was an obvious definition of a preemptive role. His next statement linked two concepts that often swirled about one another in usage and meaning. With regard to the preemptive mission, Nichols explained to the subcommittee that "this is, of course, winning the airpower battle. We have to do that before we can move on with anything else. . . . The nation which wins the airpower battle can go on and win the war. The nation which loses the airpower battle could never win the war, because they are out of business." This was a meaningful conclusion from the perspective of an associated assumption: that airpower could indeed achieve such an outcome in a war without support from other military forces. Whether this was an accurate—or even widely accepted outside the Air Force—statement was open to interpretation. LeMay chimed in and offered to the subcommittee: "Mr. Chairman, I think it is generally conceded by all military personnel in this day and age, you must win the airpower battle, gain air superiority, before you can conduct any other type of military operation." This was a significant assumption that, as was the case with Nichols' statement to similar effect, was quite open to debate. What was clear, however, was that preemption was at the top of the list when it came to SAC's charge during a war with the Soviet Union.[40]

After the testimony, LeMay clarified what was said before the Senate subcommittee, offering changes to the testimony. Nichols' statements on preemption were part of the updates.[41] These changes, however, did not alter the substantive conclusions or arguments of the original testimony. Specifically, the testimony that concerned preemption was rewritten to read: "The first task is to prevent the launching of an atomic attack against this country."[42] A handwritten comment that appeared on the original transcript of the testimony stated, "Insert in place of deletion on p. 20: 'to prevent the launching of an atomic attack on this country'[.]" Immediately above that appeared the statement: "18 May corrections by . . . Gen LeMay[.]"[43] The SAC commander was intent on specificity when it came to the question of preemption—he wanted exact language that reflected his thinking. Alongside the issue of specificity was the question of general interest in the topic; based upon this rewrite, it was clear that preemption remained among the more important issues for LeMay.

A public lecture to the American Ordnance Association on May 23 provided another example of LeMay's continued advocacy for first strikes. In that instance, however, it was in an oblique manner. In reference to SAC, LeMay told his audience that "this is the long-range nuclear striking arm of the Air Force, with the capability of reaching directly the sources of enemy air power and his air bases deep within his nation as well as industrial areas, should it be required. SAC, then, is the global expression of American air power." The notion that SAC was able to attack "the sources of enemy air power" and airfields was not a random point. To launch attacks against an opponent's air forces meant to deprive him of the use of those forces. LeMay then explained that "our medium jet bomber, the B-47, and our heavy jet bomber, the B-52, through the use of in-flight refueling, have ranges limited only by the physical endurance of the men who fly them. No target site on the face of the earth is beyond their reach." The range of SAC's assets made the command different from any military force that had theretofore existed. As a result, SAC could make a definitive act of preemption a viable option—if it could get past Soviet air defenses. That was not guaranteed, and a successful Soviet defense could have negated LeMay's efforts at preemption or a retaliatory response. But Soviet air defense was not LeMay's primary topic on May 23; he was focused on the offense, saying, "These bombers [B-47s and B-52s] constitute the force which would be, in time of war, the first to strike in the decisive Air Power Battle we have outlined. By systematic reduction of enemy airdromes, with the aircraft and materiel they hold, they could reduce the weight of possible attack on this country." LeMay's words, though somewhat veiled, nonetheless made his argument for preemption. If SAC bombers attacked an airbase where Soviet—or any nation's— bomber aircraft were still located, it would almost certainly be the case that U.S. forces struck first. On one hand, the bombers were still on the base and not in the air; on the other hand, it lessened "the weight of possible attack on this country," a statement that indicated the foe's attack had, in all practical likelihood, not yet occurred. LeMay's message was not a gentle suggestion that per- haps retaliation was not SAC's preferred aim; he had directly— though carefully—made clear what he preferred.[44]

During this time, other matters competed for and drew LeMay's attention. One of those was to ensure the command had the right people to carry out its functions. In a letter on June 6, 1956, the chief of staff told LeMay that there had been an exami- nation "of the Air Force promotion programs to determine the advisability of expanding, continuing, or eliminating the spot promotion program."[45] The rank advancement system was a performance-based promotion system that bypassed evaluation through a traditional promotion board and process. LeMay used it as an incentive program to encourage excellence in what was once a floundering organization. The program represented one of the few special rewards SAC could offer to its members for peak performance—and gave them a tangible reason to serve and remain in a command with a challenging mission. This was an important program for LeMay and SAC. Unlike much of the military promotion system in the Cold War U.S. military, it afforded more immediate performance results than were typically found. Without it, SAC was subject to the normal channels for promotion; if it were eliminated, SAC would lose an element of what made it a unique place to serve. To that end, there were problems ahead.

Those problems quickly became apparent as Twining told LeMay in his letter, "As you know, the requirement to end this program has been forecast in the past but without our being able to determine any specific date for such termination. The results of this review indicate that the spaces involved cannot be supported after 1 January 1960." In other words, the program had an expiration date. After an explanation of the reasoning behind the conclusion of the program, Twining declared, "We can no longer reserve temporary promotion vacancies for the exclusive use of any one command. . . . All spot promotion spaces, therefore, must be vacated and returned to this headquarters by 1 January 1960."[46]

LeMay responded to Twining on February 6, 1957. LeMay confirmed his command's obedience with the directive, but also pointed out its detrimental impact on SAC: "I have directed my staff to comply with your letter of 6 June, but the serious adverse effects to the combat potential of this command and the Air Force that will be caused by any phasedown of the Spot Promotion Program require that I tell you of my grave concern." Tying the issue of promotion to combat preparation, LeMay told Twining, "It is my considered opinion that the value of the Spot Promotion Program, in terms of national security, far outweighs the other factors involved. We should not permit a 'business as usual' attitude in our promotion systems when considering these few officers who represent the major combat capability of the Air Force." LeMay's words questioned the wisdom of Twining's decision, putting them on opposite sides of the issue. There was a mutual respect between the two men, but in this case LeMay did not see the larger concern as Twining, who was focused on more administrative issues, saw it.[47] Instead, LeMay had a different perspective:

> In calling attention to the effect that this action will have on the capability of this command to carry out its assigned mission, I am addressing myself to an Air Force problem which should receive your personal attention. In light of the program Headquarters, USAF, has initiated to attract and retain the best qualified officers in the strike force in order to achieve maximum combat capability, I question that we can now afford to take a step that will assuredly detract from the capability of the only force able to bear effectively upon the air power battle target system of the enemy.[48]

It was classic LeMay; he focused on the issue of doing the job assigned to him and remained fixed on the operational matters. His primary job was to be ready to fight a nuclear war, and what the chief of staff was directing him to do would infringe on that mission. LeMay was also a dutiful officer, however, and he did as directed. But he knew how to express his dissent without crossing the line into disrespect—and could do so forcefully. This instance was, however, an extreme case of that approach. LeMay argued to Twining that

> the necessity of maintaining a high level of combat capability was reiterated in the current USAF Program Guidance, which states in part: 'Success in the initial phase of a general war will determine the ultimate outcome of the war and the parameters of any following strategy. Every effort must be made, therefore, to insure that the United States is in a position to win the initial phase. The *forces,* equipment and stocks *needed to fight and win* this phase *must be in being on D-Day. There can be no compromise with the top priority which these means must receive'* [emphasis added]. I am in hearty concurrence with this philosophy. When action required to attain the posture indicated in the above objective is analyzed, one cannot help but appreciate the great individual responsibilities that are carried by the combat crews of this command—responsibilities unmatched in the history of the military.[49]

LeMay's plea to Twining was an uncomplicated one: SAC would suffer as a result of the proposed change to the promotion program and, hence, the nation's defense would subsequently be weakened. At the same time, LeMay viewed SAC as more important than other aspects of the U.S. defense structure and thus in need of special treatment. LeMay concluded his letter to Twining:

"I cannot help but feel that it is the responsibility of all of us to face this issue so vital to national security and to provide the incentives that are absolutely necessary for this command to attain this goal. If this cannot be accomplished within the framework of existing public law, then I believe that Congress should be so informed."[50] This was a strong statement, even for LeMay. What made it more intriguing was that he left out any mention of who in the chain of command needed to be satisfied on the matter and, if not, who would make the notification to Congress. LeMay was an astute enough practitioner of policy-level decision-making to understand that ambiguity in such matters did not usually lead to positive outcomes. It was, however, also out of character for LeMay to make veiled threats to his superior, particularly a man he respected as much as he did Twining. Nonetheless, there was ambiguity in LeMay's conclusion. What was more certain was the sense from LeMay's response to Twining that the SAC commander was under pressure. Even for SAC, there were limitations.

LeMay and Twining faced other issues in the fall of 1956. One of the more important matters involved the development of additional bases and the production of new aircraft for SAC. In a letter to Twining on September 21, 1956, LeMay wrote that "I am deeply concerned that, because of a shortage of time and funds, our proposed new bases will not be capable of accepting B-52 [bombers] and KC-135 [aerial refueling tankers] aircraft scheduled for production from FY [Fiscal Year] 1959 through FY 1962."[51] In the latter half of the 1950s, SAC undertook a program to increase the capability of its fleet and build more bases on which to house it—a process known in SAC as dispersal. The technique was an attempt by the command to frustrate the Soviets' ability to successfully target and strike SAC assets, particularly in the scenario of a surprise attack, which was a major concern in the defense community in that era. Dispersal of the fleet would make it more difficult for the Soviets to disarm the United States and eliminate its ability to respond during a nuclear war.

LeMay then moved into the specifics of the issue with Twining: "The ceiling placed on the FY 1957 and prior years' Military Construction Programs leaves approximately $900-million of authorized items unfunded."[52] The funding cap on building projects was the root problem, however. One of the resultant issues that would exist in subsequent years, in LeMay's eyes, was also an issue: "Furthermore, the ceiling placed on the FY 1958 Military Construction Program for SAC items precludes our programming adequate facilities to support the aircraft deployment and utilization shown in PD 58–1, Supplement 1, for end position FY 1960." This meant that the new structures associated with the operation of SAC's aircraft were not going to be ready when called for. LeMay's argument was not inconsequential; without the necessary infrastructure, the ability to operate aircraft would be constrained. The question that hung over the matter was whether LeMay's argument and desire were reasonable ones. LeMay moved on to the more specific problem of actually constructing the facilities in question: "In addition to the problem of funds limitations, I am concerned about the short lead time allowed in our programming cycle for the FY 1958 Military Construction Program for end position FY 1960 for new bases, especially in cold climates. It is physically impossible under our present procedures to locate acceptable sites, plan, program and construct complete bases in the time period for items in the FY 1958 Military Construction Program to be completed and ready to meet the FY 1960 end position."[53] LeMay was at once a person of thought and a pragmatic administrator; this instance elucidated his ability to be honest about those problems. He had, however, a tendency to focus on the solution while failing to understand circumstances beyond those immediately within his purview. If it did not impact SAC, it was not his problem. In one sense this was a valuable trait that allowed LeMay to focus on his mission and his problems. In another sense, this side of LeMay's nature was a detrimental one that provided fodder for a reputation of single-mindedness. To a certain degree and based on this situation, it was an accurate characterization.

LeMay achieved much of what he set out to do. When it came to accomplishing specific tasks or meeting goals, his pragmatic nature paid off. He took that practical approach in the September 21 letter to Twining in which he proposed some courses of action to resolve the problems LeMay brought up in the letter. The first of LeMay's proposals would "divert sufficient money to construction from other sources to insure having bases, aircraft and personnel in proper phase as complete packages." Omitted, however, was exactly where those funds were to come from; this was a specific example of how LeMay could plow forward without giving at least a nod to attendant issues.[54]

The next item on LeMay's list of suggestions carried a greater degree of detail, but it also entailed a need for specific actions: "Increase lead time in programming cycle for construction of new bases so the installations can be ready in phase with aircraft production. We should identify bases required for end position FY 61 and FY 62 and long lead time items such as real estate procurement should be added to the proposed FY 1958 Military Construction Program." LeMay's final proposal would have solved the problem if it worked, but it would have required assistance from levels well above Twining: "Survey our present backlog of unfunded authorization and support a deficiency appropriation to catch up on funding and construction of essential facilities authorized in prior programs."[55] Congressional funding was not a guaranteed solution. Taking such a route would have been time consuming and would have required a great deal of coordination among the Air Force, Department of Defense, and Congress itself. It was far from an easy solution.

In a letter of November 15, 1956, Twining responded with a calm and professional tone that did not share the vigor of LeMay's September 21 letter: "Your recommendations for funding and programming actions to insure proper phasing of base construction and B-52/KC-135 production and deployment, which were outlined in your letter of 21 September 1956, have been studied and the results of our studies are outlined below." It may as well have been a warning to LeMay about the outcomes of his requests—though all was not lost. Twining explained both the wisdom and folly of the SAC commander's thinking: "In line with your recommendation, means are being investigated for providing supplemental guidance which will permit programming long lead-time construction items in adequate time for completion of required facilities in phase with production and deployment schedules. . . . The diversion of funds to construction from other Air Force appropriations is not feasible. Although the construction program is certainly a major bottleneck at the present time, all other Air Force appropriations are fully programmed and diversion could only be at the expense of high priority procurements." In other words, there was no available money to move without consequences—consequences that Twining seemed unwilling to accept. As chief of staff, he was the final military authority in the Air Force, and all decisions that involved Air Force matters beyond SAC's sole control called for Twining's oversight. Twining explained his rationale: "As pointed out in the following paragraph, the limiting factors in the Construction

Appropriation are both construction capability and funding limitations. To obtain supplemental appropriation in FY 1957 would require full-scale presentation to the Appropriation Committees and probably to the Armed Services Committees of the Congress. The best that we could hope for would be additional appropriation late in the fiscal year, probably not before May and June." In Twining's opinion, even if they could get approval, the money would not get to the Air Force in a timely fashion. The chief of staff pointed out to the SAC commander, "This in effect would simply compound the problem for FY 1958 since any additional appropriation would not be available for contract award until July at best. Since we are already planning to request increased appropriation to more nearly approach our contract award capability for FY 1958, the supplemental approach this year would not be of any material assistance."[56] The statement laid bare the fact that LeMay's thoughts in his letter to Twining on September 21 did not take into account some critical issues. Though LeMay was a shrewd administrator of SAC, he was also parochial when it came to some matters. That was a problematic weakness for LeMay.

Twining offered a higher-level perspective on the issue, telling LeMay, "It is apparent that total military construction requirements are so great that they exceed even the present construction capability of the Air Force." Though funding was never as robust as LeMay wanted during his time at SAC, it was less common to see such a clear statement of constraint from the chief of staff directed at SAC. But Twining's next words gave reason for optimism: "Although the amount of funds available for construction during FY 1956 and FY 1957 have served to artificially restrict the development of momentum in construction capability, this same condition should not occur in FY 1958 with the increased appropriation anticipated."[57]

From the chief of staff's informed perspective, the problem LeMay posed in his September 21 letter was likely to work itself out.

LeMay's approach to this seemingly mundane administrative matter spoke of his general demeanor—the SAC commander was given to worry. It was his nature. This trait bled into LeMay's approach to operational matters as well and may have been a contributing factor in his advocacy for preemption. The funding matter was not, however, as mundane as it appeared. The infrastructure and equipment LeMay and Twining discussed were to become the framework of the SAC force for the balance of the Cold War. In that sense, what the men debated was an important matter. It was not, however, as exciting as fighting an imminent nuclear war—but was intended to play a part in the deterrence of one. From that perspective, LeMay remained worried about an issue of strategic concern.

In 1957 LeMay entered his final months in command of SAC. He did not, however, lessen his focus on what he viewed as his mission, which included his advocacy for his common foil: preemption. LeMay's adherence to the idea was an indication of his continued fear of nuclear war and remained what he saw as the best defense.

On February 9, 1957, LeMay spoke at the Citadel, a military academy in Charleston, South Carolina. Though the speech was not given a security classification, it was an essentially military audience before which the SAC commander spoke. This was reflected in the candor with which LeMay spoke on that day:

My purpose here is to discuss with you a problem that deeply concerns everyone, whether in the military service or not. It is the problem of how to wage peace successfully, now and in the future. It is truly said that even the degree of peace we now enjoy will be lost unless the military front is continuously held by an effective deterrence force. . . . A little later on, I propose to give you SAC's definition of an effective deterrent force, and to outline SAC's ideas about what it will take to maintain that force on into the future.[58]

LeMay's assertion that SAC had its own definition of deterrence was a noteworthy point that suggested that what the command and, hence, LeMay saw as deterrence was materially different from the commonly accepted understanding of the concept. The natural questions were what was that definition, and why did LeMay single it out? He answered the first question: "We in SAC define the deterrent force to be 'an effective intercontinental nuclear air offensive force which is secure from destruction by the enemy regardless of what offensive and defensive action he takes against it. It must be of such size and composition and be alerted to such a degree that the Soviet Union will realize that an attack on the United States will mean committing national suicide.'" LeMay's definition was a fairly specific one that, unsurprisingly, highlighted a mission that mirrored SAC's purpose. This did not mean that LeMay did not sincerely believe in that approach. For LeMay, starting a war to prevent a larger war was a worthwhile venture; if one could be deterred, all the better.[59]

LeMay's definition of deterrence was not the most striking aspect of his remarks. Even more noteworthy was the invocation of an article the SAC commander had previously and closely associated with his argument for preemption: "You may be familiar with the widely discussed article entitled 'Courage or Perdition? The Fourteen Fundamental Facts of the Nuclear Age'—written by

'Ferreus' of the University of Notre Dame. To my mind, this article should be required reading for anyone concerned with the defense of this nation. If you have not read it, I commend it to you as being well worth your time and attention." LeMay had cited this same article in support of his argument for preemption to an audience of policymakers at the Quantico conference in July 1955. He now invoked the same article—without qualification of any of its arguments—to the audience at the Citadel. It was an artful way of communicating advocacy for preemption without expressly stating it.[60]

LeMay drove home the point with his Citadel audience: "In his article, Ferreus clearly outlines the modern-day military task in these words: 'The military task, briefly, consists of maintaining armaments in such quantities and of such quality that the opponent of the United States will find it impossible to solve his military problem through the employment of nuclear weapons. More particularly, he must be prevented from knocking out the American retaliatory forces through surprise blows and from delivering a substantial portion of his atomic stockpile on American targets.'" Though LeMay used the article to do his work, the SAC commander offered Ferreus' words as an implicit call for first strikes. The mission, as called for, was seeing that the foe was prevented from eliminating the U.S. military's response capability—and that meant to stop an opponent before he attacked. The point was reinforced with the article's call for preclusion of an enemy being able to dispense with positing "a substantial portion of his atomic stockpile on American targets." The only realistic manner for the preclusion of such was a preemptive strike to eliminate the possibility of it occurring in the first place. As a result, however, LeMay solidified the nature of his commentary: "In other words, Ferreus says to us in SAC: 'Now and in the future—at any hour of any day of any year—you must be ready at a moment's notice to launch a strategic bomber force, armed with nuclear weapons, capable of destroying anywhere in the world any targets that constitute a threat to the security of the United States and its allies.'" If the United States were to eliminate the Soviet bomber force with its own bombers, that meant doing so on the ground, and that meant a first strike.[61]

LeMay used someone else's words, but they fully captured the SAC commander's argument for preemption. He was not finished, however, going on to argue that

> objective planners in all military services now must start with a primary fact that air power's long arm and smashing fist can reach and utterly wipe out any targets anywhere in the world. Therefore one primary task in war—a job that must be done early—is the defeat of the enemy's air power, and particularly his long-range nuclear air arm. . . . Of course, a modern, skillfully operated continental air defense system can inflict losses upon the attacking bomber force. Such attrition will vary, depending upon the relative capabilities of offense versus defense—but a substantial part of the offensive force will always get through the defense. Therefore, the primary defensive force is actually the offensive nuclear strike force which can destroy enemy air power at its roots.[62]

This meant to eliminate the threat where it existed—on the ground at the foe's airbases. It completed LeMay's argument for preemption at the Citadel, both in the immediate and rhetorical senses.

On May 21 the SAC commander spoke at Patrick Air Force Base in Florida to a group that advised the Air Force on scientific matters.[63] The speech was significant for one reason: LeMay's time at SAC was almost over. Though he remained in the Air Force for eight years after he left SAC, in his subsequent positions he no longer commanded the airborne nuclear force. As such, he no longer directly controlled the nuclear weapons and delivery platforms that enabled a large portion of the forces that carried out U.S. nuclear policy. It was that very policy that his advocacy for preemption was intended to impact. As a result, what LeMay said on May 21 was a bookend to his remarks on preemption during his time at SAC and confirmed his continued concern over the matter.

LeMay's discourse at Patrick began with a simple preamble that belied a more complicated story: "You have asked me to discuss the operational side of air offense, with particular reference to those operational considerations which should underlie an evaluation of manned bombers in comparison with strategic missiles. I welcome the opportunity to do this."[64] There was a larger story behind the question of bomber aircraft piloted by an aircrew vis-à-vis unmanned rockets in SAC, however. LeMay was not opposed in theory to missiles being fielded in the SAC nuclear force; simultaneously, he was not a proponent of having such systems replace crewed aircraft until the missile had verified its worth.

LeMay had in fact made statements at the Citadel that supported that assertion, telling the audience that "we must spare no effort in the development of reliable intercontinental missiles. . . . President Eisenhower directed some time ago that the development of the intercontinental ballistic missile be given first priority among all programs in which the Department of Defense is engaged. The Strategic Air Command is in complete agreement with this policy." However, what the SAC commander said next was entirely representative of his own thinking: "You may wonder why SAC urges continued improvement and expansion of the manned bomber force and its bases, concurrently with strenuous efforts to develop the intercontinental guided missile. Don't we intend to replace manned bombers with missiles? Each program costs billions. Why the expensive duplication?" These were legitimate questions, and LeMay assuaged the heady concerns for the audience at the Citadel: "The answer is: as soon as the missile qualifies as a reliable weapons system there won't be any duplication—but until it so qualifies, the missile is not actually a deterrent." Whether his critics agreed was one matter, but the documentary evidence suggested LeMay did desire to bring missiles into use at SAC—he simply had caveats to that desire. Those concerns equally spoke to LeMay's worry about the unknown.[65]

Nonetheless, LeMay reiterated his primary emphasis in nuclear war to his audience in Florida. His explanation contained what amounted to the nation's actual nuclear policy, as it was enforced. This was given LeMay's plain influence on targeting within SAC as the organization's commander and the centrality of SAC targeting to the definition of U.S. priorities in a nuclear war. LeMay offered that "the objective of our national defense policy is deterrence. In the public mind—both ours and the Soviets'— deterrence is rooted in fear of nuclear devastation of population centers. However, in the professional military mind—again, both ours and the Soviets'—deterrence is measured in terms of ability to destroy the enemy's means of long-range delivery of nuclear weapons."[66] This was a definition of preemption at a basic level. Taking away an adversary's ability to launch a nuclear strike meant striking first, before it had been launched. By the time LeMay neared his departure from SAC, the organization was indeed the preemptive weapon he sought during his nearly nine years in charge of the U.S. nuclear command.

The End at SAC

LeMay left SAC in a much different condition than he found it. By the time he left for Washington in the summer of 1957, SAC had become essentially the command he set about to build when he arrived in 1948. The command possessed the ability to quickly carry out a large-scale nuclear war in a fairly successful manner. Beyond that, LeMay left behind one of his most trusted confidants, Thomas Power. LeMay had known Power since World War II, and he was one of the SAC commander's most valued understudies. Power's elevation to command of SAC ensured that what LeMay had organized became institutionalized.

LeMay was a larger-than-life figure in the sense that he initiated many of the programs, processes, standards, and, certainly, enduring mentality of the organization. LeMay defined SAC, and it came to define him. Without SAC, LeMay had only a minor role in the Cold War; with SAC, LeMay defined much of the American experience during the Cold War.

Conclusion

O n July 1, 1957, Curtis LeMay departed SAC after almost nine years in command and became the vice chief of staff of the Air Force. It was a promotion in terms of position for LeMay but a downgrade in terms of status; he was no longer a commander. He now was essentially in a senior staff officer role, which was one for which he had not necessarily prepared. Being a commander— especially with his history, background, and influence—was much different from being a staff officer. As commander, LeMay usually got what he wanted, at least within SAC. As a staff officer, influence, administrative processes, and long-cultivated personal relationships often determined the success or failure of matters. While LeMay had excelled in these arts during his time at SAC, once he became the vice chief LeMay was forced to gain new influence in an environment he did not control. He was mostly starting over. But for SAC and the United States, LeMay's record stood.

LeMay was clear: he believed in preemption as the best possible solution to the problem of a nuclear war that could result in the destruction of U.S. cities and the deaths of many citizens— the same outcomes he had produced in Japan during World War II. LeMay was neither angel nor demon; he was a pragmatist that saw an opening. If that meant he had to drop the first bombs in a nuclear war to protect his country—at least in his estimation— then so be it.

It was that pragmatism that drove LeMay to this possible solution to nuclear war and his advocacy for preemption. For as disciplined as he appeared and as he expected his command to be, LeMay could not regulate his own concerns about nuclear war. However, fear did not exclusively carry negative outcomes. Had LeMay not held the fear he did—and acted upon it in the manner he did—the Cold War could have been a different conflict. It was unlikely, however, that the Cold War could have been substantially more peaceful in its exercise and outcome. For that, perhaps LeMay's concern was not only well founded but also well heeded and exercised. As a result, the Cold War never became a hot war. In many ways, the United States owes this to LeMay's fears and his pragmatic response to them. That LeMay advocated for a policy of nuclear preemption—and ending a war before it was fully under way—was in keeping with those fears. Whether such a policy, and any plan to conduct such warfare, would have been effective is counterfactual. Thankfully, it will never be known how such an event would have turned out.

LeMay's advocacy for preemption had several deeper meanings and impacts. The United States was not as interested in the destruction of cities and the killing of civilians during the early Cold War—at least not as initial targets—as has been commonly conceived. Whether this meant the United States was any more or less aggressive cannot be answered in binary "yes or no" terms; what was clear from this, however, was that the United States, via LeMay, had a palpable concern that an attack could come and sought a means by which to assuage it. This suggested that U.S. actions during the early Cold War were motivated more by concerns for national safety than international dominance.

But even worries over national safety led LeMay and the United States to extremes. Had a nuclear war begun because the United States dropped the first nuclear weapons, the nation might have been safer, but it also would have had been branded as the antagonist. The United States would have sacrificed the use of its most cherished values as key weapons in the ongoing battle with the Soviets in winning the struggle for public support and opinion. To do so probably would have been fatal to the larger U.S. cause.

LeMay's efforts, however, came to naught. His advocacy never resulted in a wholesale alteration to the publicly declared nuclear policy of the United States. Nonetheless, LeMay's decision to advocate for preemption was, despite its extremity, an attempt to do something to stop what he knew would be a terrible war. To be alive and criticized was, in the SAC commander's estimation, better than to be dead. His rationale was, like the man himself, pragmatic. He was a military commander whose duty it was to win a nuclear war. Policy was left to those in Washington—though LeMay wanted his opinion heard. The record was clear on LeMay's advocacy for first strikes in the face of an imminent war. LeMay was simply interested in ensuring that a discussion on that policy, right or wrong, could be had.

Notes

A note on sources drawn from the Library of Congress: During the course of researching this manuscript, some of the box numbers in the LeMay Papers were renumbered. The box numbers provided here are those current as of the time of access and may differ from those currently in use. The author has retained either digital images or hard copies of the documents used.

Chapter 1. Reasons for Fear

1. In his book, *American Airpower Strategy in Korea, 1950–1953*, historian Conrad Crane argues that, "In Korea the new U.S. Air Force was forced to conduct an unexpected type of war in an unexpected place" (page vii in Crane's book). This study finds resonance with Crane's argument, and the argument herein made about LeMay's frustration in understanding the necessity of supporting certain operations found its origin in Crane's argument.

2. Phillip S. Meilinger, *Hoyt S. Vandenberg: The Life of a General*, (Publication city unknown: Air Force History and Museums Program, 2000), 106. This edition is a new imprint; the Indiana University Press published the original.

3. Harry R. Borowski, *A Hollow Threat: Strategic Air Power and Containment before Korea*, (Westport: Greenwood Press, 1982), 148–49; LeMay held three titles during his time at SAC. From his time of appointment on 19 October 1948 until June of 1953, LeMay held the title of Commanding General. From June of 1953 until 31 March 1955 LeMay's official title was that of Commander. Beginning on 1 April 1955 until his departure from SAC, LeMay and all officers who would subsequently hold the position were titled Commander in Chief, the shorthand for which was "CINCSAC." Source: Command Historian's Office, Headquarters Strategic Air Command Key Personnel 1946–1992, (Offutt Air Force Base: United States Strategic Command, 1999), 3. Throughout this book, reference will be made to LeMay serving as "commander" of SAC during periods that his official title was otherwise. The term "commander" is a distinction that identifies the individual with legal responsibility for the unit they command, a separate distinction than afforded by their title, which in LeMay's case changed during his tenure.

Therefore, despite what his duty title may have been, LeMay was always the commander of SAC. As a result, reference to LeMay in this book as commander does not necessarily connote such as his duty title and is a general reference to the positional authority he exerted under the law.

4. Ibid., 149; General George Kenney commanded SAC from its creation in 1946 until LeMay's assumption of the command in 1948.

5. Ibid., 149.

6. Ibid., 149.

7. Ibid., 149.

8. Walter J. Boyne, *Beyond the Wild Blue: A History of the United States Air Force, 1947–2007*, (New York: Thomas Dunne Books, St. Martin's Press, 2007), 103.

9. Library of Congress, Manuscript Reading Room, Papers of Curtis E. LeMay, Box B-103, folder entitled "DIARY," Notes on Visit to Topeka AFB, 10 December 1948, pages 1–2 (no page number on first page).

10. Library of Congress, Manuscript Reading Room, Papers of Curtis E. LeMay, Box B-103, folder entitled "DIARY," Notes on Visit to Kearney AFB, 13 Dec 1948, page 2 (no page number on first page).

11. Ibid, 3.

12. Library of Congress, Manuscript Reading Room, Papers of Curtis E. LeMay, Box B-103, folder entitled "DIARY," Notes on Visit to Carswell AFB, 16 DEC 1948, page 1 (no page number of first page).

13. Ibid, 1–2.

14. Ibid, 2.

15. Ibid, 3.

16. For a discussion of the need for overseas bases see: Bernard C. Nalty, ed., *Winged Shield, Winged Sword: A History of the United States Air Force*, (Washington, D.C.: Air Force History and Museums Program, United States Air Force, 1997), 68. While the Nalty text does argue that the need to for overseas bases was driven by a requirement to support not just the shorter range bombers, such as the B-47, but also to stage the B-36, primary source documentation suggests that LeMay was intent also on launching the B-36 directly against Soviet targets from bases in the United States.

17. Boyne, 108.

18. Library of Congress, Manuscript Reading Room, Papers of Curtis E. LeMay, Box B-103, folder entitled "DIARY," Notes on Visit to Carswell AFB, 16 DEC 1948, page 3.

19. Ibid, 4.

20. Library of Congress, Manuscript Reading Room, Papers of Curtis E. LeMay, Box B-61, folder entitled "VANDENBERG" (this folder is listed under "Vandenberg, Hoyt S." in the LOC finding aid), letter from LeMay to Vandenberg, 14 January 1949.
21. Ibid.
22. Ibid.
23. Ibid.
24. Within LeMay's papers at the Library of Congress, Box B-103, there are several "Reports of Inspection." These documents detail the findings of inspections at SAC bases. While it is not known whether or not LeMay personally made these inspections, they nonetheless provide insight as to the perspective that was informing LeMay's perception of the command. It is possible these inspections were related to future basing concerns for SAC units potentially moving to these locations, but this aspect is not clear.
25. Library of Congress, Manuscript Reading Room, Papers of Curtis E. LeMay, Box B-103, folder entitled "DIARY", "Report of Inspection, Smokey Hill AF Base, Kansas, 24 March 1949".
26. Library of Congress, Manuscript Reading Room, Papers of Curtis E. LeMay, Box B-103, folder entitled "DIARY", "Report of Inspection, Mountain Home AFB, Idaho, 4 May 1949".
27. Walton S. Moody, Building a Strategic Air Force, (Washington, D.C.: U.S. Government Printing Office, 1995), 233.
28. Ibid.
29. Ibid.
30. Gregg Herken, The Winning Weapon: The Atomic Bomb In The Cold War 1945–1950, (New York: Alfred A. Knopf, 1980), 312–14.
31. Ibid., 312.
32. Ibid., 319.
33. John Lewis Gaddis, Surprise, Security, and the American Experience, (Cambridge: Harvard University Press, 2004), 61.
34. Library of Congress, Manuscript Reading Room, Papers of Curtis E. LeMay, Box B-192, folder B-3111, Letter from LeMay to Vandenberg, dated 12 December 1949.
35. Ibid.
36. Ibid.
37. Ibid.
38. Ibid.

39. Library of Congress, Manuscript Reading Room, Papers of Curtis E. LeMay, Box B-192 (updated box number; previous box was B-195), document B-3476, Letter from Vandenberg (signed by Fairchild) to LeMay, dated 1 FEB 1950.

40. Ibid.

41. Gaddis, John Lewis, and Paul Nitze. "NSC 68 and the Soviet Threat Reconsidered." *International Security*, Vol. 4, no. 4 (Spring, 1980): 164–176.

42. Ibid., 170.

43. Ibid., 172.

44. Meilinger, *Hoyt S. Vandenberg*, 193. For the discussion of whether or not LeMay had knowledge of NSC-68 or read it, thanks to Sebastian Lukasik of Air Command and Staff College for the inspiration for this verbiage.

45. Proceedings, Commanders Conference, 25, 26 & 27 April, 1950, page 203. Record stored at: NARA, Record Group 341, RG 341, Headquarters U.S. Air Force, Office of the Chief of Staff, Vice Chief of Staff Executive Service Division, General Files 1950–1953, box 1. This record was accessed through George Washington University's National Security Archive online document site. The web address for this document, at the time of access in September, 2008, was: http://www.gwu.edu/~nsarchiv/nukevault/special/doc03b.pdf.

46. Ibid., 222–224 and quote from 224.

47. Ibid., 224.

48. Ibid., 225.

49. Ibid., 225.

50. Ibid., 225–226

51. Ibid., 226–227.

52. Ibid., 227.

53. Ibid., 227.

54. Ibid., 227.

55. Ibid., 227–28. With regard to LeMay's reference to sites "Able, Baker, and Charlie", although the source document does not make clear to exactly what sites LeMay was referring, it is likely that he was referring to US nuclear weapons storage sites as a comparison to similar such sites in the Soviet Union.

56. Ibid., 228.

57. Ibid., 228.

58. Ibid., 231.

59. Library of Congress, Manuscript Reading Room, Papers of Curtis E. LeMay, Box B-103, folder entitled "LeMAY DIARY #1, I JAN 50 to 30 JUN 50," Commanding Generals Diary Mqy [sic] 25–26 1950.

60. Library of Congress, Manuscript Reading Room, Papers of Curtis E. LeMay, Box B-103, folder entitled "LeMAY DIARY #1, I JAN 50 to 30 JUN 50," Commanding Generals Diary June 26 1950.

61. Ibid.

62. Ibid.

63. Library of Congress, Manuscript Reading Room, Papers of Curtis E. LeMay, Box B-103, folder entitled "LeMAY DIARY #1, I JAN 50 to 30 JUN 50," Commanding Generals Diary 27 June 50.

64. Ibid. LeMay's office diary refers to General Montague by two spellings, both incorrect: Montigue and Montique, both incorrect. However, based on the circumstances, context and subsequent memorandum from July 20th, 1950, it is clear these were references to Robert Montague.

65. Library of Congress, Manuscript Reading Room, Papers of Curtis E. LeMay, Box B-196 (B-7220), MFR from General Kissner, dated 24 July 1950.

66. Ibid.

67. Ibid.

68. Ibid.

69. Ibid.

70. Library of Congress, Manuscript Reading Room, Papers of Curtis E. LeMay, Box B-195 (B-5324/6), Letter from LeMay to Vandenberg, dated 30 June 1950.

71. Ibid.

72. Ibid.

73. Moody, 340.

74. Conrad C. Crane, *American Airpower Strategy in Korea, 1950–1953*, (Lawrence: The University of Kansas Press, 2000), 37.

75. For the telephone conversation, see: Library of Congress, Manuscript Reading Room, Papers of Curtis E. LeMay, Box B-103, folder entitled "LeMAY DIARY #2 1 JUL 50 to 30 DEC 50", Transcript of Telephone Conversation, General LeMay and General Ramey, 1 July 1950.

76. Ibid.

77. Ibid.

78. Library of Congress, Manuscript Reading Room, Papers of Curtis E. LeMay, Box B-103, folder entitled "LeMAY DIARY #2 1 JUL 50 to 30 DEC 50", Transcript of telephone conversation, General LeMay and General Nugent, 1 July 1950.

79. Ibid.

80. Ibid.

81. Ibid.

82. Ibid.

83. Ibid.
84. Library of Congress, Manuscript Reading Room, Papers of Curtis E. LeMay, Box B-103, folder entitled "LeMAY DIARY #2 1 JUL 50 to 30 DEC 50", Transcript of telephone conversation, General LeMay and General Norstad, 1 July 1950.
85. Ibid.
86. Ibid.
87. Ibid.
88. Ibid.
89. Ibid. The term "Air Staff" refers to the group of senior officers that surround and support the Chief of Staff in various functional and staff areas, such as operations, personnel, logistics, intelligence and immediate staff support.

Chapter 2. When It Became Real

1. Library of Congress, Manuscript Reading Room, Papers of Curtis E. LeMay, Box B-103, folder entitled "LeMAY DIARY #2 1 JUL 50 to 30 DEC 50", Commanding Generals Diary for 10 July 50, page 1.
2. Ibid.
3. Ibid., 2.
4. Ibid., 2.
5. Eric Schlosser, *Command and Control: Nuclear Weapons, the Damascus Accident, and the Illusion of Safety* (New York: Penguin Books, 2013), 93–94.
6. Quotation of Truman cited by James Forrestal in Richard Rhodes, *Dark Sun: The Making of the Hydrogen Bomb*, (New York: Simon and Schuster, 1996), 326.
7. Library of Congress, Manuscript Reading Room, Papers of Curtis E. LeMay, Box B-103, folder entitled "LeMAY DIARY #2 1 JUL 50 to 30 DEC 50", Commanding Generals Diary for 10 July 50, page 2.
8. Ibid.
9. Ibid.
10. Library of Congress, Manuscript Reading Room, Papers of Curtis E. LeMay, Box B-103, folder entitled "LeMAY DIARY #2 1 JUL 50 to 30 DEC 50", Commanding General's Diary for 28, 29, 30 September 1950. This entry was identified in the document as taking place on 30 September.
11. Library of Congress, Manuscript Reading Room, Papers of Curtis E. LeMay, Box B-103, folder entitled "LeMAY DIARY #2 1 JUL 50 to 30 DEC 50", Commanding General's Diary for 2 October 1950.
12. Library of Congress, Manuscript Reading Room, Papers of Curtis E. LeMay, Box B-103, folder entitled "LeMAY DIARY #2 1 JUL 50 to 30 DEC 50",

Excerpts from an interview of General LeMay by Mr. McNeil, Scripps-Howard Papers, 1015, 20 October 1950, page 1–2.

13. Ibid., 3.

14. Library of Congress, Manuscript Reading Room, Papers of Curtis E. LeMay, Box B-103, folder entitled "LeMAY DIARY #2 1 JUL 50 to 30 DEC 50", Commanding General's Diary, 2 November 1950.

15. Library of Congress, Manuscript Reading Room, Papers of Curtis E. LeMay, Box B-103, folder entitled "LeMAY DIARY #2 1 JUL 50 to 30 DEC 50", Memorandum for the Record, 6 November 1950.

16. Library of Congress, Manuscript Reading Room, Papers of Curtis E. LeMay, Box B-103, folder entitled "LeMAY DIARY #2 1 JUL 50 to 30 DEC 50", Commanding General's Diary, 6 November 1950.

17. Library of Congress, Manuscript Reading Room, Papers of Curtis E. LeMay, Box B-103, folder entitled "LeMAY DIARY #2 1 JUL 50 to 30 DEC 50", Commanding Generals Diary, Tuesday 28 Nov.

18. Ibid.

19. Library of Congress, Manuscript Reading Room, Papers of Curtis E. LeMay, Box B-103, folder entitled "LeMAY DIARY #2 1 JUL 50 to 30 DEC 50", Commanding Generals Diary, 3 Dec 50. Based on the context of this entry, it appears to have been crafted by LeMay's Aide-de-Camp, Paul Carlton, as with entirety of entries for this period. Carlton's speculation, while simply that, can be considered reliable as he spent a great deal of personal time with LeMay and knew the man well. It does not imply, however, that it was anything more than speculation.

20. Library of Congress, Manuscript Reading Room, Papers of Curtis E. LeMay, Box B-103, folder entitled "LeMAY DIARY #2 1 JUL 50 to 30 DEC 50", Commanding Generals Diary for 6 Dec 50.

21. Conrad Crane, *American Airpower Strategy in Korea, 1950–1953*, (Lawrence: University of Kansas Press, 2000), 93.

22. Strategic Air Command History, January–June 1951, Call # K416.01, Vol. 1, page 22, IRIS # 501949, in the USAF Collection, AFHRA, Maxwell AFB, AL.

23. Library of Congress, Manuscript Reading Room, Papers of Curtis E. LeMay, Box B-103, folder entitled "LeMAY Diary 1951 #3", MEMORANDUM FOR RECORD, Visit to Headquarters, USAF, on 2 and 3 January, 1951, memorandum dated 3 January 1951.

24. Library of Congress, Manuscript Reading Room, Papers of Curtis E. LeMay, Box B-103, folder entitled "LeMAY Diary 1951 #3", MEMORANDUM FOR GENERAL LeMAY, 11 January 1951, page 1 of the memorandum.

25. National Security Archive (George Washington University), Wampler NATO NHP Collection, Box #18, National Security Archive Documents (Folder Name: LeMay, Burke NSS), National Security Archive-Washington D.C.

26. Ibid.

27. Strategic Air Command History, January–June 1951, Call # K416.01, Vol. III (Supporting Documents), Exhibit 47 (letter from LeMay to Twining, 5 April 1951), IRIS # 501951, in the USAF Collection, AFHRA, Maxwell AFB, AL. The meeting with "the Secretary" to which LeMay refers in the letter to Twining was confirmed to be with Finletter by cross-referencing with LeMay's office diary, which for the 26th of March 1951 stated: "with the conference with Secretary Finletter taking place at 4:00 on that afternoon." For this entry from LeMay's office diary see: Library of Congress, Manuscript Reading Room, Papers of Curtis E. LeMay, Box B-103, folder entitled "LeMAY Diary 1951 #3", Gen LeMay's Diary, entry for 26 March 1941 [should read 26 March 1951, but was incorrectly entered as 1941].

28. Strategic Air Command History, January–June 1951, Call # K416.01, Vol. III (Supporting Documents), Exhibit 47 (letter from LeMay to Twining, 5 April 1951), IRIS # 501951, in the USAF Collection, AFHRA, Maxwell AFB, AL.

29. Phillip S. Meilinger, "Getting to the Target: The Penetration Problem in the Strategic Air Command during the 1950s," *Airpower History* 61, no. 3 (2014): 38–49. This citation drawn from page 44.

30. Ibid., 44.

31. Library of Congress, Manuscript Reading Room, Papers of Curtis E. LeMay, Box B-103, folder entitled "LeMAY DIARY 1951 #3," Commanding Generals Diary for 5 April 51.

32. Crane, *American Airpower Strategy in Korea, 1950–1953*, 70.

33. Library of Congress, Manuscript Reading Room, Papers of Curtis E. LeMay, Box B-103, folder entitled "LeMAY DIARY 1951 #3," Commanding Generals Diary for 17 Apr 51.

34. Library of Congress, Manuscript Reading Room, Papers of Curtis E. LeMay, Box B-103, folder entitled "LeMAY DIARY 1951 #3," Commanding Generals Diary for 24 Apr 51.

35. Crane, *American Airpower Strategy in Korea, 1950–1953*, 70–72.

36. Library of Congress, Manuscript Reading Room, Papers of Curtis E. LeMay, Box B-103, folder entitled "LeMAY DIARY 1951 #3," Commanding Generals Diary for 30 April 51.

37. Strategic Air Command History, January–June 1951, Call # K416.01, Vol. 1, page 53–54, IRIS # 501949, in the USAF Collection, AFHRA, Maxwell AFB, AL.

38. Library of Congress, Manuscript Reading Room, Papers of Curtis E. LeMay, Box B-103, folder entitled "LeMAY DIARY 1951 #3," Commanding Generals Diary for 26 Apr 51.

39. Strategic Air Command History, January–June 1951, Call # K416.01, Vol. 1, page 54, IRIS # 501949, in the USAF Collection, AFHRA, Maxwell AFB, AL; regarding the unresolved nature of the selection of a general officer as referenced in Vandenberg's message from the 26th of April, LeMay's office diary from the 7th, 8th and 9th of May referred to the unsettled nature of the question of who was to be assigned to that duty. For this entry see: Library of Congress, Manuscript Reading Room, Papers of Curtis E. LeMay, Box B-103, folder entitled "LeMAY DIARY 1951 #3," Commanding Generals Diary for 7, 8, 9th May 51.

40. Library of Congress, Manuscript Reading Room, Papers of Curtis E. LeMay, Box B-103, folder entitled "LeMAY DIARY 1951 #3," Commanding Generals Diary for 2 May 51.

41. Library of Congress, Manuscript Reading Room, Papers of Curtis E. LeMay, Box B-103, folder entitled "LeMAY DIARY 1951 #3," Commanding Generals Diary for 18–20 May 51. This entry in LeMay's office diary is not actually titled on this page, but is part of the larger sequence of the "Commanding Generals Diary." The dates were handwritten at the top of the page.

42. Library of Congress, Manuscript Reading Room, Papers of Curtis E. LeMay, Box B-197, Letter from LeMay to White, 7 May 1951. In the upper right-hand corner of first page of the letter is the number B10934/4.

43. Library of Congress, Manuscript Reading Room, Papers of Curtis E. LeMay, Box B-103, folder entitled "LeMAY DIARY 1951 #3," Commanding Generals Diary for 7, 8, 9th May 51.

44. Library of Congress, Manuscript Reading Room, Papers of Curtis E. LeMay, Box B-103, folder entitled "LeMAY DIARY 1951 #3," Commanding Generals Diary for 10 May 51.

45. Library of Congress, Manuscript Reading Room, Papers of Curtis E. LeMay, Box B-103, folder entitled "LeMAY DIARY 1951 #3," Commanding Generals Diary for 7, 8, 9th May 51.

46. Library of Congress, Manuscript Reading Room, Papers of Curtis E. LeMay, Box B-103, folder entitled "LeMAY DIARY 1951 #3," General LeMay's Diary for: 23 June; 24 June; 25 June. The data for this paragraph was separately drawn from LeMay's office diary under the three dates listed.

47. Strategic Air Command History, January–June 1951, Call # K416.01, Vol. 1, pages 50–52, IRIS # 501949, in the USAF Collection, AFHRA, Maxwell AFB, AL.

48. Library of Congress, Manuscript Reading Room, Papers of Curtis E. LeMay, Box B-103, folder entitled "LeMAY DIARY 1951 #3," General LeMay's Diary for 27 June.

49. Library of Congress, Manuscript Reading Room, Papers of Curtis E. LeMay, Box B-103, folder entitled "LeMAY DIARY 1951 #3," General LeMay's Diary for: 27 June; 28 June; 29 June; and 30 June.

50. Crane, *American Airpower Strategy in Korea, 1950–1953*, 59.

51. Library of Congress, Manuscript Reading Room, Papers of Curtis E. LeMay, Box B-103, folder entitled "LeMAY DIARY 1951 #3," General LeMay's Diary for: 1 July; 2 July; 3 July; and 4 July. Use of the material from these dates in not necessarily in order by date, but the records from these dates are generally brief.

52. Library of Congress, Manuscript Reading Room, Papers of Curtis E. LeMay, Box B-103, folder entitled "LeMAY DIARY 1951 #3," General LeMay's Diary, see the period ranging from 5 July to 9 July; see 10 July for departure from the United Kingdom.

53. Russell F. Weigley, *The American Way of War: A History of United States Military Strategy and Policy* (Bloomington: Indiana University Press, 1977), 400. (Paperback Edition through Indiana University Press)

54. Ibid.

55. Strategic Air Command History, July–December 1951, Call # K416.01, Vol. 1, page 192, IRIS # 501958, in the USAF Collection, AFHRA, Maxwell AFB, AL.

56. Ibid., 193.

57. Ibid., 194.

58. Ibid., 194–95.

59. Ibid., 196–97.

60. Library of Congress, Manuscript Reading Room, Papers of Curtis E. LeMay, Box B-103, folder entitled "LeMAY DIARY 1951 #3," Command Generals Diary for 10 Sept 51.

61. Strategic Air Command History, July–December 1951, Call # K416.01, Vol. 1, page 196–97, IRIS # 501958, in the USAF Collection, AFHRA, Maxwell AFB, AL.; For LeMay's location on the day of the conference see: Library of Congress, Manuscript Reading Room, Papers of Curtis E. LeMay, Box B-103, folder entitled "LeMAY DIARY 1951 #3," Command Generals Diary for 10 Sept 51.

62. Strategic Air Command History, July—December 1951, Call # K416.01, Vol. 1, page 229–30, IRIS # 501958, in the USAF Collection, AFHRA, Maxwell AFB, AL.

63. Ibid., 230.

64. Ibid., 230.

65. Ibid., 210–12.

66. Ibid., 234.

67. Library of Congress, Manuscript Reading Room, Papers of Curtis E. LeMay, Box B-103, folder entitled "LeMAY DIARY 1951 #3," Command Generals Diary for 8 through 15 October; for Twinning, Eaker, and Spaatz's presence on the trip, see: Library of Congress, Manuscript Reading Room, Papers of Curtis E. LeMay, Box B-103, folder entitled "LeMAY DIARY 1951 #3," Command Generals Diary for 18 Oct 51.

68. Strategic Air Command History, July–December 1951, Call # K416.01, Vol. 2, page 2, IRIS # 501959, in the USAF Collection, AFHRA, Maxwell AFB, AL.

69. Ibid., 2–3.

70. Ibid., 3.

Chapter 3. Pressing Ahead

1. Library of Congress, Manuscript Reading Room, Papers of Curtis E. LeMay, Box B-103, folder entitled "LeMAY Diary #4 1952", DIARY, General LeMay's trip of 7, 8, and 9 Jan 52, to Washington, Newark, Langley and Maxwell (C-97 acft), page 1 (no page number visible on page 1).

2. "Strategic Air Operations" by Gen. Curtis LeMay, 9 Jan 52, page 2 (page number obscured at the bottom of the page), Call # K239.716252-110, IRIS # 1005753, in the USAF Collection, AFHRA, Maxwell AFB, AL.

3. Ibid., 2.

4. Ibid., 3.

5. Ibid., 5 (page number obscured at the bottom of the page).

6. Ibid., 4. The transcript of LeMay's remarks lists the three tasks as though LeMay was to read them out-loud.

7. The transcript of the lecture does not make precisely clear whether or not the address was offered solely to the Air War College or to Air University, the Air War College's parent organization, as a whole. Based on some of the contextual facts, such as the accompanying sheet certifying the transcript, it is most likely the lecture was delivered solely to the Air War College; see: "Role of the Air Power in Future War" by Honorable Thomas K. Finletter, 8 April 52, Call # K239.716252-99, IRIS # 00918289, in the USAF Collection, AFHRA, Maxwell AFB, AL.

8. Ibid., 10–11.

9. Ibid., 11.

10. "Question Period for Mr. Finletter's Lecture," 8 April 52, page 1, Call # K239.716252-99, IRIS # 00918289, in the USAF Collection, AFHRA, Maxwell AFB, AL. This document was found within the same folder as the

associated lecture, but did not have its own call number or IRIS number. The transcript for the question and answer period was not itself dated, but the folder was dated. The call number and IRIS number used for this citation came from the folder in which this document was found.

11. Ibid., 2.

12. Library of Congress, Manuscript Reading Room, Papers of Curtis E. LeMay, Box B-103, folder entitled "LeMAY Diary #4 1952", Commanding Generals Diary for 16 April 52[,] 17 April 52.

13. Library of Congress, Manuscript Reading Room, Papers of Curtis E. LeMay, Box B-103, folder entitled "LeMAY Diary #4 1952", RECORD OF TELE-PHONE CONVERSATION: From Maj. Gen. Landry, Aide to the President, to Gen. LeMay, 15 April 1952.

14. Library of Congress, Manuscript Reading Room, Papers of Curtis E. LeMay, Box B-103, folder entitled "LeMAY Diary #4 1952", Commanding Generals Diary for 16 April 52[,] 17 April 52.

15. Library of Congress, Manuscript Reading Room, Papers of Curtis E. LeMay, Box B-103, folder entitled "LeMAY Diary #4 1952", Commanding Generals Diary for 20 May 52.

16. Library of Congress, Manuscript Reading Room, Papers of Curtis E. LeMay, Box B-103, folder entitled "LeMAY Diary #4 1952", Commanding Generals Diary for 27 thru 31 Aug. . . . (This diary entry heading, at the top of the page, reads "Commanding Generals Diary for 2 Sept. The specific entry quoted is down the page and listed as above mentioned.)

17. Library of Congress, Manuscript Reading Room, Papers of Curtis E. LeMay, Box B-103, folder entitled "LeMAY Diary #4 1952", Commanding Generals Diary for 2 Sept (item 1).

18. Ibid., (item 2).

19. Library of Congress, Manuscript Reading Room, Papers of Curtis E. LeMay, Box B-103, folder entitled "LeMAY Diary #4 1952", DIARY 5–11 September 52: (first paragraph).

20. Ibid., (fifth paragraph).

21. Ibid., (sixth paragraph).

22. Ibid., (seventh paragraph).

23. Library of Congress, Manuscript Reading Room, Papers of Curtis E. LeMay, Box B-103, folder entitled "LeMAY Diary #4 1952", *NOTES FOR GENERAL LeMAY,* 11 September 1952.

24. Library of Congress, Manuscript Reading Room, Papers of Curtis E. LeMay, Box B-103, folder entitled "LeMAY Diary #4 1952", DIARY 14–22 September 52.

25. Ibid.

26. Ibid.
27. Commanders' Conference, 15, 16, 17 October, 1952, Vol. 2 (Held at Eglin Air Force Base), Call #K 168.15-10, IRIS #1028827, in the USAF Collection, AFHRA, Maxwell AFB, AL. This document is an excerpt, recently declassified upon request of the author.
28. Ibid.
29. Ibid.
30. Library of Congress, Manuscript Reading Room, Papers of Curtis E. LeMay, Box B-103, folder entitled "LeMAY Diary #4 1952", MEMORANDUM FOR GENERAL LeMAY, 25 October 1952, pages 4–6.
31. Library of Congress, Manuscript Reading Room, Papers of Curtis E. LeMay, Box B-103, folder entitled "LeMAY Diary #4 1952", Commanding Generals Diary for 24 Nov 52.
32. Library of Congress, Manuscript Reading Room, Papers of Curtis E. LeMay, Box B-103, folder entitled "LeMAY Diary #4 1952", Commanding Generals Diary for 28 Nov 52.
33. Library of Congress, Manuscript Reading Room, Papers of Curtis E. LeMay, Box B-103, folder entitled "LeMAY Diary #4 1952", Commanding Generals Diary for 15 Dec 52.
34. Library of Congress, Manuscript Reading Room, Papers of Curtis E. LeMay, Box B-199, folder entitled "B-22149", letter from LeMay to Vandenberg, 5 December 1952.
35. Ibid.
36. Library of Congress, Manuscript Reading Room, Papers of Curtis E. LeMay, Box B-93, folder entitled "American Legion—Invitations & Speeches", sub folder entitled "CRUSADE FOR FREEDOM Speech Minneapolis, Minnesota 6 Dec 52 (American Legion)", cover page of LeMay's remarks. Within LeMay's remarks script there are numerous instances of hand-written additions, changes, and underlining included in the manuscript. In the interest of originality, care has been taken to cite only the typed text and avoid citation of hand-written additions, changes, or underlining.
37. Ibid., 2–3.
38. Ibid., 3.
39. Ibid., 3–4.
40. Ibid., 4–5.
41. Ibid., 5–6.
42. Library of Congress, Manuscript Reading Room, Papers of Curtis E. LeMay, Box B-199, folder entitled "B-22845", letter from LeMay to White, 3 January 1953.

43. Ibid.

44. Library of Congress, Manuscript Reading Room, Papers of Curtis E. LeMay, Box B-200, folder entitled "B-23376", letter from White to LeMay, 21 JAN 1953.

45. Library of Congress, Manuscript Reading Room, Papers of Curtis E. LeMay, Box B-104, folder entitled "LeMAY DIARY #5 1953", COMMANDING GENERAL'S DIARY[:] OVERSEAS TRIP, entry for Monday 16 Feb 53.

46. Library of Congress, Manuscript Reading Room, Papers of Curtis E. LeMay, Box B-61, folder entitled "VANDENBERG" (listed as Vandenberg, Hoyt S. in the LoC finding aid), letter from Vandenberg to LeMay, 26 March 1953.

47. Ibid.

48. Ibid.

49. Ibid.

50. Library of Congress, Manuscript Reading Room, Papers of Curtis E. LeMay, Box B-61, folder entitled "VANDENBERG" (listed as Vandenberg, Hoyt S. in the LoC finding aid), letter from LeMay to Vandenberg, 6 April 1953.

51. Ibid.

52. Ibid.

53. Ibid.

54. Library of Congress, Manuscript Reading Room, Papers of Curtis E. LeMay, Box B-104, folder entitled "LeMAY DIARY #5 1953", Commanding Generals Diary for[:] 6–7 May 53.

55. Library of Congress, Manuscript Reading Room, Papers of Curtis E. LeMay, Box B-104, folder entitled "LeMAY DIARY #5 1953", Memo for Record, 8 May 1953.

56. Library of Congress, Manuscript Reading Room, Papers of Curtis E. LeMay, Box B-69, folder entitled "MISCELLANEOUS 1953", subfolder entitled "Speech—Institute of Aeronautical Sciences[,] Los Angeles[,] 15 July 53", script of LeMay's remarks, 15 July 1953, cover page of LeMay's remarks.

57. Ibid., 2.

58. Ibid., 6.

59. Ibid., 15.

60. Ibid., 15.

61. Ibid., 25.

62. Library of Congress, Manuscript Reading Room, Papers of Nathan F. Twining, Box 121, folder entitled "Top Secret File (1)[,] 1952–57", MEMORANDUM FOR THE CHIEF OF STAFF, U.S. AIR FORCE, 21 Aug 53 (the date is listed in top right corner and again on page two near a signature block for "Col Whisenand", though it is unclear if this is the date the memorandum was pro-

duced or approved, or otherwise; context—and the author's best guess—is that this date is the date on which the memo was approved for forwarding to the Chief of Staff), page 1 (first page does not have a page number).

63. U.S Air Force, "GENERAL ROBERT MERRILL LEE." http://www.af.mil/AboutUs/Biographies/Display/tabid/225/Article/106458/general-robert-merrill-lee.aspx (accessed June 30, 2016).

64. Library of Congress, Manuscript Reading Room, Papers of Nathan F. Twining, Box 121, folder entitled "Top Secret File (1)[,] 1952–57", MEMORANDUM FOR THE CHIEF OF STAFF, U.S. AIR FORCE, 21 Aug 53, page 1 (first page does not have a page number).

65. Ibid.

66. Library of Congress, Manuscript Reading Room, Papers of Nathan F. Twining, Box 121, folder entitled "Top Secret File (1)[,] 1952–57", *MEMORANDUM BY THE CHIEF OF STAFF, U.S. AIR FORCE* to the JOINT CHIEFS OF STAFF on *THE COMING NATIONAL CRISIS*, 3 Sept 1953 (the date is listed in top right corner, though it is unclear if this is the date the memorandum was produced or approved, or otherwise; context—and the author's best guess—is that this date is the date on which the memo was approved by the Chief of Staff, Nathan Twining), page 1–4 (no page number provided on the first page).

67. Ibid.

68. Ibid., 6.

69. Ibid., 6.

70. Ibid., 7.

71. Library of Congress, Manuscript Reading Room, Papers of Curtis E. LeMay, Box B-201, folder entitled "B-30786", letter from Hansell to LeMay, 9 October 1953, page 1 and 2 (no page number listed on the first page). Jerry Martin, formerly the United States Strategic Command Historian, provided the information regarding SATTS.

72. Ibid., 1–2.

73. Ibid., 1–2.

74. Library of Congress, Manuscript Reading Room, Papers of Curtis E. LeMay, Box B-201, folder entitled "B-31472", message FOR LEMAY OR POWER FROM SELSER, 14 NOV 53. This message is date stamped with a marking that appears to say "14 NOV 53", though the year is somewhat obscured at the top of the marking. Based on a hand-written marking farther down the page and near the Date Time Group, which reads "Nov 53", it is quite certain this document was sent and/or received on 14 November 1953. Additionally, the message traffic was printed entirely in capital letters. For the

purposes of this passage, much of the capital letters have been changed to lower case to assist in the ease of reading.

75. Library of Congress, Manuscript Reading Room, Papers of Curtis E. LeMay, Box B-69, folder entitled "MISCELLANEOUS 1953", subfolder entitled "AMERICAN ORDNANCE ASSOCIATION[,] PITTSBURGH, PENNA[,] 7 December 53", text of remarks and subfolder cover, page 3 of text of remarks and subfolder cover (the text of the remarks are not dated, but given the date on the subfolder—as well as on a program of the event, it is circumstantially clear that the date of the event was December 7, 1953. Some of the section herein quoted was hand underlined in the text of the remarks. For clarity and accuracy, that underlining has not been replicated in the cited material).

76. Ibid., 3–9 (at points in this document there were additional handwritten marks such as underlining or the crossing out of words).

77. Ibid., 30.

Chapter 4. Clarity in Expression

1. The belief that the briefing was classified was derived from the fact that the transcript was classified and the information discussed by LeMay certainly would have been classified, given the nature of his remarks. See: Library of Congress, Manuscript Reading Room, Papers of Curtis E. LeMay, Box B-201, folder entitled B-33815 (This folder contains more than one document, including LeMay's remarks at the National War College on 28 January 1954, which is the document cited here. The transcript in question has the handwritten marking "B-33815/3" on its coversheet.), transcript of "THE STRATEGIC AIR COMMAND By General Curtis LeMay", Presented at The National War College, Washington, D.C., 28 January 1954.

2. Ibid.

3. Ibid., 1. The words " . . . trends and . . ." were hand written into the transcript immediately above a word that had been crossed out. While it is unclear exactly who made this change or when it was made, the possibility exists that LeMay and/or his staff made the change during the process of reviewing the transcript sometime after the delivery of the remarks. The words " . . . trends and . . ." are used as though they were typed into the transcript.

4. Ibid., 1–2.

5. Ibid., 5.

6. Ibid., 5–6 of the transcript.

7. Library of Congress, Manuscript Reading Room, Papers of Curtis E. LeMay, Box B-201, folder entitled B-33815 (this folder contains more than one document, including LeMay's remarks at the National War College on 28

January 1954—which included the question and answer period transcript, which is the document cited here. The remarks transcript in question has the handwritten marking "B-33815/3" on its coversheet.), "QUESTION PERIOD" appended to the transcript of "THE STRATEGIC AIR COMMAND By General Curtis LeMay", Presented at The National War College, Washington, D.C., 28 January 1954. Page 1 of the "QUESTION PERIOD".

8. Ibid., 1–2.

9. Library of Congress, Manuscript Reading Room, Papers of Curtis E. LeMay, Box B-69, folder entitled "MISCELLANEOUS 1954", subfolder entitled "SOCIETY OF AUTOMOTIVE ENGINEERS[,] Detroit, Michigan[,] 4 March 1954" (this subfolder contained more that one document, including the text of the remarks cited here—General Curtis E. LeMay's address before S.A.E., Detroit, Michigan[,] 4 March 1954), transcript of General Curtis E. LeMay's address before S.A.E., Detroit, Michigan[,] 4 March 1954. Cover page and page 1 of the transcript (the cover page and page 1 are not numbered); the context of exactly who LeMay's audience was on this date was determined by a separate document in the subfolder: letter from John A.C. Warner to LeMay, March 8, 1954.

10. Ibid.

11. Ibid., 1–4.

12. Ibid., 4–5.

13. Ibid., 5, 7. The word "and" from page 8 of the transcript, which appears after the word "scientific" and before "technical" in the transcript and in the quotation used here, appeared as though it was handwritten into the cited transcript. It is not known who wrote this into the transcript and when, but is being used as though it were a last-minute edit to the transcript.

14. Ibid., 5–11.

15. Ibid., 5–11.

16. Ibid., 11–13. In the text of LeMay's remarks the word "back" is conspicuously crossed out with two drawn lines. The difference in the meaning of his statement with the deletion of this word is tremendous. With the term "back" included in his statement, LeMay's argument clearly connotes an act of retaliation. With the term removed, as it is in the transcript, the statement leaves open the possibility of preemptive action. It is unclear how the eventual remarks were delivered, whether done so with the term "back" mentioned or without it. The bracketed term is included in the text here in an effort to provide full disclosure and to offer the reader context for the use of a bracketed term. It is unknown who might have crossed out the word.

17. Ibid., 12.

18. Library of Congress, Manuscript Reading Room, Papers of Curtis E. LeMay, Box B-69, folder entitled "MISCELLANEOUS 1954", subfolder entitled "BILLY MITCHELL AWARD[,] Waldorf-Astoria Hotel[,] New York[,] 12 MAY 1954", General Curtis E. LeMay's Acceptance Remarks, Billy Mitchell Award[,] Waldorf-Astoria Hotel, New York[,] 12 May 1954. Cover Page-2 (page 1 not numbered). Context of exactly what award was being presented derived from cover page of remarks; context of who the recipient of the award was derived from page 1.

19. Ibid., 4.

20. Library of Congress, Manuscript Reading Room, Papers of Curtis E. LeMay, Box B-69, folder entitled "MISCELLANEOUS 1954", subfolder entitled "ARMED FORCES CHEMICAL ASSOCIATION[,] Washington, D.C.[,] 21 MAY 1954". Pages 5–6.

21. Library of Congress, Manuscript Reading Room, Papers of Curtis E. LeMay, Box B-201, folder entitled "B-36492", letter from LeMay to Chief of Staff, United States Air Force, 28 MAY 1954.

22. Library of Congress, Manuscript Reading Room, Papers of Curtis E. LeMay, Box B-201, folder entitled "B-36933", letter from LeMay to Frank Everest, 11 June 1954.

23. Library of Congress, Manuscript Reading Room, Papers of Curtis E. LeMay, Box B-201, folder entitled "B-36933", study attached to letter from LeMay to Everest (letter dated 11 June 1954), study entitled "USAF FORCE COMPOSITION 1958, 1965", study stamped 14 JUN 1954, page 1 of study (page 1 is not marked).

24. Ibid.

25. Ibid.

26. Ibid., 2.

27. Ibid., 2.

28. Gregg Herken, *Counsels of War*, (New York: Alfred A. Knopf, 1985), 96.

29. Library of Congress, Manuscript Reading Room, Papers of Curtis E. LeMay, Box B-201, folder entitled "B-36933", study attached to letter from LeMay to Everest (letter dated 11 June 1954), study entitled "USAF FORCE COMPOSITION 1958, 1965", study stamped 14 JUN 1954, page 2 of study.

30. Library of Congress, Manuscript Reading Room, Papers of Curtis E. LeMay, Box B-69, folder entitled "Miscellaneous 1954", subfolder entitled "Plattsburgh[,] 31 Aug 1954", subfolder entitled "PLATTSBURGH", script of remarks, page 4. The script itself was not marked with a date or location of remarks. However, given the word "Plattsburgh" and the date "31 Aug 1954" on the initial subfolder, as well as the title "PLATTSBURGH"

on the subsequent subfolder where the remarks were contained, it was fairly clear the remarks were almost certainly delivered on August 31, 1954 at Plattsburgh. This belief was further reinforced by a document, what was apparently a copy of some sort of telegram or teletype message, addressed to Mr. Clyde Lewis in Plattsburgh, in the initial subfolder. The communiqué to Lewis stated, "Confirming our conversation this morning General LeMay will arrive Plattsburgh evening of 30 August and will spend the following morning with you looking over housing sites, Air Force Base, etc. He will attend luncheon 31 August and depart shortly thereafter." For the communiqué, see subfolder entitled "Plattsburgh[,] 31 Aug 1954", telegram or teletype from COMMANDER STRATEGIC AIR COMMAND to MR. CLYDE LEWIS.

31. Ibid. Additionally, the "e" in "remembered" was essentially invisible on the script. Therefore, to ensure clarity, it was considered as an "add" and mentioned as such in the text.

32. Ibid., 4–5.

33. Ibid., 5.

34. Ibid., 6–7.

35. Library of Congress, Manuscript Reading Room, Papers of Curtis E. LeMay, Box B-104, folder entitled "COMDR'S DIARY #6 1954", NOTES FOR THE COMMANDER, 2 September 1954, page 1 (pages are not numbered in this document). This document has been here treated as essentially a memorandum from the signed author, Brigadier General Montgomery, to LeMay, though the document is not formally addressed to LeMay. The document is, however, informally addressed to LeMay, having been titled "NOTES FOR THE COMMANDER."

36. Ibid.

37. *Foreign Relations of the United States*, 1955–1957, Volume XIX, National Security Policy, eds. William Klingman, David S. Patterson, and Ilana Stern (Washington: Government Printing Office, 1990), Document 9, "Report by the Technological Capabilities Panel of the Scientific Advisory Committee", page 41.

38. Ibid., 41n1.

39. Ibid., 41n1.

40. Ibid., 41–42.

41. Library of Congress, Manuscript Reading Room, Papers of Curtis E. LeMay, Box B-202, folder entitled "B-43903", letter from LeMay to Chief of Staff, United States Air Force, 21 MAR[CH] 1955, page 1 (page 1 is not marked).

42. Ibid.

43. Ibid.
44. Ibid., 2.
45. Ibid., 2.
46. Ibid., 2.
47. Library of Congress, Manuscript Reading Room, Papers of Curtis E. LeMay, Box B-92, folder entitled "Commercial Club of Chicago 23 March 1955", script of remarks, page 1–2 (the first page is not numbered). The script of remarks did not specifically bear a label that directly indicated they were delivered at the event mentioned in the title of the folder in which they were found—other than the fact that they were found in the aforementioned folder. The script did, however, include a statement in the first paragraph of the remarks that read, "It is a pleasure to meet with the Commercial Club of Chicago . . .". The words " . . . Commercial Club of Chicago . . ." were, however, crossed out and above them hand-written the words "Annual Conference of Engineers and Architects". After consulting with military historian, Dr. Sebastian Luka-sik, it was determined that the script was likely used at the Commercial Club of Chicago event, given the original text concerning the audience and the title of the folder in which it was found. Additionally, it was also determined that it was possible the script was reused for another event—seemingly the mentioned Annual Conference of Engineers and Architects.
48. Ibid., 2.
49. Ibid., 17–18. Additionally, the word "people", cited in this quote, was crossed out and the word "populations" was hand-written above it. The bracketed insertion of "populations" is intended to reflect this.
50. Ibid., 18.
51. Ibid., 18–19.
52. Ibid., 19.
53. Ibid., 20.
54. Ibid., 20–21.
55. Ibid., 21.
56. Library of Congress, Manuscript Reading Room, Papers of Curtis E. LeMay, Box B-202, folder entitled "B-45384", letter from Harold L. George to LeMay, 10 May 1955, page 1 (page numbers not listed on the document).
57. Foreign Relations of the United States, 1955–1957, Volume XIX, National Security Policy, eds. William Klingman, David S. Patterson, and Ilana Stern (Washington: Government Printing Office, 1990), Document 10, "Editorial Note" (taken from page 56).
58. Library of Congress, Manuscript Reading Room, Papers of Curtis E. LeMay, Box B-202, folder entitled "B-45384", letter from Harold L. George to LeMay, 10 May 1955, page 2 (page numbers not listed on the document).

59. Ibid., 1. The formatting of this block quote has been altered slightly, however the verbiage and spirit of the formatting remains to true to the source.

60. Library of Congress, Manuscript Reading Room, Nathan F. Twining Papers, container number 3 (listed as "BOX 3" in the finding aid), folder entitled "Daily Log JL 1955", CHIEF OF STAFF' DAILY LOG[:] Thursday, 14 July 1955. For LeMay's being at the Pentagon, it was assumed that given the words "General LeMay" next to a particular time on the "CHIEF OF STAFF', DAILY LOG", this was a clear indication of the SAC commander's presence there—particularly given the context of other appointments on the log.

61. Dwight D. Eisenhower Presidential Library, Papers of Chester R. Davis-Assistant Secretary of Army-1955 to 1956, Box 3, materials from the 1955 Secretaries' Conference. The materials referenced for this citation were the "Agenda, Saturday 16 July" and the "Program" for the conference, which included a directory of attendees, their lodging location, and phone extension. The directory of names was used to determine who was in attendance at the conference. This material was provided by mail by the Eisenhower Library.

62. Library of Congress, Manuscript Reading Room, Papers of Curtis E. LeMay, Box B-202, folder entitled "B-46839", REMARKS BY GENERAL CURTIS E. LeMAY AT QUANTICO—15 JULY 1955, page 1–2 of the remarks (first page not numbered). It is unclear whether LeMay delivered the remarks on the 15th or 16th of July, as some documents indicate him as speaking on the 16th (for one example where LeMay is scheduled for the 16th, see: Library of Congress, Manuscript Reading Room, Nathan F. Twining Papers, container number 3 ((listed as "BOX 3" in the finding aid)), folder entitled "Daily Log JL 1955", agenda for BUSINESS SESSIONS[,] 1955 SECRA-TARIES' CONFERENCE[,] "INTERNATIONAL RESPONSIBILITIES OF THE DEPARTMENT OF DEFENSE" ((this document appears to be the third page in a package that carried the subject line: Secretaries' Conference, 14–17 July 1955, Marine Corps School, Quantico, Virginia)) while the script states the 15th. Though this was a minor discrepancy in the records, it did not impact the greater content therein. Additionally, there was more than one transcript and/or script of remarks for this particular event at the Library of Congress. This copy was selected for use in this publication, as it was "marked-up," and gave it the appearance as the most likely to have been used in LeMay's actual remarks. Thus, these remarks were likely to most closely reflect what LeMay actually said on that occasion.

63. Library of Congress, Manuscript Reading Room, Papers of Curtis E. LeMay, Box B-202, folder entitled "B-46839", REMARKS BY GENERAL CURTIS E. LeMAY AT QUANTICO—15 JULY 1955, page 4–5.

64. Ibid., 5–7.
65. Ibid., 7–8.
66. Ibid., 22–23.
67. Ibid., 23–24.

Chapter 5. Strong until the End

1. Library of Congress, Manuscript Reading Room, Papers of Curtis E. LeMay, Box B-202, folder entitled "B-46843", Letter from Frank Armstrong to LeMay, 18 JUL 1955, page 1 (first page not numbered).
2. Ibid., 1–2.
3. Ibid., 2.
4. Ibid., 2.
5. Ibid., 2.
6. Ibid., 2.
7. Ibid., 2.
8. Ibid., 2.
9. Ibid., 2–3.
10. Library of Congress, Manuscript Reading Room, Papers of Curtis E. LeMay, Box B-202, folder entitled "B-47055", letter from LeMay to Frank Armstrong, 26 July 1955, page 1 (first page of the letter is not numbered).
11. Ibid., 1.
12. Ibid., 1–2.
13. Ibid., 2.
14. Ibid., 3.
15. Library of Congress, Manuscript Reading Room, Papers of Curtis E. LeMay, Box B-202, folder entitled "B-49454", letter from LeMay to Chief of Staff[,] United States Air Force, 1 NOV 1955, page 1 (first page is not numbered).
16. Ibid., 1–2; the term "Unit Equipped" referred to the number of aircraft assigned.
17. Library of Congress, Manuscript Reading Room, Papers of Curtis E. LeMay, Box B-69, folder entitled "misc 1955", subfolder entitled "Harvard Adv Management Club—N.Y.—6 Dec 1955", script of remarks (the cover of the script carries the handwritten title "New York = Harvard Adv. Mgmt Club—Dec 1955"), page 1–2 (first page of the script is not numbered).
18. Ibid., 2–3.
19. Ibid., 3.
20. Ibid., 7.
21. Ibid., 7–8.

22. Ibid., 8–9.

23. Ibid., 9.

24. Library of Congress, Manuscript Reading Room, Papers of Curtis E. LeMay, Box B-202, folder entitled "B-50703", letter from Anderson to LeMay, 21 December 1955, page 1 (first page is not numbered).

25. Library of Congress, Manuscript Reading Room, Papers of Curtis E. LeMay, Box B-202, folder entitled "B-51863", script of remarks, held in a bound packet entitled "REMARKS[,] GENERAL CURTIS E. LeMAY[,] AT COMMANDER'S CONFERENCE[,] WRIGHT PATTERSON AFB—JANUARY 1956", page 1 of the script of remarks (first page is not numbered). The reference to "United States AF" appeared originally in the script of remarks as "United States Air Force", however, the words "Air" and "Force" were crossed out and rewritten above those words as the letters "A" and "F". This document contained no clear indication of the exact date in January 1956 on which the conference occurred. For accuracy purposes, it is simple cited and referred to having occurred in January 1956.

26. Ibid., 1–2.

27. Ibid., 2.

28. Ibid., 2.

29. Ibid., 3.

30. Library of Congress, Manuscript Reading Room, Papers of Curtis E. LeMay, Box B-60, folder entitled "TWINING", letter from Twining to LeMay, 4 February 1956, page 1 (first page is not numbered). The exact identities of Dulles and Lodge, though their full names are not provided, are assumed given the context of this letter and the specificity of LeMay's reference to " . . . 'Ambassador Henry Cabot Lodge' . . ." during his remarks at Quantico. Though LeMay referred to a " . . . January . . ." meeting in his Quantico remarks and Twining referred to a " . . . February . . ." meeting in his letter, the meeting was almost certainly the same one, as both refer to the discussion of aggression's definition.

31. Ibid.

32. For the source document behind the Quantico remarks, see: Library of Congress, Manuscript Reading Room, Papers of Curtis E. LeMay, Box B-202, folder entitled "B-46839", REMARKS BY GENERAL CURTIS E. LeMAY AT QUANTICO—15 JULY 1955, page 22–23.

33. Library of Congress, Manuscript Reading Room, Papers of Curtis E. LeMay, Box B-60, folder entitled "TWINING", letter from Twining to LeMay, 4 February 1956, page 1 (first page is not numbered).

34. Ibid., 2.

35. Library of Congress, Manuscript Reading Room, Papers of Curtis E. LeMay, Box B-60, folder entitled "TWINING", letter from LeMay to Twining, 8 February 1956.

36. Library of Congress, Manuscript Reading Room, Papers of Curtis E. LeMay, Box B-71, script of "ADDRESS BY GENERAL CURTIS E. LeMAY AT UNIVERSITY OF NOTRE DAME[,] 22 February 1956", address contained in a spiral bound booklet with plastic covers, page 1–12 (page 1 not numbered). The script was in all-capitalized letters, which made it difficult to differentiate between proper terms, capitalized words, and lowercase text. For the purposes of this quote, the term "Award for Patriotism" was considered capitalized and thus appears that way in the passage here quoted. Nonetheless, this may not have been the proper title of the award and the capitalization may have been erroneous. This is an assumption on the part of this author. For LeMay's remarks at Quantico, July 1955, see: Library of Congress, Manuscript Reading Room, Papers of Curtis E. LeMay, Box B-202, folder entitled "B-46839", REMARKS BY GENERAL CURTIS E. LeMAY AT QUANTICO—15 JULY 1955, page 23–24.

37. Report of Proceedings, Hearing held before Subcommittee on the Air Force of the Committee on Armed Services[,] "PRESENT AND PLANNED STRENGTHS OF THE UNITED STATES AIR FORCE[:] *Strategic Air Command*", Call # K146.6201-43 V.1 PT.1, page 1, IRIS # 01118078, in the USAF Collection, AFHRA, Maxwell AFB, AL.

38. Ibid., 2–3.

39. Ibid., 3.

40. Ibid., 15–20. The transcript contained, among others, some interesting handwritten remarks and markings on page 20 (as well as the back-side of page 19, though they are subsequently and separately addressed in this manuscript); these included the statement "Reword" to the left of the paragraph which contained Nichols' discussion of " . . . the BRAVO or blunting task." Above the same paragraph was handwritten the statement—and this was as best as could be determined from reading the handwriting, "to prevent the launching of the atomic attack on [though the term " . . . on . . ." may not actually be there—it was difficult to decipher what exactly the handwriting said and this is a best guess] this country . . . ," which appeared above Nichols' statement " . . . the BRAVO or blunting task. The blunting task is to destroy the Soviet atomic forces on the ground . . . ," a statement which itself had handwritten brackets around it. To the right of most of the paragraph in question was what appeared to be a larger bracket, to the right of which appeared a check mark. Additionally, next to LeMay's statement on the same page in question,

on the left side of his statement, appeared handwritten brackets; at the same time, LeMay's statement had handwritten quotation marks on both ends. To the right of that paragraph was an undecipherable (at least in the photo-copied version of this document) handwritten remark. Exactly to what all of these markings referred or were meant to communicate was not perfectly clear—in an immediate sense. More sense will be made of them in a subsequent discussion in this manuscript.

41. "GENERAL LEMAY TESTIMONY, VOLUME 1, APRIL 25" (within the IRIS Public Record this document is titled: "GEN LEMAY'S TESTI-MONY"), Call # K146.6201-46, page unnumbered but entitled "*GA-65 CHRONOLOGY*" (this page precedes the pages that specifically enumerated the changes to the testimony), IRIS # 01118101, in the USAF Collection, AFHRA, Maxwell AFB, AL.

42. Ibid., 1. This is not the original testimony, despite the title of the document, but rather the changes to the original testimony. This document has its own unique Call # and IRIS # when compared to the original testimony.

43. Report of Proceedings, Hearing held before Subcommittee on the Air Force of the Committee on Armed Services[,] "PRESENT AND PLANNED STRENGTHS OF THE UNITED STATES AIR FORCE[:] *Strategic Air Command*", Call # K146.6201-43 V.1 PT.1, back-side of page 19 of the document on file at AFHRA (this page faces page 20), IRIS # 01118078, in the USAF Collection, AFHRA, Maxwell AFB, AL.

44. Library of Congress, Manuscript Reading Room, Papers of Curtis E. LeMay, Box B-71, script of "GENERAL CURTIS E. LeMAY'S Address before AMER-ICAN ORDNANCE ASSOCIATION[,] Philadelphia, Pennsylvania[,] 23 May 1956, page 9–10. This address was contained in a spiral bound packet with what appeared to be a plastic cover.

45. Library of Congress, Manuscript Reading Room, Papers of Curtis E. LeMay, Box B-60, folder entitled "Twining", letter from Twining to LeMay, 6 June 1956, page 1 (first page not numbered).

46. Ibid., 1–2.

47. Library of Congress, Manuscript Reading Room, Papers of Curtis E. LeMay, Box B-60, folder entitled "Twining", letter from LeMay to Twining, 6 FEB 1957, page 1 (first page not numbered).

48. Ibid.

49. Ibid., 1–2.

50. Ibid., 2

51. Library of Congress, Manuscript Reading Room, Papers of Curtis E. LeMay, Box B-60, folder entitled "Twining", letter from LeMay to Twining, 21 SEP

1956, page 1 (first page unmarked). This letter was actually attested to (it is not actually "signed," in a traditional sense—see the following) by Major General Francis H. Griswold, SAC's second in command, during a period of unavailability by LeMay. Above LeMay's signature block, at the end of the letter, it was typed or stamped "FOR AND IN THE ABSENCE OF"; Beneath LeMay's signature block was typed or stamped Griswold's signature block, which identified who authorized the letter on LeMay's behalf. In other words, Griswold "signed" the letter in LeMay's stead.

52. Ibid.
53. Ibid.
54. Ibid.
55. Ibid., 1–2.
56. Library of Congress, Manuscript Reading Room, Papers of Curtis E. LeMay, Box B-60, folder entitled "Twining", letter from Twining to LeMay, 15 November 1956, page 1–2 (pages do not appear marked with page numbers).
57. Ibid., 2.
58. Library of Congress, Manuscript Reading Room, Papers of Curtis E. LeMay, Box B-71, script of remarks [contained inside an unmarked, apparently plastic folder], LeMay address at the Citadel, 9 Feb 57, page 3–4. The location of the speech was determined using statements on page 1 of the script, whereon LeMay addresses "General Clark, members of the faculty, and students . . ." and later states "The very fact of your presence on this Citadel campus. . . ." The location of the speech was further corroborated by a letter that was binder-clipped to the script (inside the front cover, to the remarks themselves) and addressed to "Lieutenant Colonel Jones," LeMay's "Aide-de-Camp . . ." (Jones eventually served as the Chairman of the Joint Chiefs of Staff from 1978 to 1982). The letter was from "JOHN D. GORHAM, JR.," whose signature block indicated he was a "Professor of Air Science." The letter to Jones was written on letterhead for the "DEPARTMENT OF AIR SCIENCE[,] AFROTC DETACHMENT 765[,] THE CITADEL[,] CHARLESTON, SOUTH CAROLINA." The letter stated that "Inclosed [sic] you will find General Lemay's Speech which you requested we forward." The letter then went on and expressed to Jones a "Thank you for your efforts in our behalf which certainly added to the luster of General Lemay's visit." Based on all of this, the location was clear. In terms of the date of the speech, on the first page of the script itself, in the upper right corner, was handwritten "9 Feb 57." Given the context and the date of the letter, "12 February 1957," it is likely the "9 Feb 57" date is accurate, as the

remarks were probably being returned to LeMay's staff following a proximate visit. Thus, the date of "9 Feb 57" makes sense. For the letter from
Gorham to Jones, see: Library of Congress, Manuscript Reading Room,
Papers of Curtis E. LeMay, Box B-71, letter from Gorham to Jones, binder
clipped to the script of remarks (LeMay address at the Citadel, 9 Feb 57
[date of LeMay's remarks]), letter [from Gorham to Jones] dated 12 February 1957.

59. Ibid., 7–8.
60. Ibid., 7–9.
61. Ibid., 9–10.
62. Ibid., 9–10, 14–15, 16–17.
63. Library of Congress, Manuscript Reading Room, Papers of Curtis E.
    LeMay, Box B-203, folder entitled "B-60725", speech entitled "THE OPER-
    ATIONAL SIDE OF AIR OFFENSE", given at Patrick Air Force Base, Flor-
    ida, 21 MAY 1957, cover page of remarks.
64. Ibid., 1.
65. Library of Congress, Manuscript Reading Room, Papers of Curtis E. LeMay,
    Box B-71, script of remarks [contained inside an unmarked, apparently
    plastic folder], LeMay address at the Citadel, 9 Feb 57, page 26–28.
66. Library of Congress, Manuscript Reading Room, Papers of Curtis E.
    LeMay, Box B-203, folder entitled "B-60725", speech entitled "THE OPER-
    ATIONAL SIDE OF AIR OFFENSE", given at Patrick Air Force Base, Flor-
    ida, 21 MAY 1957, page 2 of the remarks.

Bibliography

Primary Sources

Anderson, Frederick L. *Papers of Frederick L. Anderson.* Stanford, CA: Hoover Institution.

Davis, Chester R. *Papers of Chester R. Davis, Assistant Secretary of Army, 1955–1956.* Abilene, KS: Dwight D. Eisenhower Presidential Library.

Klingman, William, David S. Patterson, and Ilana Stern, eds. *Foreign Relations of the United States, 1955–1957.* Vol. XIX, *National Security Policy.* Washington, DC: Government Printing Office, 1990.

LeMay, Curtis E. *Papers of Curtis E. LeMay, 1918–1969.* Washington, DC: Library of Congress.

Records Groups 341, 342. College Park, MD: National Archives and Records Administration.

Strategic Air Command Historical Branch. *Strategic Air Command History.* 3 vols. Offutt Air Force Base, NE: Strategic Air Command, 1951.

Twining, Nathan F. *Papers of Nathan F. Twining, 1924–1960.* Washington, DC: Library of Congress.

United States Air Force. *The United States Strategic Bombing Surveys Summary Report.* Montgomery, AL: Air University Press, 1987.

United States Air Force Collection. Montgomery, AL: Air Force Historical Research Agency.

Vandenberg, Hoyt S. *Papers of Hoyt S. Vandenberg, 1942–1954.* Washington, DC: Library of Congress.

Secondary Sources

Books

Abella, Alex. *Soldiers of Reason: The Rand Corporation and the Rise of the American Empire.* Boston: Mariner Books, 2009.

Alperovitz, Gar. *Atomic Diplomacy: Hiroshima and Potsdam: The Use of the Atomic Bomb and the American Confrontation with Soviet Power.* London: Pluto Press, 1994.

Armitage, M. J., and R. A. Mason, eds. *Air Power in the Nuclear Age.* Urbana: University of Illinois Press, 1983.

Arnold, Henry Harley. *Global Mission.* New York: Harper and Brothers, 1949.

Bacevich, Andrew J. *The Limits of Power: The End of American Exceptionalism.* New York: Metropolitan Books, 2009.

Beisner, Robert L. *Dean Acheson: A Life in the Cold War.* Oxford: Oxford University Press, 2006.

Biddle, Tami Davis. *Rhetoric and Reality in Air Warfare: The Evolution of British and American Ideas about Strategic Bombing, 1914–1945.* Princeton: Princeton University Press, 2002.

Borgiasz, William S. *The Strategic Air Command: Evolution and Consolidation of Nuclear Forces, 1945–1955.* Westport, CT: Praeger, 1996.

Borowski, Harry R. *A Hollow Threat: Strategic Air Power and Containment before Korea.* Westport, CT: Greenwood Press, 1982.

Botti, Timothy J. *Ace in the Hole: Why the United States Did Not Use Nuclear Weapons in the Cold War, 1945 to 1965.* Westport, CT: Greenwood Press, 1996.

Boyne, Walter J. *Beyond the Wild Blue: A History of the United States Air Force, 1947–2007.* New York: Thomas Dunne Books, St. Martin's Press, 2007.

Cate, James Lea, and Wesley Frank Craven. *The Army Air Forces in World War II.* 7 vols. Washington, DC: Office of Air Force History, 1983.

Clodfelter, Mark. *Beneficial Bombing: The Progressive Foundations of American Air Power, 1917–1945.* Omaha: University of Nebraska Press, 2011.

———. *The Limits of Air Power: The American Bombing of North Vietnam.* New York: Free Press, 1989.

Coffey, Thomas M. *Iron Eagle: The Turbulent Life of General Curtis LeMay.* New York: Avon Books, 1988.

Crane, Conrad C. *American Airpower Strategy in Korea, 1950–1953.* Lawrence: University Press of Kansas, 2000.

———. *American Airpower Strategy in World War II: Bombs, Cities, Civilians, and Oil.* Lawrence: University Press of Kansas, 2016.

———. *Bombs, Cities, and Civilians: American Airpower Strategy in World War II.* Lawrence: University Press of Kansas, 1993.

D'Este, Carlo. *Patton: A Genius for War.* New York: Harper Collins, 1995.

Douhet, Giulio. *The Command of the Air.* Washington, DC: Office of Air Force History, 1983.

Gaddis, John Lewis. *The Long Peace: Inquiries into the History of the Cold War.* New York: Oxford University Press, 1987.

———. *Strategies of Containment: A Critical Appraisal of American National Security Policy during the Cold War.* Oxford: Oxford University Press, 2005.

———. *Surprise, Security, and the American Experience.* Cambridge: Harvard University Press, 2004.

———. *The United States and the Origins of the Cold War, 1941–1947.* New York: Columbia University Press, 1972.

———. *We Now Know: Rethinking Cold War History.* Oxford: Clarendon, 1998.

Gordin, Michael D. *Five Days in August: How World War II Became a Nuclear War.* Princeton: Princeton University Press, 2007.

Hasegawa, Tsuyoshi. *Racing the Enemy: Stalin, Truman, and the Surrender of Japan.* Cambridge: Harvard University Press, 2006.

Herken, Gregg. *Brotherhood of the Bomb: The Tangled Lives and Loyalties of Robert Oppenheimer, Ernest Lawrence, and Edward Teller.* New York: Henry Holt and Co., 2002.

———. *Counsels of War.* New York: Alfred A. Knopf, 1985.

———. *The Winning Weapon: The Atomic Bomb in the Cold War, 1945–1950.* New York: Alfred A. Knopf, 1980.

Higham, Robin, and Stephen J. Harris, eds. *Why Air Forces Fail: The Anatomy of Defeat.* Lexington: University Press of Kentucky, 2006.

Hippler, Thomas. *Bombing the People: Giulio Douhet and the Foundations of Air-Power Strategy, 1884–1939.* Cambridge: Cambridge University Press, 2013.

Kaplan, Fred. *The Wizards of Armageddon.* New York: Simon and Schuster, 1983.

Kennan, George. *Memoirs: 1925–1950.* London: Little, Brown, 1967.

Kennett, Lee. *A History of Strategic Bombing.* New York: Charles Scribner's Sons, 1982.

Kunetka, James W. *The General and the Genius: Groves and Oppenheimer—The Unlikely Partnership that Built the Atom Bomb.* Washington, DC: Regnery Publishing, 2015.

Leffler, Melvyn P. *A Preponderance of Power: National Security, the Truman Administration, and the Cold War.* Stanford, CA: Stanford University Press, 1993.

LeMay, Curtis E., and MacKinlay Kantor. *Mission with LeMay: My Story.* Garden City, NY: Doubleday, 1966.

Meilinger, Phillip S. *Hoyt S. Vandenberg: The Life of a General.* Washington, DC: Air Force History and Museums Program, 2000.

Miscamble, Wilson D. *George F. Kennan and the Making of American Foreign Policy, 1947–50.* Princeton: Princeton University Press, 1992.

Moody, Walton S. *Building a Strategic Air Force*. Washington, DC: Air Force History and Museums Program, 1996.

Nalty, Bernard C., ed. *Winged Shield, Winged Sword: A History of the United States Air Force*. 2 vols. Washington, DC: Air Force History and Museums Program, 1997.

Nutter, Ralph H. *With the Possum and the Eagle: A Memoir of a Navigator's War over Germany and Japan*. Denton: University of North Texas Press, 2005.

Olsen, John Andreas, ed. *Air Commanders*. Washington, DC: Potomac Books, 2013.

————, ed. *A History of Air Warfare*. Washington, DC: Potomac Books, 2010.

Pape, Robert. *Bombing to Win: Air Power and Coercion in War*. Ithaca: Cornell University Press, 1996.

Polmar, Norman, ed. *Strategic Air Command: People, Aircraft, and Missiles*. Annapolis, MD: Nautical and Aviation Publishing Company of America, 1979.

Rhodes, Richard. *Arsenals of Folly: The Making of the Nuclear Arms Race*. New York: Vintage, 2008.

————. *Dark Sun: The Making of the Hydrogen Bomb*. New York: Simon and Schuster, 1995.

Schaffer, Ronald. *Wings of Judgment: American Bombing in World War II*. New York: Oxford University Press, 1985.

Schlosser, Eric. *Command and Control: Nuclear Weapons, the Damascus Accident, and the Illusion of Safety*. New York: Penguin Books, 2013.

Sherry, Michael S. *The Rise of American Air Power: The Creation of Armageddon*. New Haven: Yale University Press, 1987.

Thucydides. *History of the Peloponnesian War*. Trans. Benjamin Jowett. Amherst, NY: Prometheus Books, 1998.

Tillman, Barrett. *LeMay*. New York: Palgrave Macmillan, 2007.

Weigley, Russell Frank. *The American Way of War: A History of United States Military Strategy and Policy*. Bloomington: Indiana University Press, 1973.

Williams, William Appleman. *The Tragedy of American Diplomacy*. New York: Dell, 1972.

Journal Articles

Gaddis, John Lewis, and Paul Nitze. "NSC 68 and the Soviet Threat Reconsidered." *International Security* 4, no. 4 (Spring 1980): 164–76.

Meilinger, Phillip S. "Getting to the Target: The Penetration Problem in the Strategic Air Command During the 1950s." *Airpower History* 61, no. 3 (2014): 38–49.

Index

About the Author

Trevor Albertson is an assistant professor and course director at the Air Command and Staff College at Maxwell AFB, Alabama. He earned his PhD from the University of California, Merced, and was an IGCC-UCDC Dissertation Fellow in Foreign Policy Studies. He is a former U.S. Air Force officer, federal congressional staffer, and deputy secretary of an agency of California state government. His research focuses on the political-diplomatic history of the twentieth-century United States.